Research Methods for Human Resource Management

D1478793

Increasingly, there are calls for the integration of traditional individualistic (micro) and management (macro) paradigms in human resource management studies. These calls, in concert with the increasing interest in the HRM "black box", strongly imply a need for future HR research that is more sensitive to institutional and cultural contexts, that focuses on formal and informal relationships between employees, supervisors, and HR managers, and explores the means by which these organizational participants enable and motivate one another. Multi-actor, social network, and longitudinal research practices, among others, are explored. Readers will gain insight into the advantages and disadvantages of different research methods in order to evaluate which type is most suitable to their research. This book is suitable for both advanced researchers and graduate students.

Karin Sanders, PhD, is Professor of Organisational Behaviour and Human Resource Management (HRM) at the Australian School of Business, at the University of New South Wales. Her research focuses on the process approach of HRM. She uses advanced statistical research methods to test a variety of theoretical models. Her research has been published in such scholarly outlets as the *Academy of Management, Learning & Education, Human Resource Management, Journal of Vocational Behavior, Organizational Studies, Asia Pacific Journal of Management, International Journal of Human Resource Management*, and *Group and Organization Management: An International Journal*. She is associate editor of *Evidence Based HRM*.

Julie A. Cogin, PhD, is an Associate Professor at the School of Management within the Australian School of Business at the University of New South Wales. Julie's research interests surround the HRM—performance relationship. This includes understanding how components of an HRM strategy can be configured to realize superior organizational outcomes as well as impediments to HRM professionals operating as true strategic partners. Julie is also interested in HRM research methods, the progress of the field and designing research that does not suffer from major methodological problems. Her work has been published in journals such as *Human Resource Management, International Journal of Human Resource Management, and Employee Relations*.

Hugh T. J. Bainbridge (PhD, University of Melbourne) is a senior lecturer in the School of Management, at the Australian School of Business, University of New South Wales. His research interests encompass the effectiveness of human resource practices, employee diversity, and impression formation processes relevant to individuals, groups, and organizations. His current research considers how line managers and HR specialists can improve the participation and employment quality of diverse individuals in the workforce. The results of his research have been published in the *Academy of Management Review, Journal of Applied Psychology, Analyses of Social Issues and Public Policy*, and *Asia Pacific Journal of Human Resources*.

Routledge Advances in Management and Business Studies

For a full list of titles in this series, please visit www.routledge.com

Research Methods for Human Resource Management

Edited by Karin Sanders, Julie A. Cogin, and Hugh T.J. Bainbridge

LONDON AND NEW YORK

First published 2014
by Routledge
711 Third Avenue, New York, NY 10017

and by Routledge
2 Park Square, Milton Park, Abingdon, Oxon OX14 4RN

First issued in paperback 2014

*Routledge is an imprint of the Taylor & Francis Group,
an informa business*

Library of Congress Cataloging-in-Publication Data

Research methods for human resource management / edited by Karin
Sanders, Julie A. Cogin, and Hugh T. J. Bainbridge.
      pages cm. — (Routledge advances in management and business
studies ; 58)
   Includes bibliographical references and index.
   1. Personnel management—Research.   I. Sanders, Karin.
II. Cogin, Julie A.   III. Bainbridge, Hugh T. J.
   HF5549.15.R47 2014
   658.30072—dc23
   2013029944

ISBN 978-0-415-72743-3 (hbk)
ISBN 978-1-138-88511-0 (pbk)
ISBN 978-1-315-85230-0 (ebk)
Typeset in Sabon
by Apex CoVantage, LLC

Contents

.

Figures

Tables

1 The Growing Role of Advanced Human Resource Management Research Methods

Karin Sanders, Julie A. Cogin, and Hugh T. J. Bainbridge

> After reading this chapter, we expect you to be able to:
>
> 1. Learn more about the methodological criticisms of HRM research;
> 2. Understand the social embeddedness framework to combine individual and organizational factors in understanding HRM research;
> 3. Introduce the chapters and understand the structure of this volume.

1. INTRODUCTION

Scientific progress is based on the continued evolution and interplay of theory and method. Theoretical developments suggest promising lines of inquiry and new research questions for empirical examination. Methodological advances provide improved tools with which to undertake research. Over the past two decades, major theoretical advances in Human Resource Management (HRM) research have contributed to a growing understanding of the relationship between HRM and performance. For example, Bowen and Ostroff (2004) proposed advanced theoretical models that outline how an understanding of multi-level phenomena can help to open the so-called black box. They argued that HR practices at the organizational level influence employee attitudes and behaviors on the individual level, and employee attitudes and behaviors influence performance on the organizational level.

Concurrent with these theoretical advances there has been an extensive discussion about HRM research methodology. For example, Gerhart (2008) and Huselid and Becker (2000) called for more longitudinal and experimental research as cross-sectional designs often lead to the measurement of HR practices and performance at the same time—limiting the ability to infer causality. These methodological discussions are important and have helped to shape perceptions in the HRM field about the desirability of particular methodological approaches (e.g., longitudinal versus cross-sectional designs). However, recent reviews of the HRM literature suggest that advanced research methods such as longitudinal designs, mixed methods, and multi-level modeling that are well established in fields such organizational behavior have not diffused widely into HRM research (Hoobler & Brown, 2004; Hayton, Piperopoulus, & Welbourne, 2011; Sanders, Bainbridge, Kim, Cogin, & Lin, 2012; Bainbridge, Sanders, Cogin, & Lin, under review; see Chapter 8).

This is unfortunate because *advanced research methods* can assist HRM researchers in their efforts to tackle the central challenges in the field. Well-specified research models that are based on sound theory, valid and reliable measures, and advanced analytical procedures enhance researchers' likelihood of demonstrating significant effect sizes in their examination of the HRM-performance relationship. In addition, there is evidence that studies that utilize more *advanced research methods* have a greater impact (see Chapter 8). In turn, they are more likely to enhance the possibility of generating valid answers to questions about the effectiveness of HRM, to influence future research in the field, and to create positive perceptions of the rigor of the discipline (Hayton *et al.*, 2011).

The fundamental premise of this *volume* is that sophisticated research methods provide researchers with the opportunity to enhance the quality of their investigations. We believe that as the HRM field matures, researchers need to adopt increasingly sophisticated research designs to examine progressively more complex and nuanced research questions. Thus, in this *volume*, our focus is on outlining key components of a selection of advanced research methods, the utility of such methods, and the potential modes of application on a variety of HRM research questions. Our goal is to provide a resource for emerging scholars including (research) masters and PhD students during the planning and conduct of their research.

In this introductory chapter we begin by reviewing the methodological criticisms of HRM research. We then introduce social embeddedness as a framework that can be drawn on in designing research that will address these methodological criticisms. We relate the different dimensions of social embeddedness to different research methods but leave subsequent chapters to provide more detail of each of the methods. In the last section of this chapter an overview of forthcoming chapters and their authors is presented.

2. METHODOLOGICAL CRITICISMS OF HRM RESEARCH

There is an emerging consensus in the literature that HR practices reduce employee turnover, improve job attitudes, and enhance employee and organizational productivity (Huselid, Jackson, & Schulder, 1997; Wright, Gardner, Moynihan, & Allen, 2005; Boselie, Dietz, & Boon, 2005; Combs,

Liu, Hall, & Ketchen, 2006). As a result, researchers from multiple backgrounds are studying the effects of HRM on employee and organizational performance (e.g., Paauwe, 2009). Despite this developing acceptance that HR practices are linked to performance, the HRM literature has been subject to two major criticisms concerning, (i) the strength of the relationship between HRM and performance measures, and (ii) the exact nature of the causal relationship between HRM and performance.

The Strength of the Relationship Between HRM and Performance Measures

The effect size of the relationship between HRM and performance has been a matter of some concern for many years, with researchers generally reporting only a moderately significant relationship between HRM and organizational performance. For instance, in 1995 Huselid published an article in which a correlation was reported between the degree of sophistication of HR systems and market value per employee. Five years after this publication Huselid and Becker (2000) published an article in which they indicate that the effect of one standard deviation change in the HRM system will increase an organizational market value by 10–20%. A meta-analysis by Combs *et al.* (2006) showed a correlation between high performance work systems (HPWS) and organizational performance of 0.20. Wall and Wood (2005) undertook a critical analysis of 25 of the best cited studies in reputable refereed journals and concluded that it was premature to suggest a linkage between HRM systems and organizational performance due to methodological limitations and inadequate research design.

A second concern is that the linkage between HR practices and organizational performance may not be a simple linear relationship, but rather one that consists of numerous moderating and mediating variables. In this respect, some progress has been made in uncovering the variables impacting the HRM-organizational performance relationship (Combs *et al.,* 2006). Analyzing the content of 104 empirical articles, Boselie and colleagues (2005; see also Paauwe, 2009) conclude that there are three theories that are most commonly used to explain this relationship: contingency theory; resource-based-view (RBV); and the ability, motivation, opportunities (AMO) framework. These three theories reflect different paradigms in HRM research. Contingency theory and RBV focus on the examination of HRM from a management studies perspective and are researched at the organizational level *(macro HRM)*. Researchers within this paradigm are mainly interested in the organizational performance effects. The AMO framework, with its roots in industrial and organizational psychology, is more likely to be invoked in the study of phenomena at the individual level of analysis. Such research tends to focus on the relationship between employees' perceptions of single HR practices and outcomes such as job satisfaction and organizational commitment *(micro HRM)*.

Both research traditions provide valuable perspectives for unraveling the HRM-performance relationship. For example, in addition to Bowen and Ostroff (2004; see also Ostroff & Bowen, 2000), scholars have called for research to integrate macro variables into micro research designs and micro variables into macro research designs (Lepak, Liao, Chung, & Harden, 2006; Wright & Boswell, 2002; Cogin & Williamson, in press). Such assertions call for scholars to adopt multi-level research designs that capture both within (e.g., employee differences) and between organizational variance (e.g., organizational performance).

HRM researchers are also becoming more sensitive to institutional and cultural context; formal and informal relationships between employees, supervisors, and HR managers; and the means by which these organizational participants enable and motivate one another. For instance, multi-actor, social network, and longitudinal research makes it possible to take into account the fact that employees are embedded in *relations* (social network research), *teams* and *organizations* (multi-actor research), and *time* (longitudinal). Such approaches will provide added value in opening the black box and in combining insights from the micro and macro paradigms.

The Exact Nature of the Causal Relationship Between HRM and Performance

Most HRM research suggests a positive causal relationship between HRM and performance, however many researchers (e.g., Becker & Huselid, 2006; Huselid & Becker, 2000; Wright *et al.*, 2005) argue that this body of work lacks sufficient methodological rigor to demonstrate that the relationship is indeed causal (Wright *et al.*, 2005, p. 410).

Current HRM research is predominantly characterized by cross-sectional designs (Boselie *et al.*, 2005). Unfortunately, this body of cross-sectional work generally fails to meet the three criteria Cook and Campbell (1979) view as necessary for inferring causality: (i) covariation, meaning that cause and effect should covary with each other—if the cause is absent the effect should be absent, and if the cause if present, the effect should be present; (ii) temporal precedence of the cause, meaning that the cause should exist in time before the effect; and (iii) no alternative explanations should be present, meaning that all possible third variables should be ruled out.

Reviews of the HRM literature suggest that only the first condition (a test of covariation between HR practices and organizational performance) is typically met (Wright *et al.*, 2005; Gerhart, 1999; Huselid & Becker, 1996). However, covariation is a necessary but not sufficient condition for establishing causality, and research that provides statistical evidence that a HRM system contributes to organizational performance cannot rule out the possibility of reverse causality. Guest, Michie, Sheehan, and Conway (2003) found that in some cases, correlations with past performance exceeded those with future performance, and that a drastic reduction of the relationship between HR practices and organizational performance, even to nonsignificance, occurred after controlling for past performance. Despite this, the possibility of reverse causality is rarely examined. Covariation may also occur where a third variable (the alternative explanation; so-called spurious relationships) cause both HR practices and organizational performance. For instance, good economic circumstances can promote HR practices and improved organizational performance. In order to review how the HRM literature has addressed issues of causality, Wright *et al.* (2005) reviewed empirical articles examining the relationship between HR practices and organizational performance. The most prevalent design was called post-predictive design, in which HR practices were measured after the performance period, resulting in designs where HRM actually predicted past performance (Wright *et al.*, 2005, p. 412).

In the next section we introduce the social embeddedness framework to provide direction on how future HRM research can be improved by addressing these criticisms.

3. SOCIAL EMBEDDEDNESS AND ADVANCED RESEARCH METHODS

Guest (1997), Boselie *et al.* (2005), and Paauwe (2009) emphasize the importance of well-developed theory to continued progress in the examination of HRM issues. In this section we utilize the concept of *social embeddedness* as a framework for exploring individual- and organizational-level research considerations. In so doing, it can help researchers to think about designs that bridge the micro- and macro-oriented worlds. A social embeddedness perspective points to the relevance of several advanced research methods to the study of HRM. In this section we thus review how a consideration of the social embedded nature of individuals within organizations can advance our understanding of HRM.

Following Granovetter (1985), Raub and Weesie (1990, 2000), and Sanders (2009) we argue that the social context, or *social embeddedness*, is a significant influence on employees' behavior. The extent to which a relationship is embedded can be described in terms of three dimensions of embeddedness: temporal, network, and institutional (Raub & Weesie, 1990, 2000). *Temporal embeddedness* refers to the duration and expected future length of employment relationships. *Network embeddedness* refers to the network of social relationships between employees—for example, friendship or status hierarchies. *Institutional embeddedness* refers to the formal and informal rules of an organization, such as career progression and performance appraisal systems. These three dimensions of social embeddedness provide a clear road map for advanced HR research methods, which we argue is needed to advance the HRM field. In the following discussion we outline how these three dimensions of the social embeddedness framework relate to the research methods needed within the HR field.

Social embeddedness: How does it work in practice?

Evan is a PhD candidate interested in studying talent management programs. Evan's overarching research question is, What makes talent management programs for high-potential employees effective? He has partnered with a large organization that has a talent management program in place to collect data for his PhD. After examining the literature, Evan decides to conduct preliminary interviews with participants at different stages of the program before settling on a research design for his PhD. From these interviews, Evan has three insights that influence his research design. First, Evan learns that the employees' relationships with their managers and mentors were crucial to the organization retaining participants postprogram. Second, Evan discovers that participants' commitment to their manager, team, and organization changes dramatically over different stages of the program. Third, Evan finds that although the program was well structured with learning goals established at each milestone, a significant portion of development took place informally among the cohort of participants when they met socially.

The social embeddedness of talent management participants with key stakeholders, such as their managers and mentors, thus represented an important consideration that Evan should account for in his research design when investigating the determinants of program effectiveness.

Temporal embeddedness captures both the history and the (expected) future of relationships. If a relationship has a long history, individuals have had more opportunities to gain information about each other's reliability from previous interactions and to learn from their experiences (Raub & Weesie, 1990, 2000). If the employee has more information about the trustworthiness of a colleague, it can be expected that the employee will be more willing to place trust in that individual and to take a risk (Hinds, Carley, Krackhardt, & Wholey, 2000). A shared future promotes interactions through conditional cooperation (Axelrod, 1984) where employees attempt to exercise control over the behavior of a colleague through the provision of rewards for cooperative and punishments for uncooperative behavior. With respect to the study of HRM, a consideration of temporal embeddedness highlights the value of longitudinal (where data is gathered at multiple points in time) and experimental (where variables are manipulated in a relatively controlled environment) designs. These observations provide the rationale for our chapters on longitudinal (Chapter 5) and experimental research designs (Chapter 6).

Temporal embeddedness: How does it work in practice?

Returning to the example of Evan, the PhD candidate found that employees in the talent management program experienced changes in their commitment over time while participating in the program. Initially, when employees were selected for the program, various promises were made to employees by HR managers and supervisors that enhanced commitment. Subsequently, program participants were motivated to work long hours. However, for some employees, perceived obligations from managers in regard to skill development, identification of opportunities to progress in the organization, and introductions to new networks were unfulfilled as participants transitioned through the program. For others, a positive experience during the program and afterward with mentors and job rotations built trust and reduced intentions to leave.

To capture the antecedents of talent management program effectiveness, Evan needs to undertake a longitudinal study that accounts for how commitment levels of participants change over time. Without this he cannot establish a causal relationship.

Network embeddedness relates to the number and quality of an employee's interpersonal relationships. The term relates to aspects of the structure of the networks these relationships constitute (Granovetter, 1985). Networks provide information and serve as a means for the direct and indirect rewarding of (cooperative) behaviors and direct and indirect sanctioning of (noncooperative) behaviors. Network embeddedness can be either formal or informal. Formal networks of employees refers to the structure of formal relationships that exist between designated jobs. Informal networks refers to the structure of personal relations between individuals and are not necessarily tied to the position of the jobholder. By researching the informal networks, activities both within and outside the organization can be understood. For instance, nonwork activities (e.g., going for a drink together after work) provide opportunities for employees to get to know each other better and create possibilities to reward desired behavior. Such activities also can sanction opportunistic collaboration.

Research that is responsive to network embeddedness considerations pays attention to the social interactions and personal relationships that exist between employees, line managers, and HR managers and requires multi-actor and multi-informant designs. Methodologists distinguish between such multi-actor designs and single-informant (single-respondent) and single-actor designs. A *single-informant (single-respondent) design* refers to studies in which a sole respondent provides information on both HR practices and organizational performance of one organization. A *single-actor design* refers to studies in which all respondents can be classified in one category (i.e., HR managers, or employees). These designs are problematic, as single-informant (single-respondent) designs do not permit interrater reliability indices to be calculated. For example, if you wish to measure the strength of the HRM system within an organization and collect data only from HR managers, you are likely to get a biased result (see Sanders & Frenkel, 2011).

Several other researchers have criticized the reliance that HRM research places on single-actor and single-informant designs. Gerhart *et al.* (2000) and Huselid and Becker (2000) debated the presence and implications of the use of a single respondent to assess human resource practices. Wright, Gardner, Moynihan, Park, Gerhart, and Delery (2001) demonstrated in three studies that single-informant (single-respondent) measures of HR practices contain large amounts of measurement error. Becker and Gerhart (1996; see also Becker & Huselid, 1998) showed that within single-informant designs there is inconsistency across studies regarding the specific HR practices that are included in studies of HRM and business performance. Based on a study from 14 large organizations, Gerhart *et al.* (2000) found reliabilities for single informants' assessments of different HR practices were generally below 0.50. As a result, they argue that the assessment of HR practices based on a single informant are subject to unacceptable high levels of measure error and may give rise to spurious statistical relationships, particularly if the informant exaggerates his or her own effectiveness and impact on performance (Guest, 1997; Gerhart, Wright, & McMahan, 2000; Wright *et al.*, 2001).

By contrast, multi-actor and multisource designs enhance confidence in HRM research by improving construct validity and allowing estimates of interrater reliability (Gerhart, Wright, McMahan, & Snell, 2000; Colakoglu, Lepak, & Hong, 2006). Wright *et al.* (2001) suggest that the most obvious way of reducing error due to a single-informant (single-respondent) design is by increasing the number of respondents. For example, this could mean surveying all HR or all line managers within an organization. However, obvious practical considerations may preclude researchers from accessing the entire population of potential informants. Furthermore, in line with Huselid and Becker (2000), attention should be paid to respondent knowledge, as adding poorly informed respondents may increase neither reliability nor validity. Despite these considerations, there are significant benefits that flow from both increasing the number of respondents within HRM research and ensuring that the perspectives of different actors (HR, line managers, and employees) are taken into account when assessing the HR practice-performance relationship. These benefits justify the inclusion of chapters that focus on *multi-actor research* (part of Chapter 3) and *social networks* (Chapter 4) in this text.

Network embeddedness: How does it work in practice?

In our example of Evan's PhD study, the informal networks created by participants in the talent management program were associated with participants learning new skills, gaining information, and ultimately succeeding in their careers. Collecting data on such networks would enhance Evan's research findings.

Institutional embeddedness speaks to the concept that workplace interactions are also influenced by the formal and informal rules that govern power relations between employers and employees and interactions among employees (North, 1990). Governance structures constitute the settings in which employees weigh alternatives and make decisions concerning the duration and timing of efforts expended for the organization. The content of an organization's governance structures is evident in HRM policies. Elements of formal governance structures are HR practices and policies such as remuneration policies and performance management policies.

Institutional embeddedness requires multi-level research that takes into account the context of the research. There is a growing recognition of the multi-level nature of social phenomena among social scientists of various disciplinary backgrounds. The basic problem of ignoring the multi-level structure of organizations is the misspecification of the measured level in comparison to the theoretical level. It important to consider the level of measurement, as attributing individual data to the organization or attributing organizational data to the individual has an impact on the construct validity of the research. Care is thus needed to guard against the construct validity problems if data is collected at one level and applied to another level (Rousseau, 1985). For example, Ostroff and Bowen (2000; see also Bowen & Ostroff, 2004; Klein & Kozlowski, 2000; Klein, Dansereau, & Hall, 1994) criticized the research designs most frequently used by HRM researchers. They argue that even though assumptions behind most HRM research concern elements at multiple levels, most HRM research actually utilize a single-level research design. As a result, scholars are encouraged to take into account institutional embeddedness by undertaking multi-level research. We consider multi-level research designs in Chapter 3 and also in connection to cross-cultural research in Chapter 7. Although context can be conceptualized in many ways, one of the most challenging contextual issues for HRM researchers lies in the study of cross-cultural HRM.

The different aspects of social embeddedness are interrelated in ways that highlight the benefits of taking a holistic view of methodological considerations. For example, institutional frameworks shape the temporal and social space inhabited by social actors when governance structures provide incentives for particular types and orders of social interactions. In addition, tenure or career systems (institutional embeddedness) also influence the temporal embeddedness of employee attitudes and behaviors. Employee social networks influence temporal embeddedness by shaping employees' intentions to leave the organization (and vice versa). In this way governance structures can influence temporal and network embeddedness within organizations. Recognition of this complexity provides a rationale for a chapter on multiple methods (Chapter 2), in which we outline their advantages and challenges along with their specific application to the HRM field.

> **Institutional embeddedness: How does it work in practice?**
>
> For Evan's PhD, the organization in which the talent management program operates is an important consideration. Evan may choose to examine the situational variables impacting the program's success (or failure) or the attributes of leaders responsible for its implementation.

4. OVERVIEW OF THE BOOK

Although advanced research methods utilized in other disciplines *can* and should be transferred to the study of HRM issues, the techniques *cannot* and should not be applied in the same way. The research problems examined by HRM researchers are distinct from those in other fields, and thus it is instructive to examine how such advanced research methods can be applied to the study of HR problems. Each chapter outlines the strengths and weaknesses of the different advanced research methods in relation to HRM research and provides examples of how these methods have been applied to the study of HRM problems and could be applied in the future. Although step-by-step instructions on the use of such analytical software are beyond the scope of this book, we provide suggestions for further reading. Readers of this book will gain insights into the advantages and disadvantages of the different advanced quantitative and mixed research methods and, like Evan, be able to make an informed choice as to which research method is most suitable for their research.

In Chapter 2 Hugh Bainbridge and Ilro Lee discuss the definitions, origins, and debates in *mixed methods research*. Using Johnson, Onwuegbuzie, and Turner's (2007, p. 123) definition of mixed methods research: "*Mixed methods research is the type of research in which a researcher or team of researchers combines elements of qualitative and quantitative research approaches (e.g., use of qualitative and quantitative viewpoints, data collection, analysis, inference techniques) for the broad purposes of breadth and depth of understanding and corroboration,*" they outline the advantages and challenges of mixed methods research designs before discussing how mixed methods have been used in the HRM field.

In Chapter 3 Kristiina Mäkelä, Mats Ehrnrooth, Adam Smale, and Jennie Sumelius discuss *multi-actor and multi-level research projects.* This chapter focuses on the design and implementation of such quantitative research projects using interviews, structured questionnaires, and traditional multivariate methods. In the first section of this chapter the benefits of multi-actor and multi-level research are outlined. The question of why a researcher would want to engage in collecting such data, despite the higher workload it involves, is discussed. In the second section the focus is on the design of multi-actor and multi-level research projects, covering issues that need to be considered up front when embarking on such an endeavor, including the criteria that need to be satisfied for a valid multi-level analysis. In the third section the authors focus on the implementation phase of data collection, discussing important practical issues and potential pitfalls. Throughout, they illustrate these points by using an example of a large-scale multi-actor and multi-level data collection project, "Global HRM Challenge."

In Chapter 4 Robert Kaše discusses the advantages and the disadvantages of a social network research design. In this chapter attention is paid to the explanation of social network research and why the social network perspectives and tools can be useful in HR research. In addition, attention is paid to the data gathering process and different types of social network data, such as egocentric (personal), complete affiliation (two-mode), and multiplex network data. The chapter also provides a new classification of HR-relevant social network analytical approaches and discusses its current adoption in HR research. A selection of quantitative network analysis methods (i.e., multiple regression quadratic assignment procedure, exponential random graph model, and network autocorrelation model) is then introduced in more detail to facilitate future adoption in the field.

In Chapter 5 Tim Bednall discusses the advantages and disadvantages of *longitudinal research,* such as the ability to make stronger inferences about causality, the ability to investigate whether interventions are short-lived or longstanding, and the ability to distinguish the effects of context (e.g., temporary stresses) from stable factors (e.g., gender). Furthermore, this chapter provides an overview of methodological considerations, including data collection and matching of participants, retention/attrition of participants, measurement equivalence, and the timing of assessments. The chapter also discusses strategies for collecting data and matching participants, maximizing retention rates, dealing with missing data, and testing measurement equivalence. Two specific longitudinal models (latent growth models, cross-lagged panel models) are examined in depth.

Chapter 6 focuses on *experimental (vignette) research.* The authors of this chapter are Huadong Yang and Julie Dickinson. Vignettes, also called scenarios, are short descriptions of a social situation that contain precise references to what are thought to be the most important factors in the decision-making or judgment-making process of respondents (Alexander & Becker, 1978). In this chapter vignettes are defined and described as a research tool in HRM studies. In contrast to survey studies, vignettes can be used to provide detailed descriptions of real-life situations in order to elicit respondents' responses. In addition, vignettes can be used to manipulate hypothetical factors instead of measuring the full range of variation of focal variables.

In the last research method chapter Yuan Liao, Jian-Min Sun, and David Thomas give a brief introduction to *cross-cultural research* in HRM (Chapter 7). This chapter highlights four main issues embedded in cross-cultural research—the emic versus etic approach, cross-cultural equivalence issues, level of analysis, and causal inferences. It describes each of the four issues, discusses the associated challenges in the context of cross-cultural HRM research, and recommends ways to overcome these difficulties.

Finally, Cai-Hui (Veronica) Lin and Karin Sanders balance the new research methods as discussed in the different chapters (Chapter 8). Some reflections about the added value of the research methods for the HRM field are made.

Chapters 2 to 7 follow a consistent structure. The chapters commence with a short introduction to the advanced research methodology (Section 1). Section 2 outlines the added value of the specific research method in comparison to the more traditional research from both the macro and micro paradigm. In Section 3 the strong and weak points of the specific research methods are discussed. In Section 4 examples are presented and discussed. In Section 5 a discussion and conclusion are presented. Although the different chapters mainly focus on survey and quantitative research methods, the chapters take qualitative research methods into account as well.

REFERENCES

Alexander, C., & Becker, H. (1978). The use of vignettes in survey research. *Public Opinion Quarterly, 42*, 93–104.

Axelrod, R. (1984). *The evolution of cooperation.* New York: Basic Books.

Bainbridge, H. T. J., Sanders, K., Cogin, J., & Lin, C.-H. Multiple HR practices and performance: A review of methodological choices and recommendations for the future. Manuscript submitted for publication.

Becker, B., & Gerhart, B. (1996). The impact of human resource management on organizational performance: Progress and prospects. *Academy of Management Journal, 39*, 779–801.

Becker, B. E., & Huselid, M. A. (1998). High performance work systems and firm performance: A synthesis of research and managerial implications. *Research in Personnel and Human Resources Journal, 16*, 3–101.

Becker, B. E., & Huselid, M. A. (2006). Strategic human resources management: Where do we go from here? *Journal of Management, 32*, 898–925.

Boselie, P., Dietz, G., & Boon, C. (2005). Commonalities and contradictions in research on human resource management and performance. *Human Resource Management Journal, 15*(3), 67–94.

Bowen, D. E., & Ostroff, C. (2004). Understanding HRM–firm performance linkages: The role of the "Strength" of the HRM system. *Academy of Management Review, 29*, 203–221.

Cogin, J. A., & Williamson, I. O. (in press). Standardize or customize: The interactive effects of HRM and environment uncertainty on MNC subsidiary performance. *Human Resource Management.*

Colakoglu, S., Lepak, D., & Hong, Y. (2006). Measuring HRM effectiveness: Considering multiple stakeholders in a global context. *Human Resource Management Review, 16*, 209–218.

Combs, J., Liu, Y., Hall, A., & Ketchen, D. (2006). How much do high-performance work practices matter? A meta-analysis of their effects on organizational performance. *Personnel Psychology, 59*, 501–528.

Cook, T. D., & Campbell, D. T. (1979). *Quasi-experimental design: Design and analysis issues for field settings.* Skokie, IL: Rand McNally.

Gerhart, B. (1999). Human resource management and firm performance: Measurement issues and their effect on causal and policy inferences. In P. M. Wright, L. D. Dyer, J. W. Boudreau, and G. T. Milkovich (Eds.), *Research in personnel and human resources management* (Vol. 25, pp. 31–51). Greenwich, CT: JAI Press.

Gerhart, B. (2008). Review essay: The growth of international human resource management. *International Journal of Human Resource Management, 19,* 1989–1994.

Gerhart, B., Wright, P. M., & McMahan, G. C. (2000). Measurement error in research on the human resources and firm performance relationship: Further evidence and analysis. *Personnel Psychology, 53,* 855–872.

Gerhart, B., Wright, P. M., McMahan, G. C., & Snell, S. A. (2000). Measurement error in research on human resources and firm performance: How much error is there and how does it influence effect size estimates? *Personnel Psychology, 53,* 803–834.

Granovetter, M. S. (1985). Economic action and social structure: The problem of embeddedness. *American Journal of Sociology, 91,* 481–510.

Guest, D. (1997). Human resource management and performance: A review and research agenda. *International Journal of Human Resource Management, 8,* 263–276.

Guest, D., Michie, J., Sheehan, M., & Conway, N. (2003). A UK study of the relationship between human resource management and corporate performance. *British Journal of Industrial Relations, 41,* 291–314.

Hinds, P. J., Carley, K. M., Krackhardt, D., & Wholey, D. (2000). Choosing work group members: Balancing similarity, competence and familiarity. *Organizational Behavior and Human Decision Processes, 81,* 226–251.

Hayton, J. C., Piperopoulos, P., & Welbourne, T. M. (2011). Celebrating 50 years: 50 years of knowledge sharing: Learning from a field moving forward. *Human Resource Management, 50,* 697–714.

Hoobler, J. M., & Brown, J. N. (2004). An analysis of current human resource management publications. *Personnel Review, 33,* 66–676.

Huselid, M. A. (1995). The impact of human resource management practices on turnover, productivity, and corporate financial performance. *Academy of Management Journal, 38,* 635–672.

Huselid, M. A., & Becker, B. E. (1996). Methodological issues in cross-sectional and panel estimates of the human resource–firm performance link. *Industrial Relations, 35,* 400–422.

Huselid, M. A., & Becker, B. E. (2000). Comment on "Measurement error in research on human resources and firm performance: How much error is there and how does it influence effect size estimates?" by Gerhart, Wright, McMahan, and Snell. *Personnel Psychology, 53,* 835–854.

Huselid, M. A., Jackson, S. E., & Schuler, R. S. (1997). Technical and strategic human resource management effectiveness as determinants of firm performance. *Academy of Management Journal, 40,* 171–188.

Johnson, R. B., Onwuegbuzie, A., & Turner, L. (2007). Toward a definition of mixed methods research. *Journal of Mixed Methods Research, 1*(2), 112–133.

Klein, K. J., Dansereau, F., & Hall, R. J. (1994). Levels issues in theory development, data collection and analysis. *Academy of Management Review, 19,* 195–229.

Klein, K. J., & Kozlowski, S. W. J. (2000). *Multilevel theory, research, and methods in organizations: Foundations, extensions, and new directions.* San Francisco: Jossey-Bass.

Lepak, D. P., Liao, H., Chung, Y., & Harden, E. E. (2006). A conceptual review of human resource management systems in strategic human resource management research. In J. Martocchio (Ed.), *Research in personnel and human resource management* (Vol. 25, pp. 217–271). Greenwich, CT: JAI Press.

North, D. C. (1990). *Institutions, institutional change and economic performance.* Cambridge: Cambridge University Press.

Ostroff, C., & Bowen, D. E. (2000). Moving HR to a higher level: HR practices and organizational effectiveness. In K. Klein & S. W. J. Kozlowski (Eds.), *Multilevel theory, research, and methods in organizations: Foundations, extensions, and new directions* (pp. 221-266). San Francisco: Jossey-Bass.

Paauwe, J. (2009). HRM and performance: Achievements, methodological issues and prospects. *Journal of Management Studies, 46,* 129–142.

Raub, W., & Weesie, J. (1990). Reputation and efficiency in social interactions: An example of network effects. *American Journal of Sociology, 96,* 626–654.

Raub, W., & Weesie, J. (2000). The management of durable relations. In J. Weesie & W. Raub (Eds.), *The management of durable relations: Theoretical models and empirical studies of households and organizations* (pp. 1–32). Amsterdam: Thela Thesis.

Rousseau, D. M. (1985). Issues of level in organizational research: Multi-level and cross-level perspectives. In L. L. Cummings & B. Staw (Eds.), *Research in Organizational Behavior,* 1–37.

Sanders, K. (2009). Cooperative behaviors in organizations. In R. L. Morrison & S. L. Wright (Eds.), *Friends and enemies in organizations: A work psychology perspective* (pp. 101–121). Basingstoke: Palgrave Macmillan.

Sanders, K., Bainbridge, H. T. J., Kim, S., Cogin, J., & Lin, C.-H. (2012, August). *Strategic human resource management research: A content analyses.* Paper presented at the 73rd annual meeting of the Academy of Management, Boston, MA.

Sanders, K., & Frenkel, S. (2011). HR-line management relations: Characteristics and effects. *International Journal of Human Resource Management, 22,* 1611–1617.

Wall, T., & Wood, S. (2005). The romance of HRM and business performance, and the case for big science. *Human Relations, 58,* 429–62.

Wright, P. M., & Boswell, W. R. (2002). Desegregating HRM: A review and synthesis of micro and macro human resource management research. *Journal of Management, 28,* 247–276.

Wright, P. M., Gardner, T. M., Moynihan, L. M., & Allen, M. R. (2005). The relationship between HR practices and firm performance: Examining causal order. *Personnel Psychology, 58,* 409–446.

Wright, P. M., Gardner, T. M., Moynihan, L. M., Park, H. J., Gerhart, B., & Delery, J. E. (2001). Measurement error in research on human resources and firm performance: Additional data and suggestions for future research. *Personnel Psychology, 54,* 875–902.

2   Mixed Methods in HRM Research

Hugh T. J. Bainbridge and Ilro Lee

After reading this chapter, we expect you to be able to:

1. Learn more about the origins of mixed methods research and how it is defined;
2. Understand the strengths and challenges associated with mixed methods;
3. Recognize key aspects of the design and implementation of mixed methods;
4. Appreciate how mixed methods are utilized to address HRM issues via representative mixed methods HRM research.

---

1. INTRODUCTION

Social science research is often characterized as involving a dichotomous choice between quantitative and qualitative modes of inquiry. HRM research is no different in this respect. Each approach has particular features that offer distinct benefits to the researcher. Quantitative research draws upon numeric data gathered using structured and validated data collection instruments to test hypotheses about the relationships between variables. Objectivity is prized and the relationships among measures are reported on the basis of statistical significance (Patton, 1996). This allows researchers to test theories and develop generalizable findings that can be applied to other populations. In contrast, qualitative research is more oriented to data collection approaches that provide information about context and allow a deeper understanding of phenomena. Subjectivity is assumed and research is designed to take into account multiple perspectives. Qualitative methods are thus especially conducive to exploratory modes of inquiry, theory development, and rapid refinements to capitalize on unanticipated opportunities for data collection and analysis (Johnson & Christensen, 2004).

Quantitative and qualitative designs are, however, not the only choices available to researchers. Increasingly, interest is growing in a third path—a mixed methods approach. A mixed methods approach is based on the premise that a choice between a quantitative and a qualitative design is unnecessary and assumes that both approaches can be combined to allow researchers to draw upon the respective strengths of each. Consequently, mixed methods pose some interesting questions for the conduct of HRM research. Johnson, Onwuegbuzie, and Turner (2007, p. 128) encapsulate the most central of these in the question, "Do the qualitative dominant, quantitative dominant, and pure mixed methods research need separate sets of designs?" Their affirmative answer suggests that researchers should evaluate, in a structured way, the merits of these different approaches to study design as an initial step in the research process.

Although many good overviews of mixed methods are available, these resources are relatively general in their orientation or developed for specialized (non-HRM) fields of enquiry. Few resources exist specific to the requirements of HRM researchers considering mixed methods designs. Such discipline-specific resources are needed to (i) provide guidance on how to evaluate the suitability of mixed methods in one's research program, and (ii) allow the most to be made of a promising research approach. In this chapter we thus aim to provide an accessible introduction to mixed methods and to contextualize this discussion with reference to HRM issues. In Section 1 we provide an overview of mixed methods by charting its origins and outlining debates over its definition. In Section 2 we discuss the specific advantages of mixed methods and the potential problems to be considered and mitigated. In Section 3 we describe important mixed methods design considerations and outline how these have been addressed by HRM researchers. In Section 4 we conclude by reflecting on the HRM literature and suggesting future directions and opportunities for mixed methods HRM research.

Origins, Definitions, and Debates in Mixed Methods Research

The beginnings of what is now known as mixed methods research is often attributed to the influence of several early researchers in the field. Campbell and Fiske's (1959) work is credited as one of the studies that spurred interest in measuring the same traits with multiple methods and outlined how a convergence of findings from multiple methods enhances confidence that variance in the measured traits is not simply a representation of variance due to the method. Following this, Jick (1979) articulated how qualitative and quantitative methods could be mixed for the purpose of triangulation. Triangulation, as discussed by Denzin (1978), refers to efforts to improve the accuracy and comprehensiveness of research findings by combining multiple data sources and/or methodologies. This work popularized the principle that a better understanding of a phenomenon can be gained from multiple perspectives compared to a single perspective. A few years later, Greene, Caracelli, and Graham (1989) described five categories of mixed methods studies and offered research design considerations for each category. Further developments in the field occurred in the 1990s as Morse (1991) published a system of notation for mixed methods research that is now in widespread use and Steckler, McLeroy, Goodman, Bird, and McCormick (1992) outlined four ways for integrating qualitative and quantitative methods to incorporate research strategy and design considerations. However, while researchers have considered the combination of multiple methods for some time, much of what is now known as mixed methods research can be attributed to developments in the field during the last two decades. During this time there has been a significant growth in research that utilizes a mixed methodology and also in the literature dedicated to the definition and explication of what constitutes mixed methods research (see for examples, Creswell, 1994, 2002; Creswell, Plano Clark, Guttmann, & Hanson, 2003; Greene & Caracelli, 1997; Johnson & Onwuegbuzie, 2004; Leech & Onwuegbuzie, 2009; Maxwell & Loomis, 2003; McMillan & Schumacher, 2001; Morgan, 1998, 2006; Morse, 1991, 2003; Onwuegbuzie & Johnson, 2004; Tashakkori & Teddlie, 1998, 2003b; Teddlie & Tashakkori, 2006).

Within this expanding mixed methods literature, a major area of debate has centered on efforts to develop a formal definition of mixed methods research. Thurston *et al.* (2008) argued that there is no unified definition of mixed methods and the choice of mixing multiple methods within the same paradigm or between paradigms is dependent on the fit between the research question and methods. This position is in opposition to other researchers (e.g., Creswell & Plano Clark, 2007; Tashakkori & Teddlie, 1998) who have attempted to specify general characteristics of mixed methods research. However, in recent years greater consensus has been achieved on the features of mixed methods research and the aspects that distinguish it from other approaches. While the debate is by no means settled, there is increasing agreement that a mixed methodology is one that utilizes at least one quantitative and one qualitative approach (e.g., interviews and a survey). This conceptualization is considered to be the most descriptive of what constitutes mixed methods research as it is consistent with the central premise of combining the distinct advantages offered by quantitative and qualitative approaches (Creswell & Plano Clark, 2007). Drawing upon these debates, in a recent review of the mixed methods literature Johnson *et al.* (2007) surveyed leading authorities in mixed methodology to identify common elements across the working definitions of mixed methods held by these researchers. Based on this research, Johnson *et al.* (2007, p. 123) provide the following definition of mixed methods, which we adopt in this chapter.

Mixed methods research is the type of research in which a researcher or team of researchers combines elements of qualitative and quantitative research approaches (e.g., use of qualitative and quantitative viewpoints, data collection, analysis, inference techniques) for the broad purposes of breadth and depth of understanding and corroboration.

2. MIXED METHODS: STRENGTHS AND CHALLENGES ASSOCIATED WITH THE APPROACH

Over the past decade, several researchers in the HRM field have called for the greater use of mixed methods (e.g., Boselie *et al.*, 2005; Kiessling & Harvey, 2005). Such calls for research are based on the belief that a combination of quantitative and qualitative approaches allows research that is superior to that which is based on a single method. The mixed methods literature (e.g., Creswell & Plano Clark, 2007; Johnson & Onwuegbuzie, 2004) suggests several reasons why this expectation may be well founded.

Strengths of Mixed Methods Research

First, mixed methods promise access to the best of both quantitative and qualitative "worlds" by allowing the researcher (i) to compensate for a weaknesses in one method via the other, and (ii) to draw on the complementary strengths of quantitative and qualitative approaches. For example, quantitative designs facilitate the modeling of complex relationships between variables and allow findings to be more readily generalized beyond the study at the expense of depth of analysis. By contrast, the depth of understanding provided by qualitative research reveals underlying processes governing complex phenomena at the cost of external validity. Combinations of qualitative and quantitative approaches thus enable a researcher to provide both the depth and the breadth of explanation that constitute high-impact research. In so doing, mixed methods are particularly likely to be beneficial in assessing complex research problems that cut across cultural, institutional, regional, and moral dimensions because such problems require both depth and breadth of explanation (Kiessling & Harvey, 2005). Second, mixed methods allow research problems to be addressed that are inaccessible with a single method (Tashakkori & Teddlie, 2003a). For example, a hypothetical research project whose stated aim is to test a theory of the relationship between characteristics of high performance work systems (HPWS) and the performance of Vietnamese organizations is likely to require aspects of both qualitative research to facilitate theory building and quantitative research directed at theory testing. Consequently, combining the two approaches through a mixed methodology would be appropriate in order to allow the researcher to generate theory grounded in data and to provide an initial verification of that theory. Third, mixed methods allow a more comprehensive and insightful description of study phenomena. Stronger inferences can generally be made from data gathered utilizing mixed methods (Teddlie & Tashakkori, 2003) and greater confidence can be held in the results (Johnson & Christensen, 2004). For example, collecting line managers' perceptions of HRM implementation and combining these with a survey of HR managers' and employees' perceptions of the extent to which these HR practices are implemented will provide a more complete understanding of the change process. Fourth, there is evidence that mixed methods are positively associated with measures of research impact. In a recent study Molina-Azorin (2012) found that mixed methods articles receive, on average, a greater number of citations than articles that utilize a single method. This finding held when citations were measured either in terms of average citations per year or their cumulative total. Molina-Azorin (2012) suggests that such differences in citations may arise from differences in the quality of mixed methods research versus research that utilizes a single method.

Strengths of Mixed Methods Designs in the Context of HRM Research: The Role of Social Embeddedness

Mixed methods may be especially helpful in addressing the types of research problems considered in the HRM field. Chapter 1 noted the issue of social embeddedness that is faced by HRM researchers (Granovetter, 1985; Raub & Weesie, 1990, 2000; Sanders, 2009). The complex and intertwined experience of individuals, teams, and organizations requires research designs that are capable of addressing issues of temporal, network, and institutional embeddedness as they relate to HRM research. In this respect, mixed methods are particularly helpful in assisting researchers' efforts to deal with issues of temporal embeddedness, as qualitative research can provide an understanding of dynamic processes while quantitative approaches can model change over time. For example, a researcher might undertake in-depth interviews with key stakeholders to develop an understanding of key environmental characteristics and subsequently conduct a longitudinal survey in which these characteristics are tracked as they change over time. Such investigations are particularly relevant in HRM research, where much recent attention has focused on issues of causality.

Mixed methods also provide an especially powerful way of examining both formal and informal networks between entities (network embeddedness). For example, characteristics of the formal relationship between the HR function and line managers might be studied using a mixed methodology that draws upon insights from survey and participant observation to understand how the communication style of HR specialists influences line manager perceptions of training quality. Similarly, the type and source of advice on employee management issues preferred by line managers might be examined via a social network design to identify communication patterns and frequencies, complemented by in-depth interviews with line managers to explore the content of those communications and the reasons why particular individuals were consulted.

Furthermore, mixed methods can assist researchers to understand how institutional characteristics (as they manifest in HRM practices) influence the actions of individuals and teams. Institutional embeddedness refers to the rules of an organization and the governance structures that influence attitude formation, perceptions, and behaviors of organizational actors.

Mixed methods are particularly useful in the context of multi-level designs where respondent characteristics influence the feasibility of research designs. For example, a study of the process by which corporate strategy is connected to the implementation of HRM practices might examine high-level strategy formation via in-depth interviews with difficult to access executives and senior HR managers. This could be complemented by a quantitative content analysis of email correspondence between HR and line managers.

Challenges Associated with the Utilization of Mixed Methods

The preceding discussion suggests a compelling case for the adoption of mixed methods, however HRM research based upon a mixed methodology remains surprisingly rare. Clark, Grant, and Heijtjes (2000) reviewed articles in the field of comparative and global HRM between 1977 and 1997 in 29 management journals and found only 2% utilized mixed methods. More recently, Sanders *et al.* (2012) found a similar result when reviewing research on the relationship between multiple HRM practices and performance between 1996 and 2010. Only 5% of the reviewed studies utilized mixed methods, and there was no evidence of a change in the proportion of research utilizing mixed methods over time (Sanders *et al.*, 2012).

So why are mixed methods so infrequently utilized? There are several issues that might give researchers pause. First, combining qualitative and quantitative approaches can pose significant challenges, as the combination of approaches is almost invariably a more complex undertaking than research based on a single approach. This complexity manifests in the form of increased demands on the researcher in terms of requirements for broader expertise in research methodology, greater proficiency in managing large and complex research projects, and enhanced skills in the integration of findings from multiple methods. Furthermore, because mixed methods generally involve a greater breadth of data collection and analysis, such designs are also likely to require a greater investment of time and resources to undertake. Another consideration is the expected return on this investment of time and effort. One common response to these issues of complexity and resourcing is to form teams with complementary expertise to share the workload so that a single individual is not required to be proficient in each of the research methods. However, this is not without its own problems, as larger teams bring with them their own issues in the forms of the requirement for greater communication, and the management of competing priorities, workflows, and potential interpersonal conflict. Another challenge for researchers is the "allure" of mixed methods that suggests that such research will enjoy an easier route to publication in competitive outlets. But mixed methods may not always be necessary to address one's research question. In such cases, while the utilization of mixed methods may send a signal about the researcher's commitment to the research process, it may do little to enhance the quality of the research or its publication prospects. This is especially likely if either the quantitative or qualitative component is poorly matched to the research question. Thus, clarity over the research question and an understanding of its minimum methodological requirements are useful to keep in mind before prematurely committing to a research design that is "over engineered" for its purpose.

3. DESIGNING AND IMPLEMENTING MIXED METHODS RESEARCH

A mixed methods approach benefits from a consideration of the research question at the outset and an understanding of how this question is connected to design choices. For example, should one undertake a qualitative study prior to the quantitative study or a quantitative study prior to the qualitative study? Or should the researcher aspire to undertake both studies simultaneously in the hope that the understandings flowing from each study will inform the other? In such matters, a clear identification and description of the available design choices are central to well-planned research.

Interestingly, there remains some ambiguity about the range of and nature of these mixed methods design considerations. Recently Leech and Onwuegbuzie (2009, p. 266) dwelt on this issue and noted that in the influential 1998 edition of the *Handbook of Mixed Methods in Social and Behavioral Research* "35 mixed methods research designs are presented." Concerns over this proliferation of research frameworks is also echoed by Johnson *et al.* (2007, p. 128), who observe that one of the major challenges is whether "the field [will] be able to develop a typology of mixed methods designs that can be broadly agreed upon?" To illustrate, the past 20 years have seen a proliferation of typologies advanced with the aim of organizing the mixed methods literature (see for example, Creswell, 1994, 2002; Creswell *et al.*, 2003; Greene & Caracelli, 1997; Greene, Caracelli, & Graham, 1989; Johnson & Onwuegbuzie, 2004; Leech & Onwuegbuzie, 2009; Maxwell & Loomis, 2003; McMillan & Schumacher, 2001; Morgan, 1998, 2006; Morse 1991, 2003; Onwuegbuzie & Johnson, 2004; Patton, 1990; Tashakkori & Teddlie, 1998, 2003b; Teddlie & Tashakkori, 2006). Elements of much of this body of research are, however, in broad alignment with the themes outlined in the influential contribution of Tashakkori and Teddlie (1998). They identified four general approaches to mixed methods research that are distinguished by the timing and weighting given to each method. This description has guided much subsequent research in the field (e.g., Bryman & Bell, 2003; Creswell & Plano Clark, 2007; Greene *et al.*, 1989; Molina-Azorin, 2012). Recently Molina-Azorin (2012) drew upon this research to provide a description of mixed methods research in terms of aspects of purpose, priority, implementation, and design. We draw upon this framework to discuss each of these elements and provide examples of each in connection to the HRM literature (Table 2.1).

Table 2.1 Purpose, priority, implementation, and design in HRM mixed methods research

Design consideration	Decision points	Example of decision in the HRM literature	Other HRM research examples
1. Purpose	Development	*Phase 1 Interviews with senior managers, HR managers, and employees in HR departments. Purpose—To explore intended HR practices and use it to develop a questionnaire* (Khilji & Wang, 2006, p. 1176)	Bartel (2004)
	Complementarity	*. . . we report relationships between data gathered in managerial interviews in 22 companies (1996) and data from innovation surveys of the same companies in 1995 and 1997* (Shipton et al., 2006, p. 9).	Khilji and Wang (2006)
	Expansion	*It was hoped that by studying such an organization in some depth, it would be possible to advance both our empirical knowledge of HR practices and our theoretical understanding of how HRM and performance are linked* (Truss, 2001, p. 1128).	Tsai (2006)
	Triangulation	*Following analysis of the survey results, letters were sent again to all 161 hospices, containing a brief summary of the findings and an invitation to attend a half-day workshop to discuss the findings* (Clarke, 2006, p. 194).	
2. Priority	Different status	e.g., Quantitative dominant. *There were three stages to the research, with the objective of the first stage to collect information that would inform the development of a questionnaire. The second stage of the research involved piloting the questionnaire to identify any issues or problems that might arise when administering the questionnaire. In stage 3, a revised version of this questionnaire was administered to measure the frontline employees' perceptions of HRM practices in their organizations, their level of organizational commitment and their perception of the service-orientated behaviour of frontline employees in their organization* (Browning, 2006, p. 1324).	Clarke (2006); Hatch and Dyer (2004)

		e.g., Qualitative dominant. *Given the exploratory nature of the research, we adopted a mixed-method approach (comprising in-depth interviews of managers, self-completing questionnaires, and secondary sources). Our direct sources of information were the HR managers of Indian BPOs who agreed to be interviewed* (Budhwar et al., 2006, p. 345).	Khilji and Wang (2006)
	Equal status	*Interviews and the survey method were the two main approaches used for collecting data in the study* (Tsai, 2006, p. 1517).	Tessema & Soeters (2006)
3. Implementation	Simultaneous	*In 1994, 400 questionnaires were distributed to randomly selected employees at middle manager level and below, representing around 20 per cent of the total population; 215 were completed, a response rate of 56 per cent. A two-hour focus group was held with senior members of the HR department, and 36 interviews were carried out with senior managers, HR department members, line managers and non-managerial staff. In 1996, 400 questionnaires were issued and 209 returned, a response rate of 52 per cent. A four-hour focus group was held with the HR staff, and 20 interviews carried out within the organization* (Truss, 2001, p. 1128).	Budhwar et al. (2006)
	Sequential	*Phase 1 Interviews with senior managers, HR managers and employees in HR departments. Purpose—To explore intended HR practices and use it to develop a questionnaire. Phase 2 Interviews with managers and non-managers from cross-sections of areas. Purpose—To explore implemented HR practices. Phase 3 Questionnaire survey. Purpose—To explore HR satisfaction. Phase 4 Documents review (company/magazine reports and financial statements). Purpose—To explore the organizational performance* (Khilji & Wang, 2006, p. 1176).	Clarke (2006)

(Continued)

Table 2.1 (Continued)

Design consideration	Decision points	Example of decision in the HRM literature	Other HRM research examples
4. Design	Equal status/ Simultaneous	*Firstly, we have seen the value of carrying out an analysis using multiple methods and multiple respondents. Had we merely relied on questionnaire data obtained from a single informant (the HR director, as in other studies) and carried out a quantitative analysis linking performance with human resource processes, we would have concluded that this organization was an example of an organization employing 'High Performance Work Practices' to good effect. However, employing a contextualized, case-study method has enabled us to see below the surface and tap into the reality experienced by employees, which often contrasts sharply with the company rhetoric* (Truss, 2001, p. 1128)	
	Equal status/ Sequential	*Following analysis of the survey results, letters were sent again to all 161 hospices, containing a brief summary of the findings and an invitation to attend a half-day workshop to discuss the findings. Two workshops took place approximately 12 and 14 months after survey data was collected* (Clarke, 2006, p. 194).	
	Different status/ Simultaneous	*During the interviews, the managers provided qualitative data on the firm's HRM practices and elaborated on their experiences with these practices. Apart from the qualitative information, the participants also completed a questionnaire related to a number of HR practices and policies* (Budhwar et al., 2006, p. 345)	
	Different status/ Sequential	*Interviews with managers and employees were used to guide the specification of the branch-level production function* (Bartel, 2004, p. 201).	

Purpose

Mixed methods research is characterized by four general purposes: (i) *development,* (ii) *complementarity,* (iii) *expansion,* and (iv) *triangulation* (Greene *et al.*, 1989). Mixed methods research with a *development* purpose uses the results of one method to inform the construction of the subsequent study. Such research is more likely to state its purpose as focusing on developing concepts or measures for use in another component of the research. Thus, the first study should lead to a second study that is better able to answer the problems that it is designed to assess. Often this would involve a qualitative component that considers how a concept might be operationalized through interviews with well-informed individuals. This qualitative research then supports the development of quantitative measures for use in a later survey. For example, Bartel (2004) investigated the impact of a HPWS on retail banking performance using a mixed methods approach. Initial site visits and interviews with branch managers and nonmanagerial employees revealed how feedback, recognition of good work, and incentives are used to manage employee performance by describing individual managerial differences in implementation of the practices. As the interviews identified individual managerial variance, the author formulated an equation to estimate the sales with managerial variance as a fixed effect that allowed her to interpret the coefficients of HRM variables as estimates of the HRM effect on performance.

Mixed methods with a *complementarity* purpose clarify, enhance, or illustrate the results from one method with the findings from another. Studies should thus be combined or "mixed" so that the strengths of one compensate for the weaknesses of the other (Johnson & Turner, 2003). For example, a researcher might collect archival data to study turnover intentions and find that turnover was concentrated in one specific division of the firm. Subsequent exit interviews conducted with employees who had resigned from the firm might clarify why they had left.

Expansion oriented mixed methods research provides an improved, more rounded understanding by utilizing different methods that have unique strengths in revealing different characteristics of a phenomenon. For example, a researcher might survey HR managers about their implementation plan for a new set of HRM practices before making field observations of the process by which the practices were implemented.

A *triangulation* purpose refers to studies that use different methods to examine the same phenomenon to assess the degree of convergence in the findings and corroborate the results of one study through the findings of another. Triangulation can include multiple collections of the similar data from different respondents. For example, a triangulated study of a HPWS might draw upon interviews with HR managers, line managers, and employees. Triangulation also occurs when the perspectives of different researchers are incorporated into a study. For example, an organizational behavior researcher and a strategy researcher might each observe the implementation of a HPWS in an organization. Where their interpretations of events vary, these different perspectives provide breadth and richness to the study. Where they converge, confidence in the conclusions is enhanced. In the HRM literature, Truss (2001) examined the complexities of HRM and firm-level performance using mixed methods. Unlike a typical HRM study investigating the relationship between HRM practices and firm performance, her research questions are presented to examine what HRM practices and policies are implemented in a financially successful company and how this occurs. To have a more complete understanding of high performance work practices adaptation by successful organizations, she collected data from employees of all levels of a company by conducting interviews and focus groups as well as surveys. The quantitative component allowed her to measure the perception of the formal HRM environment and establish its relationship with the financial outcomes. The qualitative component provided insights into the "reality" of the work experience of the employees, which was found to be inconsistent with the formal "rhetoric" of the company's HRM policies. Combining the two methods provided a unique opportunity to demonstrate the complex relationship between HRM practices and firm performance.

Priority

Mixed methods research is also characterized in terms of the priority that is attached to different components of the investigation. Mixed methods research often involves giving a *different status* or weight to one component of the research rather than treating each component as having *equal status* (Molina-Azorin, 2012). The decision of which method is going to take precedence is commonly based on practical considerations. For instance, conducting research that gives equal weight to qualitative and quantitative methods can pose challenges in an environment where time and resources are limited. Devoting more resources to one method while allocating less to the secondary method can aid researchers such as PhD candidates to manage such a scenario. A common example of this is the tendency for research that has a strong emphasis on a quantitative survey complemented by supporting interviews. These supporting interviews are conducted to assist with the development of survey measures, to refine the survey sample, or to explain the "main" survey findings at the project conclusion. The extent of familiarity with either method can also influence the weighting of each component. Researchers tend to lean toward the method that they know better, but including a collaborator who has dissimilar methodological experience to oneself can open up alternative possibilities for prioritization across components of the research.

Implementation

Mixed methods research can be implemented in a sequential or a simultaneous approach. A tendency toward sequential implementation choices may be a reflection of research in which the quantitative component is prioritized and supported by the collection of preliminary or follow-up qualitative data. For example, Innocenti, Pilati, and Peluso (2011) drew upon two data sources—first, a questionnaire to measure the employees' trust in management, and second, follow-up telephone interviews with HR managers of the participating firms to validate the measures and acquire further information on the implemented HRM policies and practices. The qualitative interview data enhanced the validity of the quantitative measures, but did not directly influence the conclusions drawn from the overall study.

Design

The considerations of priority and implementation that have been introduced in the two previous sections are generally considered together as the main aspects that allow for a characterization of different mixed methods designs (Creswell, 1994; Lopez-Fernandez & Molina-Azorin, 2011; Morgan, 1998; Morse, 1991; Tashakkori & Teddlie, 1998). In 1991, Janice Morse used a system of notation to represent the different mixed methods designs. In this now widely utilized system, the main or dominant method appears in capital letters (QUAN, QUAL), while the complementary method is in lowercase (quan, qual). The symbol "+" indicates studies that are conducted simultaneously, and " →" indicates where studies are conducted sequentially. Using this system, priority and implementation can be combined to specify nine distinct mixed methods designs.

- Equal status/simultaneous implementation: (1) QUAL + QUAN
- Equal status/sequential implementation: (2) QUAL → QUAN; (3) QUAN → QUAL
- Different status/simultaneous implementation: (4) QUAL + quan; (5) QUAN + qual
- Different status/sequential implementation: (6) qual → QUAN; (7) QUAL → quan; (8) quan → QUAL; (9) QUAN → qual

In the HRM field several examples of mixed methods research have recently been published that follow these designs. For example, Truss (2001) followed an *equal status/simultaneous implementation* design (i.e., [1] QUAL + QUAN). Clarke's (2006) research into HRM policies and workplace learning in healthcare followed an *equal status/sequential implementation* design (i.e., [3] QUAN → QUAL). The utilization of a *different status/simultaneous implementation* design (i.e., [4] QUAL + quan) is evident in the research of Budhwar *et al.* (2006), who utilized a mixed methods approach involving both in-depth interviews and a short 23-item question-naire to analyze the nature of HRM systems in business process outsourcing organizations operating in India. An example of a *different status/sequential implementation* design is represented by the research of Bartel (2004), who conducted an initial set of interviews before conducting an analysis of employee attitude survey data (i.e., [6] qual → QUAN). These initial interviews were justified by Bartel (2004, p. 188) based on prior methodological literature that stated the importance of establishing "(1) the appropriate measure of organizational performance given the context of the study." Bartel's (2004) interviews with managers at branches and at headquarters indicated that branches were evaluated based on sales data (primarily deposits and loans) and helped to ensure that the subsequent quantitative component of the research was properly specified.

Undertaking a mixed methods research: How does it work in practice?

Ingrid is a PhD candidate interested in HPWS in healthcare organizations. Her research question is, How is HPWS applied to healthcare workers and to what extent does an effective HPWS influence healthcare outcomes? When considering this research question, Ingrid notes the following points that are pertinent to her evolving research design.

- A review of prior research in healthcare management reveals that there has been limited examination of: (i) HPWS within healthcare organizations, (ii) HPWS in relation to healthcare professionals, and (iii) the relationship between HPWS and healthcare outcomes.
- From initial conversations with industry experts, it appears that doctors and nurses operate under separate HRM systems with distinct policies. This insight suggests that the analysis should be organized on the basis of professions rather than hierarchically.
- Quantitative measures of the key study concepts may have to be operationalized for the healthcare context as well as for the type of profession (i.e., doctors vs. nurses).
- To establish the causal relationship between HPWS and healthcare outcomes, data needs to be collected over time.

Given these considerations, Ingrid considers a *different status* two-study *sequential* approach in which a *development purpose* qualitative study (study 1) is followed by a *complementarity purpose* quantitative study (study 2). Given her time and resource constraints, she decides to utilize a case study based on a large hospital.

In study 1 she interviews two HR managers from the hospital to understand how a HPWS is applied. During these initial interviews she explores how different HR practices are implemented for doctors and nurses. Also, she learns that patient satisfaction and readmission ratings are used to measure performance of the overall hospital and each unit within the hospital. She then conducts 10 interviews with doctors and 10 interviews with nurses to investigate how they perceive the HPWS is being applied within their units. The interviews reveal that nurses' and doctors' daily activities are highly interdependent within each unit. Thus, she concludes that the unit level is the appropriate level of analysis. Finally, Ingrid uses the interview transcripts to develop scales that measure the extent to which characteristics of a HPWS are present in each hospital unit.

In study 2 Ingrid proposes a two-wave longitudinal design with a 12-month time interval in which she collects multi-actor survey data from 100 doctors and 100 nurses. From the research design perspective, study 2 is the dominant part of the overall study. The longitudinal component of her research utilizes quantitative measures of the study variables she developed from the interviews to investigate how HPWS influences doctors' and nurses' performance.

4. CONCLUSIONS

Several reviews of the HRM literature suggest a strong disposition toward quantitative research designs. For example, Boselie *et al.* (2005) found that a majority of the 104 HRM studies they reviewed utilized quantitative methods and only a small number could be categorized as either qualitative (4 studies) or as combining both quantitative and qualitative methods (2 studies). Teagarden *et al.* (1995) also identified that quantitative techniques are the norm in international HRM research, and Hayton, Piperopoulos, and Welbourne (2011) reported that quantitative studies significantly outnumbered the qualitative studies in the journal *Human Resource Management* between 2000 and 2010.

Decisions about research designs should be based on their fitness for addressing the research questions (Morse, 2003; Thurston, Cove, & Meadows, 2008). Thus, while quantitative approaches have important strengths, the extent of the imbalance identified by Boselie *et al.* (2005) suggests that HRM researchers may be overemphasizing quantitative modes of inquiry. Encouraging a more critical assessment of whether this is always the best approach for addressing a research problem may be appropriate. This critical evaluation can be assisted by a clear articulation of the merits of a mixed methods approach for the HRM field. To that end, we have sought in this chapter to define mixed methods, to identify major advantages and drawbacks, to discuss key design considerations, and to illuminate these with examples from HRM mixed methods research. We hope that the opportunities that are made apparent by such comparisons provide the impetus for future HRM researchers to address some of those gaps. In concluding this chapter we reflect on two prominent features of HRM mixed methods research. Our review of the HRM mixed methods literature indicates a strong weighting toward research with a *developmental purpose*. Development is an important consideration for many researchers, as it provides the foundation for the creation of quantitative measures of concepts. However, the emphasis on development oriented mixed methods indicates that there are opportunities for research that, for example, utilizes quantitative and qualitative approaches to provide complementary perspectives on phenomena, to expand understanding, and to triangulate the research. Such research would provide additional confidence about study relationships and address common method variance concerns. We also note an emphasis on different status, quantitative dominant designs in HRM research. Future research that utilizes qualitative dominant or equal status approaches to prioritization would allow researchers to make important contributions to the HRM field.

REFERENCES

Bartel, A. P. (2004). Human resource management and organizational performance: Evidence from retail banking. *Industrial and Labor Relations Review, 57,* 181–203.

Boselie, P., Dietz, G., & Boon, C. (2005). Commonalities and contradictions in HRM and performance research. *Human Resource Management Journal, 15,* 67–94.

Browning, V. (2006). The relationship between HRM practices and service behaviour in South African service organizations. *The International Journal of Human Resource Management, 17,* 1321–1338.

Bryman, A., & Bell, E. (2003). *Business research methods.* Oxford, UK: Oxford University Press.

Budhwar, P. S., Luthar, H. K., & Bhatnagar, J. (2006). The dynamics of HRM systems in Indian BPO firms. *Journal of Labor Research, 27,* 339–360.

Campbell, D. T., & Fiske, D. W. (1959). Convergent and discriminant validation by the multitrait-multimethod matrix. *Psychological Bulletin, 56,* 81–105.

Clark, T., Grant, D., & Heijtjes, M. (2000). Researching comparative and international human resource management. *International Studies of Management and Organization, 29,* 6–23.

Clarke, N. (2006). Why HR policies fail to support workplace learning: the complexities of policy implementation in healthcare. *The International Journal of Human Resource Management, 17,* 190–206.

Creswell, J. W. (1994). *Research design: Qualitative and quantitative approaches.* Thousand Oaks, CA: Sage.

Creswell, J. W. (2002). *Educational research: Planning, conducting, and evaluating quantitative and qualitative research.* Upper Saddle River, NJ: Pearson.

Creswell, J. W., & Plano Clark, V. L. (2007). *Designing and conducting mixed methods research.* Thousand Oaks, CA: Sage.

Creswell, J. W., Plano Clark, V. L., Guttmann, M. L., & Hanson, E. E. (2003). Advanced mixed methods research design. In A. Tashakkori & C. Teddlie (Eds.), *Handbook of mixed methods in social and behavioral research* (pp. 209–240). Thousand Oaks, CA: Sage.

Denzin, N. (1978). Sociological methods: Critical reflections and the logic of naturalistic inquiry. In N. Denzin (Ed.), *Sociological methods: A source book* (pp. 1–29). New York: McGraw-Hill.

Granovetter, M. S. (1985). Economic action and social structure: The problem of embeddedness. *American Journal of Sociology, 91,* 481–510.

Greene, J. C., & Caracelli, V. J. (1997). *Advances in mixed-method evaluation: The challenges and benefits of integrating diverse paradigms.* San Francisco, CA: Jossey-Bass.

Greene, J. C., Caracelli, V. J., & Graham, W. F. (1989). Toward a conceptual framework for mixed-method evaluation designs. *Educational Evaluation and Policy Analysis, 11,* 255–274.

Hatch, N. W., & Dyer, J. H. (2004). Human capital and learning as a source of sustainable competitive advantage. *Strategic Management Journal, 25,* 1155–1178.

Hayton, J. C., Piperopoulos, P., & Welbourne, T. M. (2011). Celebrating 50 years: 50 years of knowledge sharing: Learning from a field moving forward. *Human Resource Management, 50,* 697–714.

Innocenti, L., Pilati, M., & Peluso, A. M. (2011). Trust as moderator in the relationship between HRM practices and employee attitudes. *Human Resource Management Journal, 21,* 303–317.

Jick, T. D. (1979). Mixing qualitative and quantitative methods: Triangulation in action. *Administrative Science Quarterly, 24,* 602–611.

Johnson, R. B., & Christensen, L. (2004). *Educational research: Quantitative, qualitative and mixed approaches* (2nd ed.). Boston, MA: Pearson.

Johnson, R. B., & Onwuegbuzie, A. J. (2004). Mixed methods research: A research paradigm whose time has come. *Educational Researcher, 33*(7), 14–26.

Johnson, R. B., Onwuegbuzie, A. J., & Turner, L. A. (2007). Toward a definition of mixed methods research. *Journal of Mixed Methods Research, 1*(2), 112–133.

Johnson, R. B., & Turner, L. A. (2003). Data collection strategies in mixed methods research. In A. Tashakkori, & C. Teddlie (Eds.), *Handbook of mixed methods in social and behavioral research* (pp. 297–319). Thousand Oaks, CA: Sage.

Khilji, S. E., & Wang, X. (2006). 'Intended' and 'implemented' HRM: The missing linchpin in strategic human resource management research. *The International Journal of Human Resource Management, 17,* 1171–1189.

Kiessling, T., & Harvey, M. (2005). Strategic global human resource management research in the twenty-first century: An endorsement of the mixed-method research methodology. *International Journal of Human Resource Management, 16,* 22–45.

Leech, N. L., & Onwuegbuzie, A. J. (2009). A typology of mixed methods research designs. *Quantity & Quality, 43,* 265–275.

Lopez-Fernandez, O., & Molina-Azorin, J. F. (2011). The use of mixed methods research in the field of behavioral sciences. *Quality & Quantity, 45,* 1459–1472.

Maxwell, J. A., & Loomis, D. M. (2003). Mixed methods design: an alternative approach. In A. Tashakkori & C. Teddlie (Eds.), *Handbook of mixed methods in social and behavioral research* (pp. 241–272). Thousand Oaks, CA: Sage.

McMillan, J. H., & Schumacher, S. (2001). *Research in education: A conceptual introduction* (5th ed.). New York, NY: Longman.

Molina-Azorin, J. F. (2012). Mixed methods research in strategic management: Impact and applications. *Organizational Research Methods, 15,* 33–56

Morgan, D. L. (1998). Practical strategies for combining qualitative and quantitative methods: Applications to health research. *Qualitative Health Research, 3,* 362–376.

Morgan, D. L. (2006). Paradigms lost and pragmatism regained: Methodological implications of combining qualitative and quantitative methods. *Journal of Mixed Methods Research, 1,* 48–76.

Morse, J. M. (1991). Approaches to qualitative-quantitative methodological triangulation. *Nursing Research, 40,* 120–123.

Morse, J. M. (2003). Principles of mixed methods and multimethod research design. In A. Tashakkori & C. Teddlie (Eds.), *Handbook of mixed methods in social and behavioral research* (pp. 189–208). Thousand Oaks, CA: Sage.

Onwuegbuzie, A. J. (2003). Expanding the framework of internal and external validity in quantitative research. *Research in the Schools, 10,* 71–90.

Onwuegbuzie, A. J., & Johnson, R. B. (2004). Mixed method and mixed model research. In R. B. Johnson & L. B. Christensen (Eds.), *Educational research: Quantitative, qualitative, and mixed approaches* (pp. 408–431). Needham Heights, MA: Allyn and Bacon.

Onwuegbuzie, A. J., & Johnson, R. B. (2006). The validity issue in mixed research. *Research in the Schools, 13,* 48–63.

Onwuegbuzie, A. J., & Leech, N. L. (2007). Validity and qualitative research: An oxymoron? *Quality & Quantity: International Journal of Methodology, 41,* 233–249.

Patton, M. Q. (1990). *Qualitative evaluation and research methods: A systematic approach.* Newbury Park, CA: Sage.

Patton, M. Q. (1996). *Utilization-focused evaluation: The new century text* (4th ed.). Newbury Park, CA: Sage.

Punch, K. F. (2005). *Introduction to social research: Quantitative and qualitative approaches* (2nd ed.). Thousand Oaks, CA: Sage.

Raub, W., & Weesie, J. (1990). Reputation and efficiency in social interactions: An example of network effects. *American Journal of Sociology, 96,* 626–654.

Raub, W., & Weesie, J. (2000). The management of durable relations. In J. Weesie & W. Raub (Eds.), *The management of durable relations: Theoretical models and empirical studies of households and organizations* (pp. 1–32). Amsterdam: Thela Thesis.

Sanders, K. (2009). Cooperative behaviors in organizations. In R. Morrison & S. Wright, *Friends and enemies in organizations: A work psychology perspective* (pp. 101–121). Basingstoke: Palgrave Macmillan.

Sanders, K., Bainbridge, H. T. J., Kim, S., Cogin, J., & Lin, C.-H. (2012, August). *Strategic human resource management research: A content analysis.* Paper presented at the 73rd annual meeting of the Academy of Management, Boston, MA.

Shipton, H., West, M. A., Dawson, J., Birdi, K., & Patterson, M. (2006). HRM as a predictor of innovation. *Human Resource Management Journal, 16,* 3–27.

Steckler, A., McLeroy, K. R., Goodman, R. M., Bird, S. T., & McCormick, L. (1992). Toward integrating qualitative and quantitative methods: An introduction. *Health Education Quarterly, 19,* 1–8.

Tashakkori, A., & Teddlie, C. (1998). *Mixed methodology: Combining qualitative and quantitative approaches.* Thousand Oaks, CA: Sage.

Tashakkori, A., & Teddlie, C. (Eds.). (2003a). *Handbook of mixed methods in social and behavioral research.* Thousand Oaks, CA: Sage.

Tashakkori, A., & Teddlie, C. (2003b). The past and future of mixed methods research: From data triangulation to mixed model designs. In A. Tashakkori & C. Teddlie (Eds.), *Handbook of mixed methods in social and behavioral research* (pp. 671–701). Thousand Oaks, CA: Sage.

Teagarden, M. B., Glinow, M. A., Bowen, D. E., Frayne, C. A., Nason, S., Huo, Y. P., Milliman, J., Arias, M. A., Butler, M. C., Geringer, J. M., Kim, N. K., Scullion, H., Lowe, K. B., & Drost, E. A. (1995). Towards building a theory of competitive management research methodology: An idiographic case study of the best international human resources management projects. *Academy of Management Journal, 38,* 1261–1287.

Teddlie, C., & Tashakkori, A. (2003). Major issues and controversies in the use of mixed methods in the social and behavioral sciences. In A. Tashakkori & C. Teddlie (Eds.), *Handbook of mixed methods in social and behavioral research* (pp. 3–50). Thousand Oaks, CA: Sage.

Teddlie, C., & Tashakkori, A. (2006). A general typology of research designs featuring mixed methods. *Research in the Schools, 13*, 12–28.

Tessema, M. T., & Soeters, J. L. (2006). Challenges and prospects of HRM in developing countries: Testing the HRM–performance link in the Eritrean civil service. *The International Journal of Human Resource Management, 17*, 86–105.

Thurston, W. E., Cove, L., & Meadows, L. M. (2008). Methodological congruence in complex and collaborative mixed method studies. *International Journal of Multiple Research Approaches, 2*, 2–14.

Truss, C. (2001). Complexities and controversies in linking HRM with organizational outcomes. *Journal of Management Studies, 38*, 1121–1149.

Tsai, C-J. (2006). High performance work systems and organizational performance: An empirical study of Taiwan's semiconductor design firms. *The International Journal of Human Resource Management, 17*, 1512–1530.

3 Multi-Level and Multi-Actor Research

Kristiina Mäkelä, Mats Ehrnrooth,
Adam Smale, and Jennie Sumelius

After reading this chapter, we expect you to be able to:

1. Understand the added value of multi-level and multi-actor research as compared to more traditional (multivariate) methods: Why would a researcher want to engage in collecting such data, despite the greater complexity and workload it involves, and what are the relative strengths and weaknesses of the approach?
2. Get an overview of the design and implementation stage of multi-level and multi-actor research, including key issues that need to be considered up front as well as the strengths and weaknesses of the different choices. In particular, you will learn about considerations related to the corner-stones of multi-level research: the level of theory (where the focal unit of analysis resides), the level of measurement (from which level the data are obtained, or the "boxes"), and the level of analysis (from which level of data the influences are drawn, or the "arrows") (Mathieu & Chen, 2011);
3. Gain practical understanding of the above through firsthand experiences from a large-scale multi-level and multi-actor research project "Global HRM Challenge," carried out by the authors.

---

1. INTRODUCTION

Multi-level and multi-actor research has become increasingly sought after in management studies. This type of research involves the building of research models that cross multiple levels of analysis and the collection of data from multiple organizational actors. One significant factor contributing to the demand of such research is the growing acknowledgement that the question of how to integrate micro and macro research methods and theories is one of the most critical challenges currently facing management studies (Aguinis,

Boyd, Pierce, & Short, 2011). Huselid & Becker (2011) argue that the same is true of research in strategic HRM.

In line with the arguments for *social embeddedness* outlined in Chapter 1 of this edited volume, organizations increasingly rely on collaboration between different domains, processes, and groups of people and organizational outcomes typically require input from different parts and levels of the organization (Foss, 2007; Felin, Foss, Heimericks, & Marsden, 2012). Such complex issues are difficult to examine in a comprehensive, rigorous way without drawing on influences from different levels of analysis and rich data that considers multiple sources of antecedents and determinants (Bono & McNamara, 2011). Indeed, many HRM-related phenomena of interest are influenced by heterogeneous perceptual and attitudinal factors, which can vary significantly depending on who you ask (Denrell, Arvidsson, & Zander, 2004; Felin *et al.,* 2012; Mäkelä, Björkman, Ehnrooth, Smale, & Sumelius, 2013; Wright & Nishii, 2007).

Various qualitative methods have been developed that enable researchers to conduct a more holistic analysis and bring in contextual richness. In quantitative survey-type research, the use of multi-level and multi-actor data has traditionally been less common. However, in line with several recent calls for moving away from single-level, single-respondent, and cross-sectional designs (e.g., Peterson, Arregle, & Martin, 2012; Bono & McNamara, 2011; Chang, van Witteloostuijn, & Eden, 2010), the situation has begun to change. Interest toward multi-level research is growing rapidly in both HRM and in management research more generally (see Mathieu & Chen, 2011 for a detailed review), as is evidenced by the publication of several special issues and guest editorials in leading journals (e.g., Aguinis, Boyd, Pierce, & Short, 2011; Hitt, Beamish, Jackson, & Mathieu, 2007; Klein, Tosi, & Cannella, 1999; Peterson, Arregle, & Martin, 2012). Given that most of today's managerial challenges are multi-level and multi-actor by nature, this approach is also being purported to possess heightened practical relevance.

Advancements in multi-level research necessitate simultaneous developments in theory, measurement, design, and analysis (Mathieu & Chen, 2011). The aim of this chapter is to discuss key issues relating to the design and implementation of multi-level quantitative research (using structured questionnaires and traditional multivariate methods). While there are numerous excellent sources focusing on multi-level data analysis (e.g., Bickel, 2007; Hox, 2010; Snijders & Bosker, 2011), much less help is available in the design and implementation phases of such complex data collection endeavors—and yet, well-thought-out design and implementation are prerequisites for high-quality multi-level analysis. What is more, multi-level data can originate from a wide range of sources. Although internal and external archival data sources from different firms can be useful, our focus here is on collecting data from people within organizations, be it individual employees responding for themselves or appropriate representatives of collective organizational actors such as work groups, departments, or subsidiaries.

2. WHY MULTI-LEVEL AND MULTI-ACTOR RESEARCH: STRENGTHS AND WEAKNESSES OF THE APPROACH

The added value of pursuing multi-level and multi-actor research can be argued on both *theoretical* and *methodological* grounds, which themselves are interrelated. In terms of *theory*, there have been few attempts in management research to integrate theory at different levels of inquiry, which has meant that macro and micro research have progressed in parallel rather than informing each other. Multi-level research is seen as one important way to address this paradigmatic diversity, which has so far led to an incomplete understanding of organizational phenomena occurring at either level (Hitt, Beamish, Jackson, & Mathieu, 2007). In short, while research at the micro level too often ignores social dynamics and contextual effects at higher levels, macro research downplays behavioral, attitudinal, and perceptual processes at lower levels (Klein, Tosi, & Cannella, 1999). Multi-level research thus possesses the potential to enrich theory by creating and testing more comprehensive models of relationships and their interactions, which incorporates contextual *and* lower level effects. Accordingly, HRM scholars are being encouraged to view HRM as an integrative field of inquiry that should cut across the macro-micro divide (Huselid & Becker, 2011; Wright & Boswell, 2002).

A central tenet of multi-level research is that organizational entities exist in "nested arrangements" (Hitt *et al.*, 2007); that is to say, individuals are nested in work groups, which are nested in units, which are nested in organizations, which are nested in environments, etc. The assumption in multi-level research is that many of the outcomes we are interested in as management scholars at one level will be the result of a confluence of influences deriving from various others levels (Rousseau, 1985). This should lead us to ask important questions such as where the antecedents or determinants of the outcome variable reside (Felin & Hesterly, 2007), and what the underlying mechanisms are (Minbaeva, Foss, & Snell, 2009). Many research questions cannot be answered fully without taking stock of the locus of the independent variables (Felin & Hesterly, 2007; Bono & McNamara, 2011). Although the primary tendency is to search for basic underlying and emergent explanations at lower levels (as encouraged by the micro-foundations approach), Hackman (2003) emphasizes the importance of also seeking contextual explanations at higher levels and, by doing so, "bracketing" the main subject of study. All in all, the primary strength of multi-level research has to do with its ability to consider multiple influences at different levels of analysis simultaneously and, thus, better represent the complexity of real-life problems.

On the downside, collecting data from multiple sources is arguably an arduous task and requires both more effort and more time from the researcher than single-respondent data collection. Yet, given the complex nature of HRM issues, there are good theory-driven reasons to obtain data from different actors. For example, HRM process theory (Bowen &

Ostroff, 2004; Wright & Nishii, 2007) that has gained rapid momentum in recent years places strong emphasis on individual-level perceptions of signals communicated by the HRM system, suggesting that the extent to which these perceptions are shared determines the strength of the organizational climate. When influenced by such features as consensus, among others, it becomes clear that a thorough examination of HRM processes will necessitate the collection of data from multiple sources. This emergent focus on process theory in HRM research (e.g., Lengnick-Hall, Lengnick-Hall, Andrade, & Drake, 2009) also extends to how HRM practices and policies are implemented and enacted (Wright & Nishii, 2007). To this end, Rupidara and McGraw (2011) argue that a key-actor approach—and concomitantly multi-actor research designs—are needed to complement existing theory in order to take into account the dynamic interactions between key actors (such as subsidiary HR managers) and their context, since it is those key actors who play a significant role in shaping and influencing decisions about HRM (see Chapter 4 for a discussion of social network research and tools). Many of these sentiments are shared in the stakeholder approach to HRM (see e.g., De Winne, Delmotte, Gilbert, & Sels, 2013; Tsui, Ashford, St. Clair, & Xin, 1995), which also highlights the need to incorporate multiple actors into research designs.

Turning to the *methodological* arguments for multi-level and multi-actor research, multi-level research addresses the problems of aggregation and disaggregation that are very common in quantitative research conducted at a single level of analysis (Peterson *et al.*, 2012). This is important since findings at one level of analysis do not necessarily generalize to other levels (Klein & Kozlowski, 2000). Aggregating variables at the lower level to a higher level may lead to committing an ecological fallacy, referring to the mistaken assumption that relationships between variables at the aggregate level generalize to the individual level. Disaggregating higher level variables to the lower level, on the other hand, may involve an atomistic fallacy and produce biased statistics since it treats higher level values assigned to lower level observations as independent (Arregle, Hebert, & Beamish, 2006). Multi-level research not only enables researchers to avoid these methodological problems attributable to the nestedness of data, but with ever more sophisticated data analysis techniques also allows for more complex modeling of influences and interactions across levels of analysis. To address the issues of aggregation, intraclass correlation (ICC) values are typically calculated as important criteria for assessing the extent to which variation in the dependent variable is attributable to the different levels of analysis, including measures for both within-group variance (ICC1) and reliability (ICC2) (for more on this, see LeBreton & Senter, 2008). We advise researchers pay close attention to these important, but possibly at least partly evolving, criteria.

One of the most compelling methodological arguments for including multiple actors in quantitative research is the avoidance of common method variance (CMV), which has become a stringent requirement of highly ranked journals (Bono & McNamara, 2011; Chang *et al.*, 2010). As Chang *et al.* (2010, p. 179) state,

> [. . .] the obvious strategy is, of course, to avoid any potential CMV in the research design stage by using other sources of information for some of the key variables. In particular, if possible, the dependent variable should be constructed using information from different sources than the independent variables.

This in many, if not most, cases means using multi-actor data, potentially at different levels of analysis. Another methodological justification is that due to their perceptual nature, many constructs may get very different values depending on whom you ask (Denrell *et al.*, 2004; Mäkelä *et al.*, 2013). For example, if we wish to measure the impact of HRM practices, do we focus on those that are "intended" (and ask corporate HR), "implemented" (and ask subsidiary/unit HR and line managers), or "perceived" (and ask employees) (Wright & Nishii, 2007), or do we focus on the signals the HRM systems send and individuals interpret (Bowen & Ostroff, 2004)? As alluded to above, these differences might not only represent potential threats to validity, but might also present opportunities to examine how and to what extent these differences matter.

Having said all of this, the primary weakness of multi-level and multi-actor research is that it is a complex endeavor, and many more issues have to be considered than when conducting single-level, single-respondent studies. These difficulties, which affect both access to appropriate data and the length and cost of its collection, are the key reasons why multi-level and multi-actor research is still an exception rather than the rule. In what follows, we go through issues and considerations that we have found to be particularly important when designing and implementing multi-level and multi-actor research.

3. DESIGNING AND IMPLEMENTING MULTI-LEVEL AND MULTI-ACTOR RESEARCH

The cornerstones of multi-level research are the level of theory, the level of measurement (or data), and the level of analysis (Mathieu & Chen, 2011). The *level of theory* relates to an adequate understanding of the lower and higher level characteristics of a phenomenon (Kozlowski & Klein, 2000; Morgeson & Hoffman, 1999), while the *level of measurement* concerns where the data are drawn from or attached (the "boxes") and issues of construct validity (Chen, Mathieu, & Bliese, 2004). Finally, the *level of analysis* refers to which level data are used to test hypotheses (the "arrows"), together with aspects such as appropriate sample size (Scherbaum & Ferreter, 2009). All of these issues are important to consider at the design-phase of multi-level projects, yet they are often inadequately conducted in current research

(Yammarino, Dionne, Chun, & Dansereau, 2005; Markham, 2010). We will now go through these considerations in turn, illustrating some of the different points and challenges with practical examples from our "Global HRM Challenge" project. See Table 3.1 for more details about the project and Table 3.2 for information relating the issues discussed below to practical examples in our project.

Level of Theory

Quantitative research methods and data analysis should ideally begin and end with theory, although the reality in multi-level research is somewhat more complex, with data- and analysis-related considerations driving theory development in many cases (Bliese, Chan, & Ployhart, 2007). Nevertheless, the first important question a researcher should ask concerns the level at which the "focal unit(s) of analysis" (i.e., the entities we want to generalize about) reside (Mathieu & Chen, 2011). Only then can multi-level theory be

Table 3.1 Summary description of the "Global HRM Challenge" project

Focus of the project	• To examine the global implementation of HRM practices in the subsidiaries of multinational corporations. More specifically, we examined (i) how key HRM practices are perceived by corporate HR representatives, subsidiary HR and general managers, and employees; and (ii) how these perceptions influence different individual- and organizational-level outcomes.
Key theoretical frameworks	• HRM process theory (Bowen & Ostroff, 2004) • Process model of strategic HRM (Wright & Nishii, 2007) • Stakeholder theory (e.g., Tsui, 1987)
Sample	• 12 Nordic multinational corporations (headquartered in Finland, Sweden, and Norway) • 123 subsidiaries (approx. 10 subsidiaries in each company; approx. 30 countries in total, located across all continents) • 930 employees (managers and professionals only; approx. 10 in each subsidiary)
Survey data	Structured questionnaires with the following: (i) Corporate HR representatives, with questions pertaining to each subsidiary HR department (face-to-face interviews Sept–Dec 2008; items used for independent variables) (ii) Subsidiary HR managers (telephone interviews April–Sept 2009; items used for independent variables) (iii) Subsidiary general managers (telephone interviews April–Sept 2009; items used for independent and dependent variables) (iv) Employees (web-based survey Nov 2010–March 2011; items used for independent and dependent variables)

(Continued)

Table 3.1   (*Continued*)

Papers published	• Björkman, I., Ehrnrooth, M., Smale, A., & John, S. (2011). The determinants of line management internalisation of HRM practices in MNC subsidiaries. *International Journal of Human Resource Management*, 22(8), 1654–1671. • Björkman, I., Ehrnrooth, M., Mäkelä, K., Smale, A., & Sumelius, J. (2013). Talent or not? Employee reactions to talent identification. *Human Resource Management*, 52(2), 195–214. • Mäkelä, K., Sumelius, J., Höglund, M., &Ahlvik, C. (2012). Determinants of strategic HR capabilities in MNC subsidiaries. *Journal of Management Studies*, 49(8), 1459–1483. • Mäkelä, K., Björkman, I., Ehrnrooth, M., Smale, A. & Sumelius, J. (2013). Explaining stakeholder evaluations of HRM capabilities in MNC subsidiaries. *Journal of International Business Studies*, 44(8): 813–832. • Smale, A., Björkman, I., Ehrnrooth, M., John, S., Mäkelä, K., & Sumelius, J. (2013). A multilevel study on the organizational identification of MNC subsidiary employees. *Proceedings of the 2013 Academy of Management Meeting*, Lake Buena Vista (Orlando), Florida.

Table 3.2   Practical design and implementation issues in the "Global HRM Challenge" project

	Key practical questions that we needed to address (see more detailed descriptions in the text)
Level of theory	• What do we want to measure: e.g., intended (by corporate HR), implemented (by subsidiary HR), or perceived (by employees) all reside at different levels of analysis? • How do we address multiple research problems on multiple levels within the same set of questionnaires, all the while avoiding common method variance and other biases?
Level of measurement	• Given the matrix-type structure of the MNC, and potential geographical dispersion, how do we define a subsidiary, and how do we gain access to those subsidiaries? Nestedness was also not entirely straightforward in a matrix-type structure. • At which level do the different constructs reside? • Who are the relevant respondents for firm- and subsidiary-level constructs? • How to correctly aggregate data (composition vs. compilation)?
Level of analysis	• How to balance data requirements and access-related practical considerations? • Considering which constructs at which levels can be theoretically and methodologically linked to dependent variables, all the while keeping the number of items manageable in order to ensure maximum response rates?

built, and the level of predictor variables specified. This question immediately becomes problematic when the focus is on HRM, or HRM practices, since organizations can purposively have different HRM practices, for example, for different groups of employees (Lepak & Snell, 1999) and for different foreign operations (Rosenzweig & Nohria, 1994). In our project the HRM theorizations of Wright and Nishii (2007) and Bowen and Ostroff (2004) constituted central starting points when considering the level of theory and our subsequent focal units of analysis. Wright and Nishii (2007) argue that the focal unit will differ depending on whether we are looking at "intended" (organizational level—planned), "actual" (organizational level—implemented), or "perceived" (individual level—experienced) HRM practices. This meant that the level of theory was a particularly important (and not always straightforward) question, since for HRM practices to have an impact on performance, HRM practices must go from intended to actual to perceived and that this process "spans multiple levels of analysis, with important variance occurring at each of those levels" (2007, p. 9).

Multi-level and multi-actor projects provide an opportunity to examine a variety of research problems within the same context, problems which may reside at a different level (or across different levels), and require data from different respondents. After all, given that multi-level and multi-actor research projects are often complex and time-consuming endeavors, researchers quite pragmatically want to publish several papers out of the data set to make the investment worthwhile. While such optimal utilization of data is also sought after in single-level data collection efforts, addressing multiple research problems requires much more design work when constructing multi-level and multi-actor data sets, since potential theoretical frameworks, models, and paper ideas need to be envisioned and planned for in the design stage.

Extant research has also identified a number of other important issues in multi-level theory building, which researchers would do well to study before thinking about measurement and analysis. Whereas a closer examination falls outside the scope of this chapter, we encourage researchers to become familiar with issues such as cross-level inferences (referring to relationships between variables at one level being inferred from analyses done at a different level), isomorphism (degree of conceptual similarity across levels, see also below), bond strength, and embeddedness (for a detailed review see e.g., Rousseau, 1985; Kozlowski & Klein, 2000).

Level of Measurement

When trying to take into account the above theoretical anchors, it becomes apparent that one needs measures from a number of different actors and across different levels of analysis. Quite obviously, this is not without challenges either. Key issues with regard to the level of measurement include "the unit problem," nesting assumptions, selecting data sources, data aggregation principles, and questionnaire design and administration. We discuss each of these in more detail below.

The Unit Problem

In terms of measurement in the multi-level paradigm, one potentially troublesome issue is the "unit problem," i.e., the extent to which we can claim our units of analysis are salient and that unit membership is unambiguous (Mathieu & Chen, 2011). This is important since it allows us to develop theoretical models suited to placing constructs at one or more levels and examining their interrelationships within and across levels.

In fact, the unit problem was unexpectedly acute in our project since the question of what constitutes a subsidiary in the MNC context was problematic in many cases. Some MNCs were structured along geographical lines—in which case a subsidiary was a *country unit*; others were structured along divisional lines of business—in which case a subsidiary was a *business unit* (of which there might be several in one geographical location); and some adopted a matrix structure making it even more difficult to identify what represented the most salient unit for our project. Additionally, as any international business scholar will tell you, MNC subsidiaries can be heterogeneous across a number of different dimensions (e.g., strategy, structure, size, role, number of functions). In terms of unit membership, we also faced situations in which employees within some subsidiaries had dual reporting lines (e.g., in a matrix organization); some employees were not colocated with others; HR and/or General Managers had responsibilities for more than one subsidiary; and units (e.g., factories) had notable differences between different employee groups. In short, we were facing a complex unit problem, insofar as formal designations can often be insufficient (or even misleading) when identifying salient units. While such problems are by no means unique in the MNC context, they contribute to an amplified measurement challenge in multi-level and multi-actor research; if not considered carefully and up front, they may lead to considerable validity issues—and also to a potentially significant problem of ending up with too few units to observe. We tackled the unit problem through a series of lengthy discussions in which we negotiated subsidiary (and employee) selection criteria and access in detail with our corporate contact persons.

Nesting Assumptions

The unit membership issues above also raised questions about our assumptions of "unit nestedness," in that it was unclear how neatly employees could be assumed to be nested within subsidiaries. Although it may be virtually impossible to ensure that there are no violations of the nesting assumption in modern-day organizations—especially in MNC subsidiaries that typically operate along some form of business, functional, and/or geographical matrix—up-front attempts should be made to demonstrate that nesting assumptions are broadly valid. We can think of several examples that may cause potential issues in this regard, including those related to multiple reporting lines, colocation or noncolocation, involvement in global/virtual teams, and the existence of different employee groups within one unit.

In our project, we wanted data that enabled an examination of Bowen and Ostroff's (2004) HRM process theory, in which one of the key issues is the relationship between the HRM process as perceived by individual employees and its consequences for the collective unit climate in which the individuals are nested. In order to ensure a desirable degree of interaction/interdependence among Level 1 (employee-level) respondents while achieving enough variance, we decided on the following criteria: there should be a fairly even balance between managers with direct subordinates and professionals/specialists with no direct subordinates; the respondents should be 1–2 steps removed from the subsidiary general manager; and the respondents should be from a range of different departments/functions, but not from HR. These considerations were driven by our research objectives, but we encourage all multi-level/multi-actor researchers to engage in similar reflection since, as with the unit problem discussed above, nesting assumptions will crucially impact the validity of their research.

Selecting Data Sources

A third core issue in terms of the level of measurement is the choice of sources from which the data are directly drawn. In many cases, this is not particularly problematic: for example, employee reactions, attitudes, and behaviors are quite clearly Level 1 data (individual level), whereas subsidiary characteristics (e.g., size, age, performance) are Level 2 data (subsidiary level). However, research usually also involves other constructs where this is not entirely straightforward. For instance, returning to the process model of strategic HRM, Wright and Nishii (2007) argue for the importance of paying sufficient attention to the sources from which data on "intended," "actual," and "perceived" HRM practices are drawn. We opted to use corporate HR representatives to answer questions relating to the intended HRM practices for each subsidiary, the most senior person responsible for HR in the subsidiary to answer questions relating to actual HRM practices used in the subsidiary, and up to 10 managers and professionals to answer questions relating to perceived HRM practices.

Our project's aspiration to apply a stakeholder approach to HRM (Tsui, 1987; De Winne *et al.*, 2013) also forced us to think of meaningful, theory-driven ways in which to leverage further the use of multi-actor data. As an outcome, we asked corporate HR, subsidiary HR, and subsidiary general managers to answer questions about the similarity between parent and subsidiary HRM practices in order to study issues of alignment (Ahlvik, Höglund, Smale, & Sumelius, 2010). In addition, we asked corporate HR, general managers, and subsidiary employees to evaluate the capabilities of the subsidiary

HR department in order to shed light on the antecedents of HR capabilities (Mäkelä, Sumelius, Höglund, & Ahlvik, 2012) and the kinds of factors that influence the evaluations of key stakeholders (Mäkelä *et al.*, 2013).

In addition to being guided by theoretical considerations, collecting multi-actor data also helps to address the issue of common method variance (Podsakoff, MacKenzie, Lee, & Podsakoff, 2003). Thus, when determining which data to gather from which respondent, researchers should consider who would be most knowledgeable about the particular topic. They also should consider, however, that independent and dependent variables that are planned to be used in the same model are not constructed based on responses from the same person.

Data aggregation principles

Multi-level research and the use of multi-level constructs require researchers to consider the potential consequences of situations when a lower level variable is aggregated to form a higher level variable (Bliese, 2000). For example, aggregation can produce changes in meaning across levels, representing a serious problem in terms of construct validity (see Shenkar, 2001, for a critique on using measures of cultural difference at different levels of analysis).

Kozlowski and Klein (2000) refer to two main types of aggregation principles: composition and compilation. *Composition* refers to instances in which aggregated higher level variables (calculated by using summary statistics such as means) are believed to retain the same conceptual content and thus adequately represent their lower level counterparts. *Compilation,* on the other hand, refers to "situations where measures collected from lower-level entities combine in nonlinear, complex ways to generate a gestalt, or whole not reducible to its constituent parts" (Mathieu & Chen, 2011, p. 618). Many constructs of interest to organizational and HRM researchers, such as commitment or job satisfaction, may manifest different properties depending on whether the focus is on, for example, individual commitment or group commitment. If this is the case, group means of individual measures do not adequately represent the commitment of the group/unit (Klein & Kozlowski, 2000). In terms of aggregation, we advise researchers to also look into Chen, Mathieu, & Bliese (2004), who specify six different kinds of aggregate constructs that are important to decide upon when designing questionnaires for multi-level research.

The choice of type of constructs to include should primarily be theory driven. We opted for a number of composition-type aggregate constructs (Chen *et al.*, 2004; Mathieu & Chen, 2011), such as unit climate, and (collective) HRM process distinctiveness, consistency, and consensus (Bowen & Ostroff, 2004). We thus assumed, for example, that each individual-level perception of the HRM process "implicitly and equally contributes to the higher-level" (Mathieu *et al.*, 2011, p. 618) HRM process construct. With regard to this, we note that constructs may be "manifested using the same measures yet perhaps mean different things at different levels" (Chen *et al.*, 2004, p. 286). The extent to which the meaning of a composition-type aggregate-level HRM process construct is isomorphic with the corresponding individual-level HRM process construct (Chen *et al.*, 2004; Mathieu & Chen, 2011) was considered to be one of the interesting things to test. Bowen and Ostroff's (2004) theorization arguably implies that the HRM process construct is a fuzzy composition-type of construct (Chen *et al.*, 2004), i.e., a construct exhibiting different meanings at different levels of analyses. For instance, it could be argued that a key aspect of the HRM process construct is that it should create a social-influence effect at the aggregate-level of analysis over and above its individual-level effects.

Questionnaire Design and Administration

Based on common problems in multi-level research and our own experiences, the two issues we draw particular attention to here are questionnaire design and administration. In terms of level of measurement and questionnaire design, Kozlowski & Klein (2000) stress the importance of aligning the wording of questionnaire items with the intended level of analysis in order to avoid mixed-level referents. For example, we worded an item relating to the employee's perception of the HRM process feature of procedural justice (individual level) as *"I have enough influence over the decisions made in the performance appraisal process,"* whereas an item relating to "actual" HRM practice use (subsidiary level) was worded as *"performance appraisals are used to provide feedback on development."*

Regarding the administering of questionnaires in multi-level research, there needs to be fairly strict methodological control in terms of who answers what, how, and on behalf of what or whom. For this reason, among others, in our project we decided to conduct structured telephone interviews with the 123 subsidiary general managers and HR managers, and face-to-face interviews with the majority of corporate HR managers. The benefits of this approach in multi-level research (especially in a complex MNC empirical setting) are, firstly, that the intended entity—based on assumptions concerning key informants and unit membership, etc.—are the actual respondents. Secondly, structured interviews allow the researcher to clarify any queries about the instructions or the wording of items. This approach also helped to resolve any language-related difficulties, which was important given that it was in English and since the questionnaire was administered in about 30 countries.

Level of Analysis

Even though the level of analysis is largely dictated by theory and enabled/ hindered by the approach to measurement, it is essential to plan for it in advance. Although the development of multi-level theory in most fields of organization studies tends to be ahead of the realities of empirical data collection, the alignment of theory, data, and level of analysis is nevertheless a crucially important consideration. In fact, only 43% of a representative sample of reviewed studies in leadership published between 1995 and 2005 (Yammarino *et al.*, 2005), and only 26% of studies published in *Leadership Quarterly* between 2005 and 2010 (Markham, 2010) got this theory-data-analysis alignment right.

In practical terms, theory-data-analysis alignment is closely related to the issue of sample sizes at the various implied levels of analyses. As discussed, we planned for analyses at the level of (i) individuals across subsidiaries and MNCs (single level of analysis); (ii) MNC subsidiaries, or groups of individuals in MNC subsidiaries (a single level of analysis with some consensus-model variables aggregated); and (iii) cross-level phenomena between subsidiaries, groups embedded within subsidiaries, and individuals within them (multi-level analyses). For all of this we needed not only variables measured both at the individual and subsidiary levels of analyses, but also adequate samples sizes at both levels. Indeed, considerations of statistical power and sample size are central issues in multi-level research projects. Adequate sample size at various levels of analysis is crucial for the researcher's ability to align theory, measurement, data, and levels of analysis. Scherbaum and Ferreter (2009) recommend Level 1/Level 2 sample sizes of 30/30 or 50/20 (p. 354), and they offer the following general advice:

> As a general rule of thumb, increasing the sample size at the highest level (i.e., sampling more groups) will do more to increase [statistical] power than increasing the number of individuals in the groups (p. 352).

They also note that the former is usually also the more expensive to do in terms of time and resources, and we agree.

In the case of the "Global HRM Challenge" project, we aimed to ensure adequate sample sizes both at the subsidiary (unit) level and at the individual level. We went for 100 subsidiaries and approximately 10 individual level observations within each unit, which, based on Scherbaum and Ferreter (2009), clearly provided us with adequate statistical power. This allowed us to conduct single-level analyses both at the unit (n = 123) and individual level (n = 930), and we were also able to achieve adequate within-group interdependence and cohesion. In hindsight, our criteria for group membership (see above) should probably have been more specific, which is a good example of the empirical realities and trade-offs that all multi-level researchers frequently face. Indeed, Scherbaum and Ferreter (2009) recognize sample-size-related considerations are often empirically constrained:

> In many instances, however, it is likely that external constraints exist (e.g., work groups have a fixed number of members or there are a fixed number of work groups) that limits the range of choices for sample sizes at either level (Scherbaum and Ferreter, 2009, p. 356).

Aligning level of theory, measurement, and analysis: How does it work in practice?

Lisa is a PhD student focusing on the factors that affect the global adoption of performance management practices in multinational corporations. She is in the process of planning the data collection for her survey. First, Lisa needs to determine her unit of analysis (level of theory): is it the MNC, the subsidiary, the work group, or the individual employee? Lisa soon realizes that her answer to that question is important since it will have important implications for the levels at which the predictor variables should be, which respondents to target in the survey (level of measurement), and whether she will be able to arrive at a large enough sample in order to perform the analyses she plans to do (level of analysis). Her first idea is to examine adoption at the subsidiary level and from the perspective of alignment, perhaps between performance management practices at headquarters and subsidiaries. However, she realizes that unless she can get access to an extremely large MNC with lots of subsidiaries and convince corporate HR representatives to answer on behalf of many different subsidiaries, this approach would require access to a large number of MNCs in order to end up with a sufficient sample size. Furthermore, she is worried that the perspectives of the corporate and subsidiary HR managers might be more representative of how performance management practices are intended to be used, as opposed to whether the practices have actually been adopted—an issue that Lisa had noted as being heavily criticized in the recent literature. Instead, she decides to go with the work group (i.e., teams, departments) as the unit of analysis, and to examine the degree of alignment between the perceptions of managers and employees, who both participate actively in the performance management process but who are likely to see it from two different perspectives. She also thinks it will be easier for her to get access to multiple work groups within one multinational, and thus achieve the sample size she needs. She still has to consider several other issues, such as what is a "work group" in her study; assumptions about the nestedness of employees and managers in work groups and work groups in subsidiaries; whether the predictor variables should be at the individual, relationship, work group, subsidiary or country level; and who should answer those questions, etc., but Lisa's PhD supervisor reassures her that careful consideration at the design stage will ensure that she generates the kind of high-quality data that will allow her to reach her goal of publishing her research in highly ranked journals.

4. CONCLUSIONS

This chapter has focused on the design and implementation of quantitative multi-level and multi-actor research, outlining central issues and challenges that are generally regarded to be important. In HRM research the use of multi-level and multi-actor data is still relatively uncommon, despite a growing number of scholars arguing for the need to integrate micro and macro HRM research in order to provide a more complete understanding of various HRM-related outcomes, which, more often than not, are multi-level in nature.

We started out by arguing for the importance of pursuing multi-level and multi-actor HRM research, presenting both theoretical and methodological reasons for doing so. Our arguments are much in keeping with those delineated in Chapter 1 regarding how a social embeddedness lens is conducive for highlighting the complexity associated with HRM issues. Pertaining to theory, we discussed the concept of "nestedness" and that nestedness of individuals in work groups and units, which in turn are nested in organizations, results in outcomes at one level being ostensibly affected by influences at several different levels. We further presented methodological arguments for multi-level and multi-actor research, such as the ability to address concerns related to the aggregation and disaggregation of data and concerns related to common method variance. With this in mind, collecting data from multiple sources at multiple levels in the organization becomes imperative for those researchers wishing to develop more comprehensive models of the relationship between various HRM-related determinants and outcomes. We believe that the key for future research to enrich our understanding of various HRM issues lies in a better understanding of how the group affects the individual and how the individual affects the group. This in turn is largely contingent on researchers making the effort to adopt increasingly sophisticated research designs that allow for the development of sound theoretical linkages between the macro and micro levels.

As for matters associated with research design, we have discussed three key foundations of multi-level research—level of theory, measurement, and analysis (Rousseau, 1985; Mathieu & Chen, 2011). Although each of the "levels" are important in and of themselves, we concur with Mathieu and Chen (2011) that it is the *alignment* between them that is crucial when designing and implementing good multi-level research, and we underline the need for researchers to allocate sufficient time and attention to it. In terms of practical advice for those contemplating on embarking on multi-level and multi-actor research, we cannot overstate the importance of careful up front planning. Whereas ensuring alignment between level of theory, measurement, and analysis is one key concern, another is gaining buy-in to the data collection effort at a high level in target organizations. For those with the MNC as their research context, we urge them to deliberate carefully over "the unit problem" and the question of what a subsidiary is in the context of the target organization at the outset of the project in order to avoid encountering validity issues later on.

Bearing in mind that the context of our research was 12 MNCs with a total of 123 subsidiaries located in about 30 different countries, and that we gathered data at HQ, subsidiary management, and subsidiary employee level, we faced a considerable amount of contextual and cross-cultural complexity in the various phases of data collection. Although it was not the purpose of this chapter to elaborate on our experiences of, and approaches to, dealing with cross-cultural issues, we would emphasize that the topics discussed in Chapter 7 are also highly relevant and deserve considerable attention in the planning and implementation phases of multi-level and multi-actor data collection efforts in MNCs. To conclude, we hope the overview of some of the main concerns associated with the design and implementation of one such project, and our experiences of tackling them, will serve to encourage and guide the efforts of others looking to take on the admittedly somewhat daunting task that multi-level and multi-actor research methods inevitably present.

REFERENCES

Aguinis, H., Boyd, B. K., Pierce, C. A., & Short, J. C. (2011). Walking new avenues in management research methods and theories: Bridging micro and macro domains (Special Issue). *Journal of Management, 37*(2), 395–403.

Ahlvik, C., Höglund, M., Smale, A., & Sumelius, J. (2010). Explaining the alignment between intended vs. actual parent resemblance of HRM practices in MNCs. *Proceedings of the 11th Conference on International Human Resource Management,* Aston, UK.

Arregle, J. L., Hebert, L., & Beamish, P. W. (2006). Mode of international entry: The advantages of multilevel methods. *Management International Review, 46*(5), 557–618.

Bickel, R. (2007). *Multilevel analysis for applied research: It's just regression.* New York: The Guildford Press.

Bliese, P. D. (2000). Within-group agreement, non-independence, and reliability: Implications for data aggregation and analysis. In K. J. Klein & S. W. Kozlowski (Eds.), *Multilevel theory, research, and methods in organizations: Foundations, extensions and new directions* (pp. 349–381). San Francisco: Jossey-Bass.

Bliese, P. D., Chan, D., & Ployhart, R. E. (2007). Multilevel methods: Future directions in measurement, longitudinal analyses, and non-normal outcomes. *Organizational Research Methods, 10*(4), 551–563.

Bono, J. E., & McNamara, G. (2011). From the editors: Publishing in AMJ—Part 2: Research design. *Academy of Management Journal, 54*(4), 657–660.

Bowen, D. E., & Ostroff, C. (2004). Understanding HRM–firm performance linkages: The role of the "strength" of the HRM system. *Academy of Management Review, 29*, 203–221.

Chang, S.-J., van Witteloostuijn, A., & Eden, L. (2010). Common method variance in international business research. *Journal of International Business Studies, 41*, 178–184.

Chen, G., Mathieu, J. E., & Bliese, P. D. (2004). A framework for conducting multilevel construct validation. In F. J. Dansereau & F. Yammarino (Eds.), *Research in multilevel issues: The many faces of multilevel issues* (pp. 273–303). Oxford, UK: Elsevier Science.

Denrell, J., Arvidsson, N., & Zander, U. (2004). Managing knowledge in the dark: An empirical examination of the reliability of competency evaluations. *Management Science, 50*(11), 1491–1503.

De Winne, S., Delmotte, J., Gilbert, C., & Sels, L. (2013). Comparing and explaining HR department effectiveness assessments: evidence from line managers and trade union representatives. *International Journal of Human Resource Management, 24*(8), 1708–1735.

Felin, T., Foss, N., Heimericks, K. H., & Madsen, T. (2012). Microfoundations of routines and capabilities: Individuals, processes, and structure. *Journal of Management Studies, 49,* 1351–1374.

Felin, T., & Hesterly, W. S. (2007). The knowledge-based view, nested heterogeneity, and new value creation: Philosophical considerations on the locus of knowledge. *Academy of Management Review, 32*(1), 195–218.

Foss, N. J. (2007). The emerging knowledge governance approach: Challenges and characteristics. *Organization, 14,* 29–52.

Hackman, J. R. (2003). Learning more by crossing levels: Evidence from airplanes, hospitals, and orchestras. *Journal of Organizational Behavior, 24,* 905–922.

Hitt, M. A., Beamish, P. W., Jackson, S. E., & Mathieu, J. E. (2007). Building theoretical and empirical bridges across levels: Multilevel research in management (Special Issue). *Academy of Management Journal, 50*(6), 1385–1399.

Hox, J. J. (2010). *Multilevel analysis. Techniques and applications* (2nd ed.). New York: Routledge.

Huselid, M. A., & Becker, B. E. (2011). Bridging micro and macro domains: Workforce differentiation and strategic human resource management. *Journal of Management, 37*(2), 421–428.

Klein, K. J., & Kozlowski, S. W. J. (2000). From micro to meso: Critical steps in conceptualizing and conducting multilevel research. *Organizational Research Methods, 3*(3), 211–236.

Klein, K. J., Tosi, H., & Cannella, A. A. Jr., (1999). Multilevel theory building: Benefits, barriers, and new developments (Special Issue). *Academy of Management Review, 24*(2), 243–248.

Kozlowski, S. W. J., & Klein, K. J. (2000). A multilevel approach to theory and research in organizations: Contextual, temporal, and emergent processes. In K. J. Klein & S. W. Kozlowski (Eds.), *Multilevel theory, research, and methods in organizations: Foundations, extensions and new directions* (pp. 3–90). San Francisco: Jossey-Bass.

LeBreton, J., & Senter, J. (2008). Answers to 20 questions about interrater reliability and interrater agreement. *Organizational Research Methods, 11,* 815–852.

Lengnick-Hall, M. L., Lengnick-Hall, C. A., Andrade, L. S., & Drake, S. (2009). Strategic human resource management: The evolution of the field. *Human Resource Management Review, 19*(2), 64–85.

Lepak, D. P., & Snell, S. A. (1999). The human resource architecture: Toward a theory of human capital allocation and development. *Academy of Management Review, 24*(1), 31–48.

Mäkelä, K., Björkman, I., Ehrnrooth, M., Smale, A. & Sumelius, J. (2013). Explaining stakeholder evaluations of HRM capabilities in MNC subsidiaries. *Journal of International Business Studies, 44*(8): 813–832.

Mäkelä, K., Sumelius, J., Höglund, M., & Ahlvik, C. (2012). Determinants of strategic HR capabilities in MNC subsidiaries. *Journal of Management Studies, 49*(8), 1459–1483.

Markham, S. E. (2010). Leadership, levels of analysis, and déjà vu: Modest proposals for taxonomy and cladistics coupled with replication and visualization. *Leadership Quarterly, 21,* 1121–1143.

Mathieu, J. E., & Chen, G. (2011). The etiology of the multilevel paradigm in management research. *Journal of Management, 37*(2), 610–641.

Minbaeva, D., Foss, N., & Snell, S. (2009). Bringing knowledge perspective into HRM: Introduction to the special issue. *Human Resource Management, 48*(4), 477–483.

Morgeson, F. P., & Hofmann, D. A. (1999). The structure and function of collective constructs: Implications for multilevel research and theory development. *Academy of Management Review, 24,* 249–265.

Peterson, M. F., Arregle, J.-L., & Martin, X. (2012). Multilevel models in international business research (Special Issue). *Journal of International Business Studies, 43,* 451–457.

Podsakoff, P., MacKenzie, S., Lee, J.-Y., & Podsakoff, N. (2003). Common method biases in behavioral research: A critical review of the literature and recommended remedies. *Journal of Applied Psychology, 88,* 879–903.

Rosenzweig, P., & Nohria, N. (1994). Influences on human resource management practices in multinational corporations. *Journal of International Business Studies, 25*(2), 229–252.

Rousseau, D. M. (1985). Issues of level in organizational research: Multilevel and cross-level perspectives. In L. L. Cummings & B. M. Staw (Eds.), *Research in organizational behavior* (Vol. 7, pp. 1–37). Greenwich, CT: JAI Press.

Rupidara, N., & McGraw, P. (2011). The role of actors in configuring HR systems within multinational subsidiaries. *Human Resource Management Review, 21,* 174–185.

Scherbaum, C. A., & Ferreter, J. M. (2009). Estimating statistical power and required sample sizes for organizational research using multilevel modeling. *Organizational Research Methods,12,* 347–367.

Shenkar, O. (2001). Cultural distance revisited: Towards a more rigorous conceptualization and measurement of cultural differences. *Journal of International Business Studies, 32,* 519–535.

Snijders, T. A. B., & Boskel, R. J. (2011). *Multilevel analysis: An introduction to basic and advanced multilevel modeling* (2nd ed.). London: Sage.

Tsui, A. (1987). Defining the activities and effectiveness of the human resource department: A multiple constituency approach. *Human Resource Management, 26,* 35–69.

Tsui, A. S., Ashford, S. J., St. Clair, L., & Xin, K. R. (1995). Dealing with discrepant expectations: Response strategies and managerial effectiveness. *Academy of Management Journal, 38*(6), 1515–1543.

Wright, P. M., & Boswell, W. R. (2002). Desegregating HRM: A review and synthesis of micro and macro human resource management research. *Journal of Management, 28,* 247–276.

Wright, P. M., & Nishii, L. H. (2007). *Strategic HRM and organizational behavior: Integrating multiple levels of analysis* (CAHRS Working Paper #07–03). Ithaca, NY: Cornell University, School of Industrial and Labor Relations, Center for Advanced Human Resource Studies. Retrieved from http://digitalcommons.ilr.cornell.edu/cahrswp/468

Yammarino, F. J., Dionne, S. D., Chun, J. U., & Dansereau, F. (2005). Leadership and levels of analysis: A state-of-the-science review. *Leadership Quarterly, 16,* 879– 919.

4 Social Network Research

Robert Kaše

After reading this chapter, we expect you to:

1. Be able to recognize which HR-related research questions could be addressed with social network research;
2. Understand the potential benefits and challenges of addressing a particular research question with a social network research design;
3. Be able to determine which social network data type is most suitable for your research question;
4. Be able to evaluate applicability of different social network analyses for your research question;
5. Know what you need for implementation of your social network research design.

---

1. INTRODUCTION

Social network research incorporates theories, concepts, and methodology that acknowledge and explicitly address relational ties between actors such as individuals, groups, and organizations (Galaskiewicz, 2007; Kilduff & Tsai, 2005; Wasserman & Faust, 1994). Unlike the traditional individualist paradigm in the social sciences, where actors are assumed as agents making decisions without considering the behavior of others, social network research acknowledges the opportunities and constraints arising from the social context in which actors are embedded (Borgatti & Foster, 2003).

Social network research is most widely recognized for its structural perspective, which focuses on the social structure—the pattern of relational ties and the position of actors within it—and its implications. This emphasis enables a researcher to explore, for example, how embeddedness in networks affects the behavior of individuals in organizations (see also Chapter 1) and how various organizational contexts such as HRM systems facilitate development and dissolution of relational ties. In two classical studies, network researchers have examined how position within a social network affects individuals' power (Burkhardt & Brass, 1990) and how peer turnover in organizations affects the job satisfaction of stayers (Krackhardt & Porter, 1985). Although the emphasis on structural characteristics contributes most to the differentiation between the social network and the traditional individualist paradigm in the social sciences, the importance of relational content—properties of relational ties—should not be underestimated (Raider & Krackhardt, 2002), especially in HR research. Galaskiewicz (2007, p. 7) put it nicely: "the content of the tie matters and the cultural meaning attached . . . friend, neighbor, drinking buddy, workmate, boss, acquaintance, etc. makes a big difference."

Recently, the core social network research ideas such as primacy of relations, embeddedness, benefits of connections, and structural patterning of social life (see Kilduff & Brass, 2010) have attracted considerable attention in management and organization research. However, diffusion of these ideas among HR researchers is still relatively modest (see Kaše, King & Minbaeva, 2013). The reasons might lie in the fact that these core ideas come together with a special methods toolbox—social network analysis (SNA)—which a researcher needs to be familiar with to thoroughly understand the underlying principles and be able to develop theory along with appropriate research designs. Because this rich toolbox is not part of the standard research methods repertoire of HR researchers, the chapter discusses network data gathering approaches and introduces selected quantitative network analysis methods in order to facilitate development of research designs that better acknowledge the importance of *social embeddedness* in HR research.

2. VALUE ADDED OF SOCIAL NETWORK RESEARCH

The main difference between using methods traditionally used in HR research and social network methods is that the latter open the possibility to explicitly address social structure and content as well as other important relational flows in organizations (e.g., knowledge transfer). Research designs acknowledging the social network perspective allow a researcher to meticulously address (depending on the method used) different kinds of interdependencies between actors or other relational phenomena at various levels of analysis and explore their consequences in an organizational setting.

Similarly, as in other fields where a social network perspective has been successfully adopted, HR research could benefit from it in three ways: (1) by shedding new light on issues that have remained unsolved in the field (e.g., how individuals' perceptions of HR practices are influenced by the social context of peers); (2) by evaluating existing knowledge in the field (e.g., reexamining effect sizes of HR practices on various organizational outcomes, while controlling for effects of intraorganizational social structure);

and, most importantly, (3) by facilitating new research questions and providing opportunities for theorizing that have previously not been considered. Of course these important benefits come together with certain costs, as social network research designs usually entail challenging data gathering, incur more time and sometimes risk for analyses, raise additional ethical issues, and, for HR researchers, involve the need to climb the learning curve.

Research design features and methods introduced in this chapter become applicable for HR researchers when they start looking at organizations as networks composed of individuals and the prescribed formal and informal relationships among them (Nohria, 1992). This means that their interests also lie in examining the social structure and content of organizations and that, in addition to data on HR practices, employee characteristics, and HR-relevant outcomes, they also have to gather data on relational ties (e.g., work cooperation, communication, and trust) between individuals or groups in organizations. Similarly, social network principles can also be adopted for exploring HR systems as networks of HR practices, programs, and interventions. In this case, HR practices are viewed as actors and interdependencies between HR practices as relational ties of an HR system. Directly addressing and analyzing complex interdependencies (e.g., synergies) within HR systems could improve our understanding of their effectiveness and thus contribute to the development of macro HRM (cf. Chadwick, 2010).

3. GATHERING SOCIAL NETWORK DATA

The nature of social network data has important implications for research designs, especially when examining complete networks. The main difference between a standard HR research project and a social network study is that the former demands gathering data only on actor attributes (e.g., employees' perceptions of HR practices, their demographic characteristics, attitudes, and behaviors), while the latter also directly inquires about the actors' relational ties with other individuals (their presence/absence and quality). As a consequence, social network research designs need more time to be completed and face specific challenges related to the need to track respondents and at the same time ensure their confidentiality. If a respondent has to report her work interactions with each of her 10 colleagues, this inevitably takes more time than if she was asked only to report her overall evaluation of interactions with her colleagues. Moreover, usually individuals, who are involved in more interactions and consequently have to report more, need even more time for reporting. Therefore, we usually find single-item measures of relational ties in social network studies.

Further, since specific relational ties between individuals are observed, it is difficult to guarantee anonymity to respondents. To be able to construct a complete social network, we have to know who exactly reported a relational tie with whom, which means that we have to track individuals across their responses. The issue becomes even more challenging when we combine individual and network data from more than one source (e.g., merging demographics from company records and network data from a survey). One solution to this problem is to use multitime passwords that allow tracking of respondents (e.g., Kaše, Paauwe, & Zupan, 2009). Instead of inputting their names before starting the sociometric part of a questionnaire, respondents enter a password we provided to them. The same password is then used by respondents to enter the traditional part of the questionnaire, which can be delivered separately at a different time. In any case, it is advisable to remove the identity of respondents from the working database as soon as data has been merged together and all relevant measures have been developed.

In addition, due to the characteristics of analytical approaches for network data, where missing data is highly problematic (Kossinets, 2006), it is necessary that participation rates in network research projects are high. In network studies of organizations this situation calls for a close cooperation with the participating organizations' representatives. Strong support by top management of participating organizations by means of openly encouraging participation and allowing enough time during work time to participate in the study is often required for success of the study. However, intense collaboration with participating organizations' management during the research project could at the same time open some ethical issues that have to be carefully handled (see Cross, Kaše, Kilduff, & King, 2013).

Gathering complete social network data: How does it work in practice?

Backed by an interesting research idea and strong theoretical development, Ana has to gather complete social network data in an organization as the next step toward completing her research project. Although she read lots of literature about research design, she found it very helpful to get a list of essentials by one of her older colleagues who just finished a similar study. These were his seven points:

1. **Target organizations should be just the right size:** preferably between 50 and 200 if you examine networks of individuals.
2. **Involve a top authority and a knowledgeable operative in target organizations:** you need someone to motivate respondents and someone to support the research process from the inside.
3. **Clarify expectations before the start of the research project:** explain in advance that feedback to the organization will not contain any names of the participants.

4. **Reduce the number of sociometric questions to a minimum and gather as much data as possible from other sources:** since each sociometric question demands high levels of involvement from respondents researchers should be conservative in adding them to the questionnaire and minimize the remaining burden on respondents (e.g., by acquiring information from existing company records).

5. **Think twice about the appropriate structure/format of the data collected:** restructuring or reformatting relational data post hoc can be very complex and time consuming.

6. **Continuously track progress and use general and targeted reminders:** do interim analyses if necessary to identify potentially highly central actors who are not responding and prepare special targeted reminders for them.

7. **Take time to provide feedback to as many respondents as possible:** this offers an excellent reality check and diminishes the potential for development of power asymmetries as a result of making some of the respondents more knowledgeable about the organization's social structure than others.

Data on social networks is usually gathered by means of a survey[1] with a special section of sociometric questions. Depending on the purpose of a research project, a sociometric questionnaire usually includes at least one name generator and tentatively one or more name interpreters. *Name generator* is a data collection device for eliciting the names of a respondent's contacts (alters) that correspond to a specific relational content (e.g., a friend, someone who you turn to for advice) (Marsden, 1987; McCallister & Fischer, 1978). *Name interpreters*, on the other hand, are additional questions/items about the quality/strength of a respondent's relations with those contacts that had previously been identified with name generator (Marsden, 1987, p. 123). In a sociometric survey the respondent typically "generates" names of contacts that match the description of a specific relation the respondent has with them. These can then be further assessed with name interpreters. For example, respondents can be asked to identify coworkers with whom they communicated face-to-face in the last month. After they have identified them, they may be asked to further evaluate (interpret) the intensity and importance of their face-to-face communication with each of the selected coworkers.

The set of contacts that a respondent can select from can be determined in advance by the researcher—this is the so-called nominalist approach, where a list or roster is prepared in advance—or it can be left to the recall of the respondent—unrestricted (Laumann, Marsden, & Prensky, 1992). In organizational network research, where our interests lie mostly in exploring complete interpersonal networks in organizations, we usually determine the boundaries of the social network (and simultaneously the pool of survey participants) in advance. This approach also helps to alleviate problems of recall and recency bias, yet it can, on the other hand, inflate the number of reported relational ties.

Another decision to be made in sociometric survey design is about the number of choices (nominations) that a respondent has available in the name generator. Usually, the number of choices is not restricted—respondents can nominate as many as all the names on the list except themselves. In this way, we get a better representation of the actors' relational ties, but because they (can) report very different numbers of contacts, the list might need to be normalized to be comparable. However, in specific situations, such as peer evaluations, restriction of choices/nominations can be used (e.g., each employee has three nominations for the best performer in the work group) and has important substantive implications for results and interpretation.

Below, four of the most salient types of social network (data) that could also be used in HR research projects are discussed briefly: (1) ego (personal) networks, (2) complete networks, (3) multiplex networks, and (4) affiliation (two-mode) networks. In Figure 4.1 all four network types are graphically represented. It is interesting that methods for analyzing these types of data remain relatively disconnected. This chapter focuses on methods for analyzing complete network data, while acknowledging others.

Ego (personal) network is the social network around an individual. It consists of a focal actor *(ego),* a set of actors with whom the ego has ties *(alters),* and ties between the ego and alters along with ties among the alters themselves (Borgatti & Foster, 2003). The focus is on the features of ego networks such as the composition, size, and configuration of personal networks. The alters in an ego network also could be from beyond the boundaries of an organization. Standard sampling and statistical techniques including hierarchical linear modeling (see van Duijn, van Busschbach, & Snijders, 1999) can be used to explore ego networks. If so, it is important that the alters included in the egos' personal networks do not overlap, or that this overlap is negligible. This type of network data could be useful for HR researchers interested in exploring socialization, careers, or other areas within HR where personal networks exert important effects on the behavioral or attitudinal outcomes of individuals. For example, a researcher interested in the adjustment of newcomers could work with ego network data to examine what kind of composition, size, and configuration of newcomers' networks are related to better adjustment, along with how organizational onboarding practices and newcomers' networking behavior affect the development of newcomers' networks and in turn adjustment.

Complete (whole) network, on the other hand, consists of a finite set of actors and the relational ties between them (e.g., Wasserman & Faust, 1994). The boundaries of the network are specified in advance by the researcher, acknowledging a specific situation, context, or affiliation. The main idea is to examine all relations between actors within prespecified boundaries and ignore actors' ties beyond these boundaries. Complete network data is

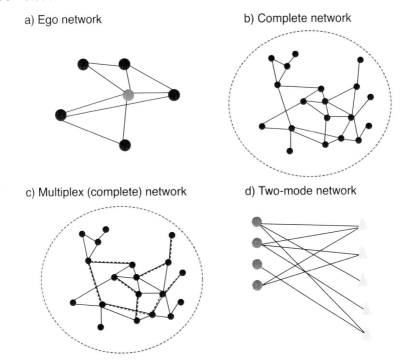

a) Ego network

b) Complete network

c) Multiplex (complete) network

d) Two-mode network

Figure 4.1   Types of social network data

Notes: * dots represent actors, lines represent ties; ** in d) triangles represent second type of actors; *** in c) double relational tie represents a multiplex ties; **** the circle in b) and c) represents the prespecified boundary of the network.

inherently multi-level and can be freely scaled up and down (e.g., to group or network level). It can also be used to explore complex interdependencies between actors included in the network. Complete network can easily be transformed into ego network; however, the alters included in such an ego network are limited to those within the prespecified boundaries and considerable overlap between alters exists. Complete network data is appropriate for research initiatives addressing relationships between HRM and intraorganizational social networks as well as the effects of social embeddedness on HR-relevant individual outcomes. For example, with complete network data a researcher can examine how individuals' experiences of compensation systems affect dyadic work cooperation or how direct face-to-face communication between peers affects their job satisfaction.

Both ego and complete networks can be explored as unidimensional (i.e., featuring only one focal relation) or ***multiplex networks,*** which consist of multiple layers or dimensions of relational content in a tie (Koehly & Pattison, 2005). For example, a network featuring both line of command

and flow of advice among the same set of actors can be considered a multiplex network. So far, more emphasis has been placed on the number of relations within a given tie between two actors (following the logic the more relations, the stronger the relational tie between individuals) than on the variability of the relational contents within the tie and the interrelatedness of these contents. Recently, Soltis, Agneessens, Sasovova, & Labianca (2013) provided a nice example of how multiplex networks can be explored in HR research. Specifically, they developed special composite relational ties such as "required advice-giving ties" (based on required workflow and advice-giving relations) to explore turnover intentions in organizations.

The last type of network we address here is **affiliation (two-mode) network.** This type of network consists of two sets of actors (e.g., people and events) and relations between them (Breiger, 1974). For example, a two-mode network could be composed of employees and HR programs, where being included in a program is the main relation under observation. A two-mode network can easily be transformed into a one-mode (complete) network. In the above-mentioned case, the strength of a relational tie between two employees in a one-mode network would be determined by the number of times they have been involved in the same HR program. Although we cannot observe actual relational ties, but only the ones based on affiliations, this type of network could be useful for HR researchers as the data can be gathered directly from company records.

At the moment, the HR field has already witnessed several contributions where researchers, in addition to individual attribute data, collected and analyzed complete social network data (Gant, Ichniowski, & Shaw, 2002; Kaše *et al.,* 2009; Soltis *et al.,* 2013); some of this research has even considered multiplex networks. There are fewer examples, on the other hand, of using ego network data and practically none of collecting two-mode network data. This is surprising because ego and two-mode network data is usually less difficult to gather and methods for analyzing it, at least for ego networks, are closer to the logic of standard approaches used in HR research. A complete tabula rasa in HR research at the moment remains longitudinal network data of any type. Considering the challenges that the HR field has been facing with gathering longitudinal HR data alone (cf. Wright, Gardner, Moynihan, & Allen, 2005), it is not realistic to expect many research projects combining longitudinal HR and (complete) network data soon (for more about longitudinal research in HR see Chapter 5).

4. ANALYTICAL APPROACHES FOR SOCIAL NETWORK DATA

In order to systematically address analytical approaches for handling social network data that could be used in HR research, a two-dimensional classification was developed. Similar to methods traditionally used in HR research, social network research methods can also be classified as *exploratory* or *confirmatory,* where exploratory methods are used to describe observed data and facilitate hypotheses development, while confirmatory methods are primarily intended to test hypotheses. Thus, the *exploratory/confirmatory* distinction represents the first dimension in our classification of social network methods relevant for HR research.

In addition, a second dimension, ranging along the *proximal* versus *distant to extant HR methods* continuum, is proposed. The rationale for proposing this dimension is that researchers are usually inclined to learn new methods that are closer to their current understanding, as more distant methods incur larger investments of time. At one end of the continuum of this dimension (i.e., proximal) we can find social network methods that follow a similar logic as statistical methods HR researchers are already familiar with and using, while at the other end we include methods whose logic is quite distant to traditional HR research (e.g., offering extensive treatment of complex interdependencies between actors). This newly proposed classification of HR-research-relevant social network analytical approaches can be found in Figure 4.2.

Exploratory SNA (lower part of Figure 4.2) is the basic building block of any social network study, as researchers have to get to know the data thoroughly before moving to confirmatory analyses. It includes both various visual representations (i.e., sociograms) of a social network or any of its parts

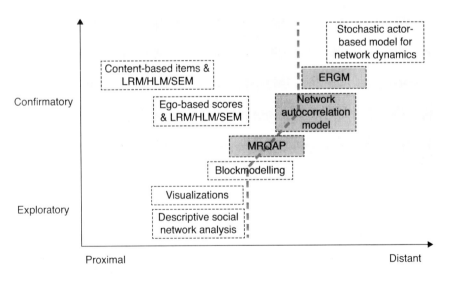

Figure 4.2 Classification of HR research relevant social network analytical approaches

Note: highlighted are confirmatory methods described in more detail in this chapter. The interrupted line illustrates the current frontier of adoption in HR research.

(e.g., with Pajek software, Batagelj & Mrvar, 1998) as well as calculation of scores/indicators describing the network, its subsection, relations, and individuals. Among the most popular indicators of overall network characteristics are network density, centralization, and diameter. As far as actors are concerned, frequency distributions of relational ties per actor as well as other more complex measures of individuals' positions in a network such as centrality or brokerage roles are usually explored. Eliciting important (cohesive) subsections of a network such as components and cliques is also a standard repertoire of exploratory SNA. All these analyses are frequently used in management and organization research when network data is collected. Moreover, some of these scores/indictors (e.g., various measures of centrality) often serve as inputs for further analyses using standard research methods such as linear regression. For more information about exploratory SNA, please refer to De Nooy, Mrvar, and Batagelj (2011), Hanneman and Riddle (2005), or Wasserman and Faust (1994).

There is another analytical technique that lies on the boundary between exploratory and confirmatory approaches—blockmodeling. It is positioned on the boundary, because it can be used both for exploring groupings among network members and for testing hypotheses about clustering in a social network. Blockmodeling is a procedure by which actors of a network are rearranged in blocks, so that those who have the same or similar relational ties to other actors (who occupy an "equivalent" position in the network) are put into the same block (Doreian, Batagelj, & Ferligoj, 2005). The procedure is often used for data reduction purposes. As a result, instead of examining individual actors and relational ties between them, we can work with blocks—groups of "equivalent" actors—and aggregated ties between them. Blockmodeling could also be used in HR research for aggregating structurally similar employees into groups or for clustering structurally similar HR practices into blocks within HR systems.

However, if an HR researcher wants to develop a research design for testing hypotheses involving patterns of relational ties in organizations, then confirmatory social network analytical approaches for complete network data (see upper part of Figure 4.2.) should be considered. Before reviewing them, we have to note that there is an essential difference between testing hypotheses about characteristics of individual actors using individual attribute data and testing hypotheses about the presence and quality of relational ties using network data. Individual attribute data is collected in vectors, whereas social network data is represented in adjacency matrices, where each row and column represent actors and the cells of the matrix depict the measured relational state between the two actors (Raider & Krackhardt, 2002, p. 68). The main challenge in testing hypotheses using network data is that the observations are systematically interdependent on one another and thus subject to network autocorrelation problem[2] (see Krackhardt, 1988).

While in standard statistical procedures observations are assumed to be independent, network data violates this assumption (biasing the standard error estimate). If traditional methods for analyzing data were used with network data, the results could be severely biased. Therefore, in order to empirically validate conceptual models defined at the relational level of analysis and using network data, statistical procedures that do not assume independence of observations should be used.

Several alternative analytical approaches have been used in management and organization research to test hypotheses in attempting to alleviate the network autocorrelation problem. The simplest approach to address research questions dealing with network and relational ties is to completely avoid network data and ask individuals about their relational ties indirectly/implicitly. For example, researchers could ask respondents to evaluate the overall strength of their ties to their coworkers on a scale from 1 to 7 or inquire about their agreement with the statement "My network is full of structural holes." Such data are then analyzed with traditional statistical approaches. This indirect approach is questionable for exploring social networks in terms of its validity.

Another way to approach the problem is to actually gather network data and use it to calculate individual scores, such as measures of individuals' network centrality, to be entered into one of the traditionally used statistical approaches (e.g., Cross & Cummings, 2004; Obstfeld, 2005; Perry-Smith, 2006). Although this approach is not inappropriate and can in specific situations be very effective (e.g., Sasovova, Mehra, Borgatti, & Schippers, 2010), it loses a large amount of information when translating/aggregating usually complete network data to the level of individuals.

Recently, substantial progress has been made in developing methods for dealing with social relations and testing hypotheses using network data (see Carrington, Scott, & Wasserman, 2005). In the remainder of the chapter analytical approaches that acknowledge interdependencies in network data and can be used to test hypotheses using cross-sectional complete network data in HR are introduced. Although several of the analytical approaches described below have already been available for some time, they remained relatively inaccessible for most management researchers until specialized software such as UCINET (Borgatti, Everett, & Freeman, 2002), SIENA (Snijders, Steglich, Schweinberger, & Huisman, 2007), and pnet (Robins, Pattison, Kalish, & Lusher, 2007) appeared. Even today these approaches are underutilized by management and HR scholars, perhaps because learning how to use these software packages demands relatively large investments of time.

Multiple Regression Quadratic Assignment Procedure

Multiple regression quadratic assignment procedure (MRQAP) is an analytical approach principally used to model a social relation (a set of dyadic relational ties) by regressing it on other relations (Krackhardt, 1988). With MRQAP one can, for example, predict the level of interpersonal advice flow in an organization as a linear function of intensity of formal communication, interpersonal trust, individuals' similarity in demographic characteristics (homophily), and physical proximity of coworkers in the office setting. Of all three confirmatory methods described in this chapter, MRQAP is the simplest one to use and adopts a logic that is most proximal to the traditional analytical approaches. In particular, the approach can be considered an analogy to a standard multiple regression analysis for relational (dyadic) data.

A defining feature of MRQAP is a special type of nonparametric test for relational data—quadratic assignment procedure (QAP) (Hubert, 1987; Krackhardt, 1988). This procedure generates a referent distribution of coefficients by simultaneously permuting rows and columns of the studied networks (matrices) in such a way that the structure of the network remains unchanged, but the order of actors in the matrices is randomly changed. The result of the procedure is a referent distribution on the basis of which the statistical significance of the correlation and multiple regression coefficients are determined.

For specifying an MRQAP model one needs a dependent relational variable (e.g., data on advice flows between pairs of coworkers within an organization) and one or more explanatory relational variables that predict it (e.g., level of interpersonal trust, intensity of communication between coworkers). Variables with individual attributes (e.g., worker's age or gender) cannot be directly entered into an MRQAP model. Rather, they first have to be transformed into variables indicating (dis)similarities and overlaps between pairs of actors (e.g., difference in workers' ages, same/different gender) or any kind of the more complex dyadic indices (see Kenny, Kashy, & Cook, 2006). Only then they can serve as an input into an MRQAP model. All variables in an MRQAP model should be one-mode, squared matrices with the same number of actors, arranged in the same order.

The simplest way to estimate an MRQAP model is to use the procedure in UCINET (Borgatti *et al.*, 2002). A result of this procedure is a report including magnitude and significance of (standardized) regression coefficients, which serves as guidance for evaluating the hypotheses. MRQAP also reports R^2; however, this overall fit indicator should be interpreted carefully as it is not always reliable.

Many examples of MRQAP use are available in the management literature (Borgatti & Cross, 2003; Kilduff, 1990; Kilduff & Krackhardt, 1994; Labianca, Brass, & Gray, 1998; Pastor, Meindl, & Mayo, 2002; Tsai, 2002; Tsai & Ghoshal, 1998) and provide a reliable background regarding how this method should be used in empirical research. In HR research, Kaše *et al.* (2009) adopted MRQAP to examine a mediation model about the effects of experienced HR practices on interpersonal relations and in turn on intrafirm knowledge transfer. They used numerous relational variables including structural, affective and cognitive relations, knowledge sharing and knowledge sourcing, as well as three dyadic indices for selected sets of experienced HR practices to specify the model. It was tested in four different organizational settings (with different overall HR systems) to cross-validate findings. There are more HR-relevant research questions that could be explored using this approach, however. For example, do experienced HR practices affect work cooperation and reciprocal help between coworkers? Does homophily (i.e., similarity of individuals' characteristics) predict similar attributions to HR practices? Which relations between coworkers act as the strongest moderators of the shared interests–dyadic knowledge transfer relationship?

MRQAP can be considered as the first step toward predicting with network (dyadic) data. In comparison to the traditional analytical approaches used in management, it already acknowledges and handles interdependencies in network data. Although we cannot use it to model structural configurations and individual actor attribute effects explicitly (this can be done with exponential random graph models, see below), MRQAP is robust against a wide variety of common network autocorrelation structures and adequately controls for them. In comparison to other social network methods, MRQAP is more suitable for use with numerical (valued) dyadic data and can be used to examine mediation. Estimation of coefficients is fast and always converges because it is not dependent on complex simulations. Furthermore, MRQAP can also be used to explore the development of relational variables over time. Finally, it should not be underestimated that using logic similar to standard linear regression, MRQAP is more accessible to the management audience, which makes the diffusion of research findings much easier.

Exponential Random Graph Models

Exponential random graph models (ERGMs), also referred to as p* models, are used to model the probability of relational ties between actors as a function of the local structural properties (i.e., the presence or absence of other relational ties around them) as well as actor and dyadic attributes (Robins, Pattison, *et al.*, 2007). An ERGM depicts a social network as a self-organizing system of relational ties between individual actors that is codetermined by social selection processes where individuals form relational ties based on certain characteristics they possess (Robins, Elliott, & Pattison, 2001). With ERGM a researcher can explore if, for instance, in the observed advice-flow network, reciprocity and transitivity occurred more often than is expected by chance. Moreover, while controlling for reciprocity and transitivity in the observed advice network, the researcher can establish if sharing an attribute with another individual will more likely result in advice flow.

The logic of ERGMs differs substantially from the extant analytical approaches in management and HR research, because it is founded on the assumptions of complex interdependencies of actors and nestedness of structural configurations within a network. The main novelty of ERGMs in comparison to traditional statistical approaches is their ability to explicitly model structural configurations of a selected network and control for these

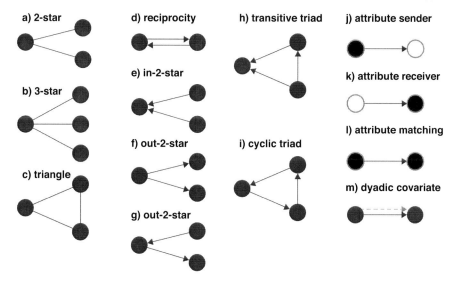

Figure 4.3   Selected configurations for ERGMs

Note: please refer to pnet user manual (Wang, Robins, Pattison, 2009) for more configurations. Items a)–c) are structural configurations for nondirected networks; items d)–i) are structural configurations for directed networks; items j)–l) represent actor effects in a directed network; item m) represents dyadic effect in a directed network.

structural effects while exploring the effects of actor and dyadic attributes on the formation of relational ties (Robins, Pattison, *et al.*, 2007; Robins, Snijders, Wang, Handcock, & Pattison, 2007).

Key elements of ERGMs are local structural properties of a network operationalized as structural configurations—small subsets of relational ties or small network substructures. There are numerous structural configurations that can be included in ERGMs (see Figure 4.3 for a graphical representation of selected configurations). For example, a configuration commonly included in ERGMs when examining networks in organizational settings is *reciprocity,* which refers to a tendency that if a tie is observed from actor A to actor B, it is likely that a tie will also be observed from B to A. Similarly, *transitive triad* configuration is also frequently modeled in intraorganizational networks. For the case of an advice-giving network, this implies that if actor A shares knowledge with actor B, and actor B shares knowledge with actor C, there will be a tendency for actor A to share knowledge with actor C. In ERGMs these structural configurations are modeled explicitly and a tendency of the network toward them is estimated with corresponding parameters.

In addition, with ERGMs we can also examine effects that feature interactions between structural characteristics and actor or dyadic attributes such as sender, receiver, matching, and dyadic covariate effects. For example, gender-sender effect in an advice network would indicate the tendency that women are more likely to provide advice to others than men, while the level of education-matching effect in the same network could show that employees are more likely to share advice with their colleagues who have the same level of education (see Figure 4.3 for a visual representation).

ERGMs can be estimated with pnet (Robins, Pattison, *et al.*, 2007) and several other software packages. For estimation, researchers need complete network data (i.e., binary adjacency matrix), which ideally should not be too large (below 200 actors) and should have no or very few missing values. In addition, they can have a set of corresponding actor attributes. The initial selection of structural configurations to be included in the model depends on our theoretical interests and selected interdependence assumption (for more about interdependence assumption see Robins, Pattison, *et al.*, 2007; Robins, Snijders, *et al.*, 2007). Usually actor and dyadic effects that are predicted to contribute to the formation of network ties are also added to the specification of the model. This part of the model should be especially interesting for HR researchers as it provides the opportunity to include HR-relevant variables.

Model estimation is based on simulations (Markov chain Monte Carlo maximum likelihood), which means that statistics of the observed network are compared with a distribution of randomly generated networks of the same size. As a consequence, estimations of ERGMs are time consuming, especially when a model includes a complex set of configurations in a large network. It frequently happens that initial selection of configurations has to be adapted to some extent to ensure a better fit of the model with the observed network.

After the model has successfully converged (which does not always happen) and the model parameters are stable, goodness of fit can be evaluated. Although there is no overall model fit measure, a range of partial indicators exists, which in the end provides a comprehensive and reliable evaluation of an ERGM. It is not rare that the model is adapted and estimated again if some of the goodness-of-fit indicators are outside of the reasonable range. Based on the final parameter estimates and their standard errors, a researcher can establish if a structural configuration, actor, or dyadic effect is present in the observed network to a greater or lesser extent than expected by chance, given all other parameter values (Robins, Pattison, *et al.*, 2007).

Although used less frequently than MRQAP, ERGMs have been adopted in management and organization research to study network exchange patterns in online communities (Faraj & Johnson, 2011) and structural logic of intraorganizational networks (Rank, Robins, & Pattison, 2010), and to showcase how they can be used for testing multi-level multi-theoretical models (Contractor, Wasserman, & Faust, 2006). However, to date we have not yet witnessed an application of ERGM in HR research.

There are several ways HR researchers could make use of this method by approaching HR practices or human capital as actor attributes, along with approaching important intraorganizational relations and flows such as work cooperation, trust, help, and knowledge transfer as networks of interest. Obviously, HR researchers will not to be primarily interested in exploring if the observed network has significantly more structural characteristics of interest than expected by chance. They can, however, make a significant contribution to the HR literature by focusing on the social selection part of the model and establishing the impact of actor attributes on the formation of relational ties, while controlling for relevant structural characteristics.

The greatest strength of ERGM is its ability to explicitly model the structural configurations. Another advantage of this analytical approach is the option to simultaneously examine endogenous (structural) and exogenous (actor and dyadic covariates) effects contributing to the formation of relational ties. Further, ERGMs are sensitive to directionality of networks and allow for a comprehensive analysis of directed networks. To conclude, there is continuing progress in the development of various ERGM applications for other types of network types such as multiplex and affiliation networks (Lusher, Koskinen, & Robins, 2012) as well multi-level networks (Wang, Robins, Pattison, & Lazega, 2013). Such progress promises even broader applicability of this approach in the future.

This analytical approach is of course not without limitations. The most important one is that ERGMs do not always converge. The new higher order structural configurations that can be added to a model specification have brought significant improvement (see Robins, Snijders, *et al.,* 2007), but this approach still remains risky for researchers. Related to this, model estimation and fine-tuning of a set of structural properties to be included in it can be highly demanding and necessitate extensive experience with fitting ERGMs. Moreover, although ERGMs implicitly assume network processes, it remains a quasidynamic approach since it does not use longitudinal network data. Finally, model estimation is time consuming and it is not unusual for a simple estimation (several are usually needed to produce a fitting model) to take hours before it is completed.

Network Autocorrelation Model

Network autocorrelation model (NAM) or network effects model is used to examine how attitudes or behaviors of individuals are influenced by their significant others through network *contagion* (Anselin, 1988; Doreian, 1989, 1990; Leenders, 2002). The model builds on the idea that individuals are embedded in networks of other people, so that their own attitudes and behaviors are shaped by considering those of people around them. For instance, NAM can be used to establish how an employee's opinion of the CEO in an organization is simultaneously determined by the opinions of coworkers along with the employee's own hierarchical position, income, and function.

The model differs from the already discussed MRQAP and ERGMs in that it does not primarily emphasize structural properties as a result, but rather examines their effects on individual attributes; it can thus be considered a social influence model (Robins, Pattison, & Elliott, 2001). The main advantage of NAM in comparison to the traditional analytical approaches in social sciences, on the other hand, is that it can, by acknowledging interdependence between actors, directly address hypothesized influence mechanisms, whereas traditional models can only explore them indirectly.

Weight matrix is a key feature of NAM, since it determines the influence mechanism under observation (Leenders, 2002). In particular, it depicts the extent of influence each alter has on the focal individual (ego). An individual's opinion in this model is thus a weighted combination of the opinions of others. By specifying the weight matrix, a researcher operationalizes the theory of social influence to be tested with the model.

There are practically unlimited ways in which the weight matrix can be operationalized (Leenders, 2002; Valente, 2005). Theoretically, any interaction or social comparison, either direct or indirect, between ego and other actors can be a source of social influence on ego provided that she can observe their behaviors or get to know their attitudes (Leenders, 2002). That is, both individuals that ego is in direct contact with (i.e., adjacent actors) and those that she is only in indirect contact with (i.e., nonadjacent actors) can exert influence on her attitudes and behaviors. Since so many options are available for operationalizing the weight matrix, it is essential to have clear theoretical guidance before specifying it and to be aware that statistical tests are available for comparing alternative (theoretically plausible) models.

For estimation of a NAM we need data about attitudes, experiences, or observed behaviors of actors within an organization; one or more weight matrices based on network data; and data about other factors observed at the individual level that could affect the attitudes and behaviors of individual actors. This means that we had already carefully operationalized our theory and used network data to specify the weight matrix. Estimation of the model using maximum likelihood method can be done with the *lnam* module within sna package in R (Butts, 2008). If equally plausible, theoretical models can be tested against each other and Akaike information criterion (AIC) can be used as a criterion for selecting the optimal one (Leenders, 2002).

NAM has been most frequently used in sociology and geography. Appearance in management research is rare (see Ibarra & Andrews, 1993, for an exception). Interestingly, it has been recently adopted for exploring an HR-related topic. In particular, Dabos and Rousseau (2013) explored how advice and friendship ties influence the opinions about psychological contract breach for competitive and noncompetitive resources. They worked with and successfully contrasted two different network influence processes (i.e., direct dyadic influence and indirect influence through the wider social structure of the organization) to show that psychological contract beliefs are developed through both mechanisms with some specificities with regard to the type of resources and relational ties involved. There are, however, many other HR-related research questions that could directly address the role of various influence mechanisms in affecting employees' experiences of HR practices or study the effects of HR-relevant factors on employees' attitudes and behaviors. For instance, Which HR actors have the strongest influence on the development of employee HR attributions? Or, How do social influence processes differ for sense-making and perceiving different HR practices?

The major advantage of the network autocorrelation model in modeling social influence processes is its flexibility, which allows a researcher to truly shape empirical models according to the theory. Further, with network auto-correlation model we can decompose social influence from the impact of other relevant factors in shaping individuals' attitudes or behaviors. It also allows for a comparison of competing social influence models and features a reliable overall fit measure for selecting the best model.

Among disadvantages one can list the fact that this approach, although addressing influence, is not truly longitudinal in that it does not acknowledge more complex interdependencies between actors and that the parameter estimating social influence is negatively biased under nearly all conditions (and especially for higher levels of the parameter and network density) (Mizruchi & Neuman, 2008). Finally, network autocorrelation model, similar to ERGM, can address only one side of social processes at a time, that is, social influence (social selection in the case of ERGMs), which leaves the important question—which of the two social processes is more salient—unanswered.

5. CONCLUSION

By describing social network data gathering and introducing the three confirmatory analytical approaches for complete network data relevant for HR research we hope that more HR researchers will recognize the potential of social network research designs and be encouraged for further learning. Interrupted line in Figure 4.2 represents the frontier of current adoption of social network methods in HR. Recent contributions to HR literature have shown that gathering and analyzing complete network data with analytical approaches such as MRQAP and NAM can also be done in HR research, and we expect to gradually see more researchers adopting these approaches to study new HR-relevant research questions. There are, however, more recent analytical approaches such as ERGMs and stochastic actor-based models for network dynamics (see Snijders, van de Bunt, & Steglich, 2010), which allow a researcher to examine the coevolution of intraorganizational social networks and individual behavior and thus effectively address the social selection and influence dilemma, yet they still remain beyond the frontier of current adoption in HR research.

ACKNOWLEDGEMENTS

The author would like to thank Saša Batistič and Zuzana Sasovova as well as the book editors for their helpful comments on earlier versions of this chapter.

NOTES

1. Ethnographic or archival data (e.g., e-mail correspondence within a company in the past three months) can also be used.
2. This problem is analogous to the one with dependence found in time series data, therefore autocorrelation, but more complex due to varying amounts of dependence of observations on one another in network data (see also Chapter 5). For example, it frequently happens in social network data that two individuals A and C are directly linked or that they both have relational ties to B (i.e., in both cases observations of A and C cannot be treated as independent), but this is not the rule for all actors in a network data set.

REFERENCES

Anselin, L. (1988). *Spatial econometrics: Methods and models.* Norwell, MA: Kluwer.
Batagelj, V., & Mrvar, A. (1998). Pajek-program for large network analysis. *Connections, 21*(2), 47–57.
Borgatti, S. P., & Cross, R. (2003). A relational view of information seeking and learning in social networks. *Management Science, 49*(4), 432–445.
Borgatti, S. P., Everett, M. G., & Freeman, L. C. (2002). *UCINET 6 for Windows: Software for social network analysis.* Harvard: Analytic Technologies.
Borgatti, S. P., & Foster, P. C. (2003). The network paradigm in organizational research: A review of typology. *Journal of Management, 29*(6), 991–1013.
Breiger, R. L. (1974). The duality of persons and groups. *Social Forces, 53*(2), 181–190.
Burkhardt, M. E., & Brass, D. J. (1990). Changing patterns or patterns of change: The effects of a change in technology on social network structure and power. *Administrative Science Quarterly, 35*(1), 104–127.
Butts, C. (2008). Social network analysis with sna. *Journal of Statistical Software, 24*(6), 1–51.
Carrington, P. J., Scott, J., & Wasserman, S. (Eds.). (2005). *Models and methods in social network analysis.* Cambridge: Cambridge University Press.
Chadwick, C. (2010). Theoretic insights on the nature of performance synergies in human resource systems: Toward greater precision. *Human Resource Management Review, 20*(2), 85–101.
Contractor, N. S., Wasserman, S., & Faust, K. (2006). Testing multitheoretical, multilevel hypotheses about organizational networks: An analytic framework and empirical example. *Academy of Management Review, 31*(3), 681–703.

Cross, R., & Cummings, J. N. (2004). Tie and network correlates of individual performance in knowledge-intensive work. *Academy of Management Journal, 47*(6), 928–937.

Cross, R., Kaše, R., Kilduff, M., & King, Z. (2013). Bridging the gap between research and practice in organizational network analysis: A conversation between Rob Cross and Martin Kilduff. *Human Resource Management, 52*(4), 627–644.

Dabos, G. E., & Rousseau, D. M. (2013). Psychological contracts and the informal structure of organizations: The effects of network centrality and social ties. *Human Resource Management, 52*(4), 485–510.

De Nooy, W., Mrvar, A., & Batagelj, V. (2011). *Exploratory social network analysis with Pajek* (2nd ed.). Cambridge: Cambridge University Press.

Doreian, P. (1989). Models of network effects on social actors. In L. C. Freeman, D. R. White, & K. Romney (Eds.), *Research methods in social analysis* (pp. 295–317). Fairfax: George Mason University Press.

Doreian, P. (1990). Network autocorrelation models: Problems and prospects. In D. A. Griffith (Ed.), *Spatial statistics: Past, present, future* (pp. 369–389). Ann Arbor: Institute of Mathematical Geography.

Doreian, P., Batagelj, V., & Ferligoj, A. (2005). *Generalized blockmodeling.* Cambridge: Cambridge University Press.

Faraj, S., & Johnson, S. L. (2011). Network exchange patterns in online communities. *Organization Science, 22*(6), 1464–1480.

Galaskiewicz, J. (2007). Editorial: Has a network theory of organizational behaviour lived up to its promises? *Management and Organization Review, 3*(1), 1–18.

Gant, J., Ichniowski, C., & Shaw, K. (2002). Social capital and organizational change in high-involvement and traditional work organizations. *Journal of Economics & Management Strategy, 11*(2), 289–328.

Hanneman, R. A., & Riddle, M. (2005). *Introduction to social network methods.* Riverside, CA: University of California.

Hubert, L. J. (1987). *The psychology of interpersonal relations.* New York: Wiley.

Ibarra, H., & Andrews, S. B. (1993). Power, social influence, and sense making: Effects of network centrality and proximity on employee perceptions. *Administrative Science Quarterly, 38*(2), 277–303.

Kaše, R., King, Z., & Minbaeva, D. (2013). Guest editors' note: Using social network research in HRM: Scratching the surface of a fundamental basis of HRM. *Human Resource Management, 52*(4), 473–483.

Kaše, R., Paauwe, J., & Zupan, N. (2009). HR practices, interpersonal relations, and intra-firm knowledge transfer in knowledge-intensive firms: A social network perspective. *Human Resource Management, 48*(4), 615–639.

Kenny, D. A., Kashy, D. A., & Cook, W. L. (2006). *Dyadic data analysis.* New York: Guilford Press.

Kilduff, M. (1990). The interpersonal structure of decision making: A social comparison approach to organizational choice. *Organizational Behavior and Human Decision Processes, 47*, 270–288.

Kilduff, M., & Brass, D. J. (2010). Organizational social network research: Core ideas and key debates. *The Academy of Management Annals, 4*, 317–357.

Kilduff, M., & Krackhardt, D. (1994). Bringing the individual back in: A structural analysis of the internal market for reputation in organizations. *Academy of Management Journal, 37*(1), 87–108.

Kilduff, M., & Tsai, W. (2005). *Social networks and organizations.* London: Sage.

Koehly, L. M., & Pattison, P. (2005). Random graph models for social networks: Multiple relations or multiple raters. In P. J. Carrington, J. Scott, & S. Wasserman (Eds.), *Models and methods in social network analysis* (pp. 162–191). Cambridge: Cambridge University Press.

72   *Robert Kaše*

Kossinets, G. (2006). Effects of missing data in social networks. *Social Networks,* 28(3), 247–268.

Krackhardt, D. (1988). Predicting with networks: Nonparametric multiple regression analysis of dyadic data. *Social Networks, 10*(4), 359–381.

Krackhardt, D., & Porter, L. W. (1985). When friends leave: A structural analysis of the relationship between turnover and stayers' attitudes. *Administrative Science Quarterly, 30*(2), 242–261.

Labianca, G., Brass, D. J., & Gray, B. (1998). Social networks and perceptions of intergroup conflict: The role of negative relationships and third parties. *Academy of Management Journal, 41*(1), 55–67.

Laumann, E. O., Marsden, P. V., & Prensky, D. (1992). The boundary specification problem in network analysis. In L. C. Freeman, D. R. White, & A. K. Romney (Eds.), *Research methods in social network analysis* (pp. 61–88). New Brunswick: Transaction Publ.

Leenders, R. T. A. J. (2002). Modeling social influence through network autocorrelation: Constructing the weight matrix. *Social Networks, 24*(1), 21–47.

Lusher, D., Koskinen, J., & Robins, G. (2012). *Exponential random graph models for social networks: Theory, methods, and applications.* Cambridge: Cambridge University Press.

Marsden, P. V. (1987). Core discussion networks of Americans. *American Sociological Review, 52,* 122–131.

McCallister, L., & Fischer, C. (1978). A procedure for surveying personal networks. *Sociological Methods and Research, 7*(2), 131–148.

Mizruchi, M. S., & Neuman, E. J. (2008). The effect of density on the level of bias in the network autocorrelation model. *Social Networks, 30*(3), 190–200.

Nohria, N. (1992). Introduction: Is a network perspective a useful way of studying organizations? In N. Nohria & R. G. Eccles (Eds.), *Networks and organizations: Structure, form, and action* (pp. 1–22). Boston, MA: Harvard Business School Press.

Obstfeld, D. (2005). Social networks, the Tertius Iungens orientation, and involvement in innovation. *Administrative Science Quarterly, 50*(1), 100–130.

Pastor, J.-C., Meindl, J. R., & Mayo, M. C. (2002). A network effects model of charisma attributions. *Academy of Management Journal, 45*(2), 410–420.

Perry-Smith, J. E. (2006). Social yet creative: The role of social relationships in facilitating individual creativity. *Academy of Management Journal, 49*(1), 85–101.

Raider, H., & Krackhardt, D. (2002). Intraorganizational networks. In J. A. C. Baum (Ed.), *The Blackwell companion to organizations* (pp. 59–74). Malden: Blackwell Publishing.

Rank, O. N., Robins, G. L., & Pattison, P. E. (2010). Structural logic of intraorganizational networks. *Organization Science, 21*(3), 745–764.

Robins, G., Elliott, P., & Pattison, P. (2001). Network models for social selection processes. *Social Networks, 23*(1), 1–30.

Robins, G., Pattison, P., & Elliott, P. (2001). Network models for social influence processes. *Psychometrika, 66*(2), 161–189.

Robins, G., Pattison, P., Kalish, Y., & Lusher, D. (2007). An introduction to exponential random graph (p*) models for social networks. *Social Networks, 29*(2), 173–191.

Robins, G., Snijders, T. A. B., Wang, P., Handcock, M., & Pattison, P. (2007). Recent developments in exponential random graph (p*) models for social networks. *Social Networks, 29*(2), 192–215.

Sasovova, Z., Mehra, A., Borgatti, S. P., & Schippers, M. C. (2010). Network churn: The effects of self-monitoring personality on brokerage dynamics. *Administrative Science Quarterly, 55*(4), 639–670.

Snijders, T. A. B., Steglich, C. E. G., Schweinberger, M., & Huisman, M. (2007). Manual for SIENA version 3. Groningen: University of Groningen, ICS. Oxford: University of Oxford, Department of Statistics.

Snijders, T. A. B., van de Bunt, G. G., & Steglich, C. E. G. (2010). Introduction to stochastic actor-based models for network dynamics. *Social Networks, 32*(1), 44–60.

Soltis, S., Agneessens, F., Sasovova, Z., & Labianca, G. (2013). A social network perspective on turnover intentions: The influence of social support and distributive justice. *Human Resource Management, 52*(4), 561–584.

Tsai, W. (2002). Social structure of "coopetition" within a multiunit organization: Coordination, competition, and intraorganizational knowledge sharing. *Organization Science, 13*(2), 179–190.

Tsai, W., & Ghoshal, S. (1998). Social capital and value creation: The role of intrafirm networks. *Academy of Management Journal, 41*(4), 464–476.

Valente, T. W. (2005). Network models and methods for studying the diffusion of innovations. In P. Carrington, J. Scott, & S. Wasserman (Eds.), *Models and methods in social network analysis*. Cambridge: Cambridge University Press.

van Duijn, M. A. J., van Busschbach, J. T., & Snijders, T. A. B. (1999). Multilevel analysis of personal networks as dependent variables. *Social Networks, 21*(2), 187–210.

Wang, P., Robins, G., Pattison, P., & Lazega, E. (2013). Exponential random graph models for multilevel networks. *Social Networks, 35*(1), 96–115.

Wasserman, S., & Faust, K. (1994). *Social network analysis: methods and applications*. Cambridge: Cambridge University Press.

Wright, P. M., Gardner, T. M., Moynihan, L. M., & Allen, M. R. (2005). The relationship between HR practices and firm performance: Examining causal order. *Personnel Psychology, 58*(2), 409–446.

5   Longitudinal Research

Timothy C. Bednall

After reading this chapter, we expect you to be able to:

1. Understand the added value of using a longitudinal research design;
2. Be able to design a longitudinal study, including the number, spacing, and timing of assessments;
3. Gain an understanding of strategies for recruiting and retaining participants;
4. Understand strategies for dealing with missing data;
5. Test the assumption of longitudinal measurement equivalence;
6. Understand the three major families of longitudinal research.

---

1. INTRODUCTION

Longitudinal research refers to studies that investigate change over time. Usually, such studies involve repeated assessments of one or more variables of interest. This chapter provides an introduction to longitudinal research designs and discusses them within a structural equation modeling (SEM) framework. It discusses methodological challenges associated with developing and testing longitudinal models, and presents strategies for overcoming them. It provides an overview and examples of three major families of longitudinal research: (1) change score models, (2) autoregressive and cross-lagged panel models, and (3) latent growth models. Applications of these basic models are discussed. Other approaches to longitudinal data analysis are also briefly reviewed.

2. WHAT IS THE ADDED VALUE OF LONGITUDINAL RESEARCH?

Longitudinal research offers numerous advantages over cross-sectional studies, in which data is collected only at a single point in time. In general, longitudinal studies allow researchers to determine *how* individuals typically change over time, including whether change is swift or gradual, and whether the rate of change remains constant. They permit researchers to determine whether other factors predict *differences* in the way that people change (Singer & Willett, 2003). For example, it may typically take new employees six months to become proficient at their jobs, but employees with a supportive mentor may achieve the same level of proficiency in less time. Compared to cross-sectional studies investigating the relationship between two variables, longitudinal studies permit stronger inferences to be made about the direction of causality (Little, Card, Preacher, & McConnell, 2009). In studies that evaluate the effectiveness of an intervention (e.g., a managerial training program), they permit researchers to assess the longevity and stability of its effects.

Another important advantage over cross-sectional studies is the ability to differentiate the impact of both time-varying and time-invariant factors. A *time-varying variable* refers to a factor that is expected to change over the course of the study. Examples of time-varying factors include an employee's workload in a given week or an employee's current mood or level of stress. Time-varying variables may also represent one-off events that occur at a specific time, such as an employee receiving negative feedback from a supervisor or experiencing conflict within the team. Conversely, a *time-invariant variable* refers to a factor that is not expected to change substantially (or at all) over the course of the study. Examples of time-invariant variables include an employee's gender, cognitive ability, and educational background. Both time-varying and time-invariant predictors may have an impact on how individuals change over time, yet often the effects of time-varying variables are short-lived and limited to the immediate context in which they occur. Longitudinal studies allow researchers to assess the relative impact and longevity of the effects of both types of predictors.

An Introduction to Longitudinal Research

Longitudinal studies offer flexibility and opportunities to make powerful inferences about the nature of change. However, such designs present numerous methodological and logistical challenges compared to cross-sectional studies. Longitudinal models are inherently more complex, and specification of such models can be trickier. Moreover, researchers must make a number of decisions about the research design, including the number and timing of assessments, how best to recruit and retain participants, how to deal with missing data, and how to ensure measurement equivalence across each assessment. This section provides an overview of designing a longitudinal study and discusses strategies for addressing each challenge.

Designing a Longitudinal Study

When designing a longitudinal study, a researcher must first make some assumptions about the hypothesized pattern of change over time. For example, is change expected to be swift or gradual? Is the rate of change expected to remain constant, or will it accelerate or decelerate? Does change occur naturally over time, or is it caused by other factors? After change occurs, is the phenomenon being studied expected to remain stable, or will it fluctuate? All of these considerations should inform the research design.

Researchers should first decide the overall *time frame* of the study, as this decision will influence the rest of the research design. Depending on the research question, this decision can be based on a number of considerations. On the one hand, the decision could reflect a researcher's ideas about the length of time needed for changes to occur. For example, the effects of networking on employees' career advancement may only become apparent after several years. Alternatively, the researcher may be interested in studying change over a specific critical period (e.g., new employees' first year on the job), or may wish to test the longevity of a phenomenon of interest (e.g., how long employees remain motivated after receiving bonus pay). Practical concerns, such as the availability of funding and other resources, will also strongly influence this decision.

The next decisions relate to the number and spacing of repeated assessments. The critical issue is to design a sequence of assessments that can appropriately model the hypothesized pattern of change (Ployhart & Vandenberg, 2009). With respect to the former issue, the *number of assessments* should provide sufficient information for the pattern of change to be reflected in the data. The data points should be able to show, for example, the direction of the change, the speed at which it occurs, whether it is linear versus nonlinear, and whether change is continuous or intermittent. In general, having more waves of data collection is desirable, as reliability and statistical power are increased, the pattern of change is easier to discern, and it is possible to test more flexible models of change (Singer & Willett, 2003). Some authors have argued that longitudinal studies should have at least *three* repeated assessments (e.g., Chan, 1998; Ployhart & Vandenberg, 2009). Studies using only two assessments suffer from at least two major shortcomings: the inability to distinguish true change from measurement error and to recognize nonlinear change.

Researchers should also consider the *spacing of assessments*. The interval between assessments should reflect the researcher's expectations about how rapidly a factor is likely to change. To track changes in something very volatile, such as a person's mood or everyday experiences, researchers may need to gather data points very frequently (see for example, Hofmann, Baumeister, Förster, & Vohs, 2012). Diary or experience sampling technologies may be useful for this purpose (Uy, Foo, & Aguinis, 2009). At the other end of the spectrum, changes in slower moving factors (e.g., an individual's attitudes and values) could be assessed less frequently. When using self-reported measures, researchers should also consider the fallibility of memory. Memories tend to become less detailed and accurate over time, and are often heavily biased by recent experiences and present attitudes (Tourangeau, 1999). As a result, if research participants are asked to describe their activities or attitudes over a long period (e.g., their average level of job satisfaction over the past six months), the information they provide may only crudely summarize what actually happened during that time.

Recruitment, Tracking, and Retention of Participants

Unlike a cross-sectional study, a longitudinal study requires that participants be contacted on multiple occasions to obtain additional data. When conducting longitudinal research, a significant risk concerns participant attrition (i.e., dropouts), which may threaten the viability of the study. To mitigate this risk, it is vital that the researchers carefully plan a *participant recruitment and retention protocol*. Several protocols have been published (e.g., Scott, 2004; Sullivan, 1996), and have described strategies for retaining participants (e.g., Cotter, Burke, Loeber, & Navratil, 2002; Leonard *et al.*, 2003; Ribisl *et al.*, 1996). While a comprehensive review of this literature is not possible, a summary of the most useful advice is presented.

The protocol should clearly define the roles and responsibilities of the entire research team (Scott, 2004). It should specify, for example, the liaison between the researchers and the organization(s) being studied, the person responsible for dealing with participant queries and troubleshooting, and the person whose role it is to obtain and/or validate incoming data. In coordinating the team, it is necessary to check that each person has the requisite knowledge and skills to fulfill the assigned role and to provide training where required. The team should meet regularly to discuss the status of the project and work together to resolve any problems that arise.

Obtaining institutional support for the study is essential. The principal investigator should make substantial efforts to cultivate a close relationship between the research team and the management of the organization being studied (Leonard *et al.*, 2003). This relationship is vital to the success of the project, as management often plays a large role in motivating and facilitating employee participation in the study. In particular, researchers should clearly explain the purpose of the study and reassure management about the likely impact the research project will have on employees' time and other resources. Initial consultation with management in developing the project (e.g., conducting focus groups with senior managers to discuss an organizational survey) may also generate initial motivation. Most importantly, management should be made aware of the *benefits* of participating. For example, benefits may include summary information about the organization and the activities of its employees, insights into how employee performance and services offered to clients can be enhanced, and greater prestige for the organization in the community.

Researchers should also make substantial efforts to engage the research participants directly. At a minimum, researchers should inform them about the reasons for the study, provide assurances about confidentiality, set clear expectations about what their continuing involvement will entail, and explain why their ongoing participation is vital. They should also be made aware of any benefits they (and their colleagues) will receive after the study is completed. For example, benefits may include greater self-knowledge and insights into how they can work more effectively. Researchers may also consider surveying employees in the first assessment about the types of benefits that would motivate them to complete the entire study (e.g., greater self-knowledge). In addition, researchers can consider *payment* as an additional incentive to recruit or retain participants. Various forms of payment exist, including lotteries or donations to a charity chosen by the participants. Another approach is to provide increasing payments in each successive wave of data collection in order to ensure ongoing motivation (Cauce, Ryan, & Grove, 1998). An alternative strategy is to provide an initial unsolicited payment to motivate continued participation by invoking norms of reciprocity (Alexander *et al.*, 2008). The aforementioned strategies can be combined with a bonus payment offer for those who complete all waves.

Another essential element of a longitudinal study is an effective *knowledge management system*, which should be used to maintain up-to-date information about study participants. This system should include a database of information to facilitate *relationship management* with participants (Cotter *et al.*, 2002). At a minimum, this database should contain information about all contact attempts with participants, including the date of the attempt, the mode of communication, whether the attempt was successful, and what was communicated. Some software packages are capable of tracking e-mail correspondence (e.g., whether e-mail has been opened, had links clicked on, or bounced), which may be helpful in studies involving online surveys. Having such information is useful, as it helps researchers build rapport in subsequent interactions and document any problems or reasons for noncompliance that may arise throughout the study.

This knowledge management system should also include a database for *participant tracking* (Ribisl *et al.*, 1996), which could include information such as alternate e-mail addresses, mobile and other telephone numbers, postal addresses, and the contact details of managers or coworkers. This information could be used to contact participants if they cannot be reached via the original channel of communication or, alternatively, to send the participants supplementary materials or incentives. In addition, participants should also be offered facilities to change their contact details if required. The database should also include sufficient identifying information to match data from the same participant across multiple assessments. For example, such information could include a unique participant number, e-mail address, date of birth, gender, postcode, and other demographic information. Some online platforms also have built-in integration with sites such as Gmail, LinkedIn, Facebook, and Amazon Mechanical Turk that may provide another means of tracking participants (Mychasiuk & Benzies, 2012). The tracking system should also be used to maintain records of participation, which can be used to follow up with participants if they appear to have dropped out.

Researchers should devise an approach for dealing with participants who have failed to respond to invitations to take part in subsequent assessments. Regardless of the available budget, researchers should generally opt to use the most inexpensive (and least invasive) methods first, before adopting more resource-intensive solutions (Ribisl *et al.*, 1996; Sullivan, 1996). For example, nonrespondents could first be contacted via follow-up e-mail reminders and short-message service (SMS) messages to participants' mobile phones. If these fail to elicit a response, then other methods of contact could be attempted, such as mailed invitations sent to participants' workplaces or contacts via telephone. While researchers should be persistent in achieving high retention, they should be careful in distinguishing difficult-to-locate versus reluctant participants (Cotter *et al.*, 2002), and respectful if participants elect to withdraw from the study.

Given that at least some attrition is almost inevitable, selecting an appropriate sample size at the outset of the study is essential. One way to do this is to first estimate the sample size required in the final wave of data collection, using either a power analysis or a simulation study (Paxton, Curran, Bollen, Kirby, & Chen, 2001). By making an educated guess about the likely attrition rate per wave of data collection, the researcher can then estimate the sample size required at the beginning of the study to achieve this number[1]. In addition, if participants have dropped out in a previous wave, it is almost always worthwhile to re-recruit them into later waves, as they can still contribute useful data. The exception is if they no longer belong to the population being studied (e.g., they have moved to another organization or have retired).

Statistical Approaches for Dealing with Missing Data

Once the final data set has been obtained, the issue then becomes how to deal with missing data. This issue cannot be ignored, as missing data may lead to incorrect inferences from the analyses. In addition, most analysis software packages will adopt a default approach for dealing with missing data, which may be suboptimal. For example, listwise deletion (i.e., analyzing only cases with complete data) is a very common, yet problematic approach. It can produce biased parameter estimates with certain types of missing data (Enders & Bandalos, 2001). Discarding partial data also substantially reduces the power of the analysis. Consequently, researchers should carefully plan and consider the implications of their strategy for dealing with missing data.

The approach undertaken should depend on the mechanism responsible for missing data, of which there are three types (Rubin, 1976). Data that are *missing completely at random* (MCAR) refers to data on a variable Y whose loss is unrelated to any of the variables in the data set, including Y itself. Data that are *missing at random* (MAR) refers to the loss of data on Y that can be predicted from other variables in the data set, but not Y itself. For example, in a study investigating job demands on multiple occasions, high job demands may lead to busy participants dropping out of the study in later waves. These dropouts may be predicted from reported levels of job demands at previous waves. If data are MAR, then information from other variables can be extrapolated to produce unbiased parameter estimates in a model. Data that are *missing not at random* (MNAR) refers to loss of data on Y that is related to levels of the variable itself. For example, in a study investigating employee bullying, bullied employees may be reluctant to answer a survey question on bullying for fear of exposing themselves to further abuse. This missing-data scenario is the most difficult to deal with.

To deal with MCAR and MAR data, the recommended strategies are the sophisticated missing data techniques, *multiple imputation* (MI) and *full-information maximum likelihood* (FIML). Both techniques have the advantage of using all of the available data when testing a model, including partial data from individuals who have left the study. Under MCAR and MAR conditions, simulation studies suggest that MI and FIML provide accurate estimates of model parameters and standard errors (Allison, 2009; Buhi, Goodson, & Neilands, 2008; Enders & Bandalos, 2001; Newman, 2003), even when data loss is large. In addition, the performance of both missing data procedures has been shown to improve when *auxiliary variables* are incorporated into the analysis (Collins, Schafer, & Kam, 2001). Auxiliary variables refer to additional measures that are not part of the model and that may be correlated with the causes of missingness or the variables that compose the model. For example, demographic (e.g., age, gender) or other employee characteristics (e.g., tenure, seniority within the organization, hours worked per week) could be used as auxiliary variables.

Dealing with MNAR data sets is trickier, but a number of strategies have been proposed (Graham, 2009). One approach is to introduce additional auxiliary variables into the missing data model using either MI or FIML. If the auxiliary variables are highly correlated with the dependent variable, this approach substantially improves the accuracy of parameter estimation (Collins *et al.*, 2001). An approach for dealing with missing data due to attrition is to measure a participant's *intention to drop out* of the study at the outset of data collection; this can later be used as an auxiliary variable in missing data analysis (Schafer & Graham, 2002). A third approach is to attempt to collect follow-up data from participants who were missing from the initial wave of data collection; this can be used to account for differences in parameter estimates between respondents and nonrespondents (Glynn, Laird, & Rubin, 1993). A final strategy is to use one of a number of sophisticated MNAR models to assess and account for the impact of different patterns of missingness (Enders, 2011), including *selection models* (Diggle & Kenward, 1994), *shared parameter models* (Wu & Carroll, 1988), and *pattern-mixture models* (Hedeker & Gibbons, 1997; Muthén, Asparouhov, Hunter, & Leuchter, 2011).

Testing Measurement Invariance of Repeated Assessments

Another methodological issue that should be considered in longitudinal studies is the measurement invariance (also known as factorial invariance) of repeated assessments. Measurement refers to the systematic assignment of numbers on variables to represent characteristics of persons, objects, or events (Vandenberg, 2000). In studies of organizations, examples of such characteristics include employee engagement, attitudes, and performance. Such characteristics are latent factors, in the sense that they are not directly observable but can be inferred through measurement. In a longitudinal design, measurement of latent factors is considered to be invariant if the relationship between the observed assessments and the factor remain consistent over time. In other words, an assessment has measurement invariance if the meaning of an observed score remains the same, regardless of when it was measured.

In measuring a latent factor, even if an identical set of items is used in repeated assessments, the relationship between each item and the factor may change. For example, "feeling like part of the family" is one of the items in Allen and Meyer's (1990) affective commitment scale. For a new employee who has had few opportunities to build professional relationships with other colleagues, this facet may not be a very important component of affective commitment. However, after the employee has been with the organization for several years, "feeling like part of the family" may better reflect the employee's level of commitment. Conversely, other items (e.g., "this organization has a great deal of personal meaning for me") may be consistent indicators of affective commitment over an employee's entire tenure.

If measurement invariance is not established, then it is ambiguous as to whether changes occurring in the observed measures reflect changes in each person's *standing* on the latent factor versus changes in the *measurement* of the factor. The assumption of measurement invariance can be tested using confirmatory factor analysis (CFA; Millsap & Olivera-Aguilar, 2012). This approach involves testing a series of four nested measurement models with increasingly stringent equivalence criteria imposed via parameter constraints. The chi-square difference test can be used to test whether the more stringent models result in significantly worse fit (Widaman, Ferrer, & Conger, 2010; Widaman & Reise, 1997). The four models include: (1) a baseline model, (2) a metric invariance model, (3) a scalar invariance model, and (4) a strict factorial invariance model.

The technical procedure for testing measurement invariance is illustrated below with an example. This procedure can be applied to a longitudinal data set using any SEM software package. It is similar to the CFA approach for testing factorial invariance across groups described in Chapter 7. Figure 5.1 presents a CFA in which a latent variable is measured on three occasions. The observed items (y_1, y_2, y_3) used to measure the latent variable are identical

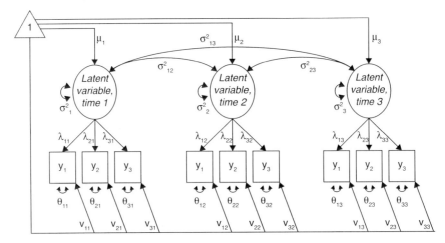

Figure 5.1   Longitudinal confirmatory factor analysis, consisting of three observed variables (y_1, y_2, and y_3) assessed over three time periods

on each occasion. The four increasingly stringent models can be fitted to Figure 5.1. A detailed description is presented below of the four models.

1. **Baseline Model** (configural invariance). In this model, the latent factor is measured across all assessments using the same items with minimal constraints. To identify the model and ensure a common metric across the latent variables, the mean of the first latent variable should be fixed to 0 ($\mu_1 = 0$) and its variance fixed to 1 ($\sigma^2_1 = 1$). The factor loadings of each first item should be constrained to be equal ($\lambda_{11} = \lambda_{12} = \lambda_{13}$) as well as the intercepts of the first items ($v_{11} = v_{12} = v_{13}$). All other parameters should be freely estimated, including latent variable means, variances and covariances, as well as factor loadings and intercepts. In addition, covariances among the error terms (θ) for the same items across assessments may be freely estimated. If this model fails to fit, the researcher should investigate the causes of misfit and respecify the model before proceeding to test the subsequent models.

2. **Metric Invariance Model** (weak factorial invariance). This model is the same as the baseline model, except the factor loadings of the same items are constrained to be equal ($\lambda_{21} = \lambda_{22} = \lambda_{23}$ and $\lambda_{31} = \lambda_{32} = \lambda_{33}$). If this invariance assumption is met, then this finding implies that the correlations among the items will remain invariant at each assessment, and that each item makes an equivalent contribution to the latent factor over time.

3. **Scalar Invariance Model** (strong factorial invariance). This model is identical to the previous model, except the intercepts of the same items

are constrained to be equal ($v_{21} = v_{22} = v_{23}$ and $v_{31} = v_{32} = v_{33}$). If this assumption is met, it implies that changes in the item scores are due to changes in the common factor rather than unilateral changes in scores on any single item. Scalar invariance is the minimum level required for latent variables to be compared across time.

4. **Strict Factorial Invariance Model.** This model is the same as the previous model, except the residual variances (i.e., error terms) of the same items are constrained to be equal ($\theta_{11} = \theta_{12} = \theta_{13}, \theta_{21} = \theta_{22} = \theta_{23}$, and $\theta_{31} = \theta_{32} = \theta_{33}$). If this assumption is met, it implies that any changes in the items are due to changes in the common factor rather than from unmodelled sources. A strict invariance model is preferred, but in some situations it may be unrealistic (Widaman & Reise, 1997). For instance, in studies of expertise (e.g., writing skill), proficiency may be measured as a set of specific components (e.g., vocabulary, grammar, sentence construction). At the beginning, the variance in ability on each component may be uniformly low (i.e., everyone starts with no knowledge). However, as general expertise improves across the entire sample, some people may become more proficient on specific components. As a result, additional variability may be introduced into each component that is not explained by the general expertise factor.

If a strong or strict factorial invariance cannot be achieved, then the researcher may consider respecifying the model to choose different items. Another strategy involves testing a *partial invariance model* (Widaman *et al.*, 2010). This approach involves diagnosing the sources of misfit in a scalar invariance model (e.g., through examination of the modification indices or residual covariance matrices), and then testing a second model in which a constrained parameter (e.g., a factor loading) is then freely estimated. The initial and partially equivalent models can then be tested in a longitudinal structural model. If the structural parameters (e.g., regression coefficients) do not differ greatly, then this outcome suggests that lack of equivalence has a negligible impact on the model results.

3. LONGITUDINAL RESEARCH DESIGNS

This section provides an introduction to three common longitudinal research designs: (1) change score models, (2) autoregressive models, and (3) latent growth curve models. Each technique and its appropriate context are described, and a basic example from the research literature is provided. Supplementary electronic materials, which include sample data sets and worked examples that can be applied in all major SEM programs, are also available. For each type of model, standard fit statistics (e.g., the chi-square test) can be used to evaluate the fit of the model to the data.

Change Score Models

Change score models are used to investigate the determinants of *change* in a dependent variable measured on two or more occasions. In other words, they allow researchers to assess the extent to which people change from an initial (baseline) assessment to a subsequent assessment. Such models could be used to assess the effectiveness of interventions in producing desired change (e.g., evaluating whether productivity increases after a new performance management system is introduced). They can also be used to assess whether nonexperimental factors are associated with change over time (e.g., whether the perceived fairness of human resource management [HRM] practices is associated with increased job satisfaction).

In a two-wave change score model, a single dependent variable (Y_2) is regressed on a baseline score (Y_1), which is called an *autoregressive* relationship. The rationale for the autoregressive relationship is that it allows the other theoretically driven predictors (X_1, X_2, etc.) to be tested as determinants of change in Y. Usually, any predictors would either be assessed between Y_1 and Y_2, or at the same time as Y_2. These predictors may be either time-varying or time-invariant variables. Such a model has been referred to as a *conditional change model* (Finkel, 1995).

The main advantage of change score models is that they may easily be tested using either multiple regression (for two-wave data) or path analysis (for three or more waves). However, they pose at least two disadvantages. First, none of the model variables or parameters depict systematic increases or decreases in the sample mean over time (Selig & Little, 2011). That is, a strong autoregressive relationship between Y_1 and Y_2 implies that each person retains their relative standing on Y compared to the rest of the sample. This relationship does not, however, indicate whether the sample has uniformly increased or decreased on Y. Second, using a regression model to adjust for a baseline measurement can sometimes produce results that are difficult to interpret (see the discussion on Lord's Paradox by Tu, Gunnell, & Gilthorpe, 2008; Wainer & Brown, 2006). Advanced applications of change score models that address these problems are discussed in McArdle (2009).

An example of a change score model is provided in Coyle-Shapiro, Morrow, Richardson, and Dunn (2002, p. 432). This study was conducted with an organization that planned to implement a policy for distributing a portion of its profits to employees as an incentive. The study investigated whether employee perceptions of the profit-sharing policy would lead to increased organizational commitment. Commitment was measured 10 months before the policy's implementation and 20 months after. In their analysis, the post-implementation measure of commitment was used as the dependent variable, which was regressed on the preimplementation measure. Other predictors included employee perceptions of the profit-sharing scheme, trust in management, and several control variables (gender, age and tenure). This analysis

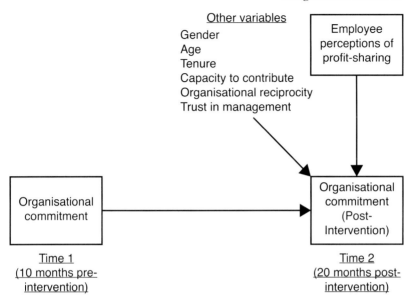

Figure 5.2   Conditional change model (adapted from Coyle-Shapiro *et al.,* 2002)

revealed that positive perceptions of profit-sharing and trust in manage-ment were associated with increased organizational commitment at Time 2. Figure 5.2 presents a depiction of the change score model used in this study.

In this model, organizational commitment is measured on two occasions. At Time 2, the effect of employee perceptions of profit sharing on change in organizational commitment is assessed.

Autoregressive and Cross-Lagged Panel Models

Panel models are similar to change score models in the sense that they examine how prior values of a variable determine its current value via an autoregressive relationship (Bollen & Curran, 2004). However, such models may also include *cross-lagged* relationships, in which prior values of a sec-ond variable determine the current value of the first variable. Cross-lagged models are useful when researchers wish to investigate the cause-effect relationship between two or more variables over time. By incorporating temporal precedence into the model and controlling for past levels of the variables, cross-lagged effects provide evidence of the *direction* of causation between two or more variables (Biesanz, 2012).

In a two-wave cross-lagged model with two factors, each variable (Y_2 and Z_2) is regressed on its baseline measurement (Y_1 and Z_1), as well as the prior values of the other variable (Z_1 and Y_1). The autoregressions provide an indication of the relative stability of individual differences in each variable over time. The cross-lagged temporal relationships also indicate how each variable influences the other variable over time. In addition, if the researcher hypothesizes a causal relationship between variables measured at a specific point in time, a directional path may be specified (e.g., Y_2 to Z_2, or vice versa). Alternatively, the researcher may allow the disturbances of Y_2 and Z_2 to covary. This relationship indicates the extent to which changes in one variable are related to changes in the other variable that are not explained by the other predictors in the model (Biesanz, 2012).

Cross-lagged panel models can also assess the effects of both time-varying and time-invariant variables. Time-varying variables may be included as covariates of each factor at each time point. With regard to time-invariant variables, there are at least three approaches to including them. Among these approaches are: (1) as a covariate of each variable on the last measurement occasion (as in a change score model), (2) as a covariate of each variable on the first measurement occasion, or (3) as a covariate of each variable on all measurement occasions. The choice of approach should depend on the nature of the covariates and the purpose of the model (Little, Preacher, Selig, & Card, 2007).

There are several issues that researchers should consider when using cross-lagged models. First, as cross-lagged models involve multiple dependent variables, they require either path analysis or full structural equation modeling to test. Second, similar to change score models, they cannot be used to depict systematic increases or decreases in the sample mean across time. In addition, models involving three or more waves of data raise additional considerations. Researchers may wish to test the assumption that the autoregressive and cross-lagged relationships remain stable over time. If the magnitude of effect sizes do not change, the model is said to be *stationary* (Cole & Maxwell, 2003). The stationarity assumption can be tested by constraining model parameters to equality and examining changes in model fit. If the constrained model results in significantly worse fit, then the stationarity assumption should be rejected (for an overview of this procedure, see Finkel, 1995). This procedure should only be applied if the interval between each wave of data collection is equal.

An example of a three-wave cross-lagged panel model is shown in Lu and Kao (2013, p. 366). This study was conducted with a sample of employees from different industries in Taiwan who were surveyed six months apart. It investigated the relationship between employees' workloads, level of work-family conflict, and job satisfaction. Significant cross-lagged relationships revealed that a high workload at baseline led to increased work-family conflict six months and one year later. The study also revealed that low job satisfaction at baseline led to increased work-family conflict six months and one year later. At each time point, significant relationships were also observed among the three variables. Figure 5.3 presents a depiction of the cross-lagged model used in this study.

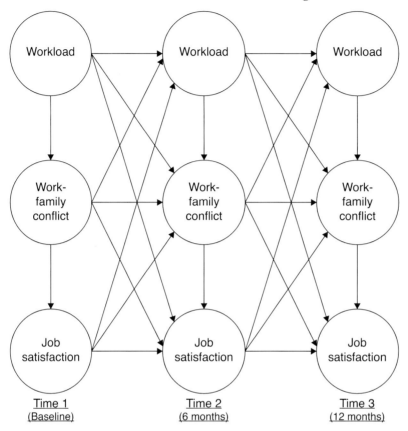

Figure 5.3   Cross-lagged panel model (adapted from Lu & Kao, 2013)

In this model, employees' workload, family-work conflict, and job satisfaction are measured on three occasions. The model depicts autoregressive and cross-lagged relationships across the three time periods. It also specifies a causal path from workload to work-family conflict to job satisfaction at each time.

Latent Growth Curve Models

Latent growth curve models (LGMs)—also referred to as latent trajectory models—are a third approach to investigating change (McArdle, 2009). Unlike change score and cross-lagged models, LGMs allows researchers to specify and test specific models of *intraindividual* change. In other words, LGMs allow researchers to specify and test models that reflect researchers' expectations about how individuals change over time. The approach involves modeling individual *trajectories* of growth (or decline) over time. Characteristics of these trajectories can be averaged across a sample to provide a descriptive summary of how a typical member of a population is expected to change.

An individual's trajectory may be thought of as a line of best fit that runs through the individual's data points that are plotted across time. A linear trajectory can be described in terms of two characteristics: (1) an intercept, representing an individual's initial standing on a variable, and (2) a slope, representing the individual's rate of linear change over time. (Nonlinear trajectories may also be depicted using additional terms.) An example of a set of linear growth trajectories is presented in Figure 5.4.

This figure depicts the level of expertise for nine employees. Expertise is measured on a scale of 0 to 5 and is assessed on four occasions. The lines represent growth trajectories for individual employees (i.e., a line of best fit through their data points). As can be seen on the graph, some employees begin with more expertise than others, and some employees increase their expertise more quickly than others. The bold line represents the "average" trajectory for the sample. This trajectory has an initial level (intercept) of 1.8 and a gradient (linear slope) of 0.2.

In an LGM, the factor being investigated must be assessed at least three times. The intercepts and slopes of each trajectory are depicted using latent variables, which load on to the observed assessments at each wave of data collection. The latent intercept is specified with factor loadings of 1 for all of the observed assessments. The latent slope is specified with factor loadings

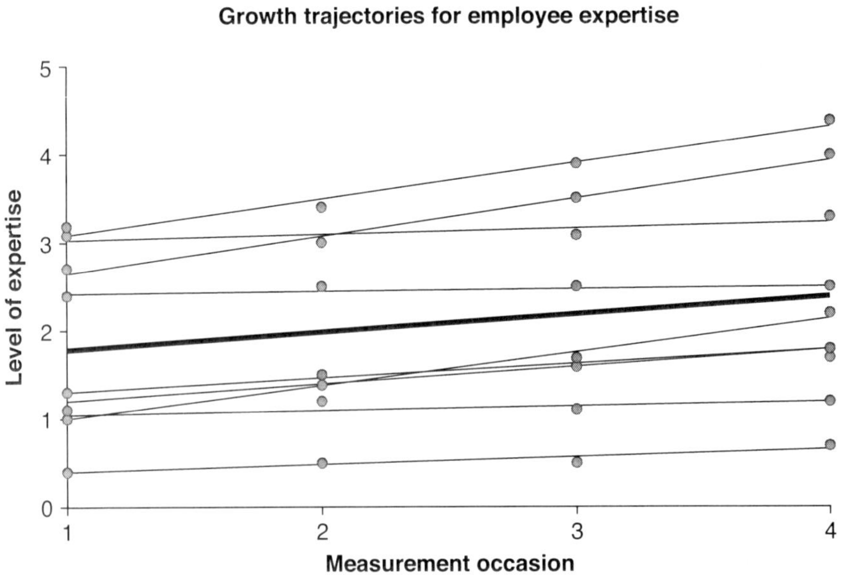

Figure 5.4   Growth trajectories for employee productivity

that reflect the timing of each assessment. Usually, these factor loadings are numbered consecutively beginning with 0 for the first assessment (e.g., 0, 1, 2, 3). If the assessments are unevenly spaced, they may follow a different sequence (e.g., 0, 3, 5, 12). The unit of time is arbitrary (e.g., the factor loadings may represent days, months, or years), but it should remain consistent within the model.

An LGM should be specified so that the means of the latent variables are freely estimated. These parameters collectively describe the trajectory of a "typical" person within the population of interest. To estimate these latent variable means, the intercepts of the observed variables must be fixed to 0. In this specification, the latent variables thus contain all of the information about the means of the observed variables.

Nonlinear change can be assessed by allowing some of the factor loadings to be freely estimated (e.g., 0, 1, λ_1, λ_2). In this configuration, at least two of the factor loadings must be fixed in order to establish a unit of time. The values of λ_1 and λ_2 can be used to assess acceleration or deceleration of change. If λ_1 and λ_2 are greater than the corresponding factor loadings for a linear model (i.e., $\lambda_1 > 2$, $\lambda_2 > 3$), this result suggests that the rate of change is accelerating over time. Conversely, if λ_1 and λ_2 are less than these factor loadings (i.e., $\lambda_1 < 2$, $\lambda_2 < 3$), this result suggests the rate of change is slowing over time (or going backwards). Nonlinear change can also be assessed by introducing additional latent variables to a basic linear slope model. For example, a quadratic trend could be tested by introducing a third latent variable with squared factor loadings (i.e., 0, 1, 4, 9).

An advantage of LGM is that it is possible to model the effects of both time-invariant and time-varying covariates. To assess the impact of time-invariant variables (e.g., cognitive ability), the latent intercept and slope variables can be regressed on the time-invariant covariates. The effects of categorical variables (e.g., gender or an experimental manipulation) can also be assessed using a multigroup model, in which separate latent variable means are calculated for each group. To assess the impact of time-varying variables (e.g., average monthly workload), assessments at each wave of data can be regressed on the time-varying covariates. An example of an LGM is provided in Wang and Shyu (2009, p. 1794). This study investigated the impact of HRM practices on labor productivity. Labor productivity was assessed yearly from 2002 to 2005 within 126 manufacturing firms. The researchers first specified a linear change model, which included two latent variables representing the initial (2002) level of productivity and a slope representing linear growth over time. This part of the analysis revealed that the average level of labor productivity increased from 2002 to 2005. In the second part of the analysis, the two latent variables were regressed on a measure of HRM practice effectiveness (as well as several other variables), which was treated as a time-invariant variable. This analysis revealed that firms with effective HRM practices had higher average levels of labor productivity in 2002. More importantly, these firms showed steeper rates of

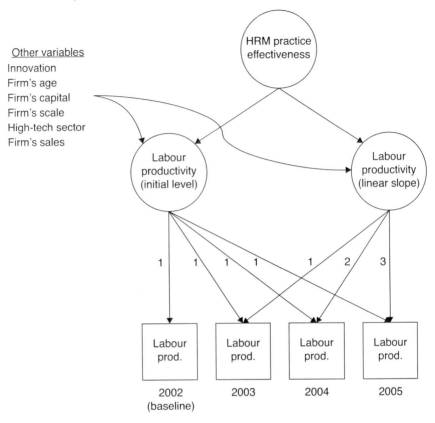

Figure 5.5   Latent growth curve model with four assessments (adapted from Wang & Shyu, 2009)

labor productivity growth in the three subsequent years. Figure 5.5 presents a (simplified) depiction of the LGM used in this study.

In this model, labor productivity is assessed on four occasions (from 2002 to 2005). Systematic change in productivity is depicted through two latent variables, representing the initial level of labor productivity and linear growth over time. The model assesses the effect of HRM practice effectiveness on these two latent variables.

4. OTHER LONGITUDINAL RESEARCH DESIGNS

This chapter provided an introduction to three families of longitudinal research designs: change score models, cross-lagged panel models, and latent growth models. Several other approaches to longitudinal data analysis are possible and may be useful to researchers investigating change.

In some cases, longitudinal models can also be analyzed using *multi-level regression* with nested data structures. For example, in a three-level model, the first level could represent individual change over time, the second level individual differences, and the third level group differences. In theory, such models should produce identical results to an LGM applied to the same data set (Hox, 2010). Although flexible, it is trickier to account for measurement error in the observed variables and assess goodness of fit. Refer to Chapter 3 in this volume for an overview of multi-level models.

Conventional LGM assumes that all individuals in the study sample are drawn from the same population. In reality, there may be unobserved subpopulations in the sample that each show very different growth trajectories. For example, one subpopulation may show linear growth in a variable over time, another may show a slower rate of growth, and a third group may reach a peak followed by a sharp decline. On occasion, an LGM will fail to converge if subpopulations are not accounted for in the analysis. *Growth mixture modelling* (Wang & Bodner, 2007) is a technique that can be used to uncover previously unknown subpopulations within a sample and estimate different growth trajectories for each group.

Various kinds of hybrid models attempt to incorporate the strengths of both panel models and LGMs. For example, *autoregressive latent trajectory models* (Bollen & Curran, 2004) allow researchers to simultaneously model both autoregressive and cross-lagged relationships, as well as systematic changes in mean scores. In addition, *state-trait-occasion models* (Cole, Martin, & Steiger, 2005) allow researchers to decompose the variance of repeated measurements into state- and trait-based variance using latent variables to depict each. Such models are useful for determining the extent to which a measure is influenced by a person's current state, as well as an underlying trait. For example, a person's level of job satisfaction may be influenced by current working conditions (e.g., it may be temporarily high if the person received positive feedback), as well as a "baseline" (i.e., trait-like) level of satisfaction. Usually, the latent variables representing states are connected via autoregressive relationships.

Survival analysis is another form of longitudinal data analysis that can be used to predict the occurrence and timing of a critical event (Singer & Willett, 2003). The technique has been used frequently in medical research to investigate factors that hasten mortality, or in engineering to predict mechanical failure. In organizational research, the same technique may be useful in studying events such as employee turnover or retirement.

Finally, while this chapter has focused on quantitative studies, there is no reason why longitudinal research cannot be conducted using *qualitative* data sets. For example, Boswell, Roehling, LePine, and Moynihan (2003) interviewed job seekers on multiple occasions during their search for a new job. Based on this interview data, they documented the factors that influenced their job choice at each stage.

Conducting a longitudinal study: How does it work in practice?

Alex is a PhD student who is investigating whether the introduction of an incentive payment system increases the performance of a sales workforce in a large retailing chain. She expects that the employees will generally begin to work harder to obtain the bonus pay, but it will take about three months for the effects to become fully apparent. Based on this assumption, she obtains sales performance data for three months.

She also expects that some employees will respond better to the new system than others. Specifically, she hypothesizes that employees who are highly customer focused will show the greatest performance increases. She reasons that such employees will be better at "upselling" additional products to the customers they serve, thereby generating higher sales revenues. Based on this hypothesis, she asks employees to self-rate their level of customer focus on a questionnaire. She uses this measure as a *time invariant* variable in her analysis. In addition, some times of year are busier than others, which will affect the volume of sales. As a result, Alex decides to record the number of walk-ins who enter the store. She uses the number of walk-ins per month as a *time-varying* variable.

Alex analyzes the data using a latent growth model, using a latent intercept to represent employees' initial sales performance and a slope to represent linear change in their performance. She finds that the slope is positive and significantly different from zero, indicating that sales performance has increased. The rate of growth is significantly higher for employees who are highly customer focused. In addition, the volume of sales was significantly higher in the months when there were many walk-in customers.

---

5. CONCLUDING REMARKS

This chapter provided an introduction to longitudinal research. It outlined several methodological considerations, including the number and timing of assessments, sampling and retention strategies, dealing with missing data, and testing measurement equivalence. It introduced three research designs: change score models, the cross-lagged panel model, and the latent growth model, and examples of each from the literature.

The choice of model should be informed by the researchers' view of how and why change occurs and the relationships between the variables of interest over time. In summary, change score models are useful when the research aim is to determine what factors are responsible for change in a factor over time. Autoregressive and cross-lagged panel models are suitable for assessing reciprocal relationships between variables over time and providing evidence of the direction of causality. Latent growth models are useful for describing individual trajectories of change and assessing how other factors influence those trajectories.

ACKNOWLEDGEMENTS

I would like to acknowledge a number of people who provided suggestions and feedback on this chapter, including David Bednall, Joanne Earl, Denise Jepsen, Yiqiong Li, and Alexa Muratore.

NOTE

1. The researchers can apply the formula, $N_1 = N_w \div (R^{w-1})$, where N_x refers to the number of participants in the xth wave of data collection, w refers to the number of waves of data collection in the study, and R refers to the expected retention rate. For example, in a three-wave study in which the required number of participants was 100 in the final wave and the expected rate of attrition was 10% in each wave, $N_1 = 100 \div (.90^{3-1}) = 123$.

REFERENCES

Alexander, G. L., Divine, G. W., Couper, M. P., McClure, J. B., Stopponi, M. A., Fortman, K. K., Johnson, C. C. (2008). Effect of incentives and mailing features on online health program enrollment. *American Journal of Preventive Medicine, 34,* 382–388.

Allen, N. J., & Meyer, J. P. (1990). The measurement and antecedents of affective, continuance and normative commitment to the organization. *Journal of Occupational Psychology, 63,* 1–18.

Allison, P. D. (2009). Missing data. In R. E. Millsap & A. Maydeu-Olivares (Eds.), *The SAGE handbook of quantitative methods in psychology* (Vol. 55, pp. 193–196). London: Sage.

Biesanz, J. (2012). Autoregressive longitudinal models. In R. H. Hoyle (Ed.), *Handbook of structural equation modeling* (pp. 459–471). New York: The Guilford Press.

Bollen, K. A., & Curran, P. J. (2004). Autoregressive latent trajectory (ALT) models: A synthesis of two traditions. *Sociological Methods & Research, 32,* 336–383.

Boswell, W. R., Roehling, M. V., LePine, M. A., & Moynihan, L. M. (2003). Individual job-choice decisions and the impact of job attributes and recruitment practices: A longitudinal field study. *Human Resource Management, 42,* 23–37.

Buhi, E. R., Goodson, P., & Neilands, T. B. (2008). Out of sight, not out of mind: Strategies for handling missing data. *American Journal of Health Behavior, 32,* 83–92.

Cauce, A. M., Ryan, K. D., & Grove, K. (1998). Children and adolescents of color, where are you? Participation, selection, recruitment, and retention in developmental research. In V. C. McLoyd & L. Steinberg (Eds.), *Studying minority adolescents: Conceptual, methodological, and theoretical issues* (pp. 147–166). Mahwah, New Jersey: Lawrence Erlbaum.

Chan, D. (1998). The conceptualization and analysis of change over time: An integrative approach incorporating longitudinal mean and covariance structures analysis (LMACS) and multiple indicator latent growth modeling (MLGM). *Organizational Research Methods, 1,* 421–483.

Cole, D. A., Martin, N. C., & Steiger, J. H. (2005). Empirical and conceptual problems with longitudinal trait-state models: Introducing a trait-state-occasion model. *Psychological Methods, 10,* 3–20.

Cole, D. A., & Maxwell, S. E. (2003). Testing mediational models with longitudinal data: Questions and tips in the use of structural equation modeling. *Journal of Abnormal Psychology, 112*, 558–577.

Collins, L. M., Schafer, J. L., & Kam, C.-M. (2001). A comparison of inclusive and restrictive strategies in modern missing data procedures. *Psychological Methods, 6*, 330–351.

Cotter, R. B., Burke, J. D., Loeber, R., & Navratil, J. L. (2002). Innovative retention methods in longitudinal research: A case study of the developmental trends study. *Journal of Child and Family Studies, 11*, 485–498.

Coyle-Shapiro, J. A. M., Morrow, P. C., Richardson, R., & Dunn, S. R. (2002). Using profit sharing to enhance employee attitudes: A longitudinal examination of the effects on trust and commitment. *Human Resource Management, 41*, 423–439.

Diggle, P., & Kenward, M. G. (1994). Informative drop-out in longitudinal data analysis. *Applied Statistics, 43*, 49–93.

Enders, C. K. (2011). Analyzing longitudinal data with missing values. *Rehabilitation Psychology, 56*, 267–288.

Enders, C. K., & Bandalos, D. L. (2001). The relative performance of full information maximum likelihood estimation for missing data in structural equation models. *Structural Equation Modeling: A Multidisciplinary Journal, 8*, 430–457.

Finkel, S. E. (1995). *Causal analysis with panel data* (Vol. 105). Thousand Oaks, CA: Sage Publications, Inc.

Glynn, R. J., Laird, N. M., & Rubin, D. B. (1993). Multiple imputation in mixture models for nonignorable nonresponse with follow-ups. *Journal of the American Statistical Association, 88*, 984–993.

Graham, J. W. (2009). Missing data analysis: Making it work in the real world. *Annual Review of Psychology, 60*, 549–576.

Hedeker, D., & Gibbons, R. D. (1997). Application of random-effects pattern-mixture models for missing data in longitudinal studies. *Psychological Methods, 2*, 64–78.

Hofmann, W., Baumeister, R. F., Förster, G., & Vohs, K. D. (2012). Everyday temptations: An experience sampling study of desire, conflict, and self-control. *Journal of Personality and Social Psychology, 102*, 1318–1335.

Hox, J. J. (2010). *Multilevel analysis: Techniques and applications*. New York: Routledge.

Leonard, N. R., Lester, P., Rotheram-Borus, M. J., Mattes, K., Gwadz, M., & Ferns, B. (2003). Successful recruitment and retention of participants in longitudinal behavioral research. *AIDS Education and Prevention, 15*, 269–281.

Little, T. D., Card, N. A., Preacher, K. J., & McConnell, E. (2009). Modeling longitudinal data from research on adolescence. In R. M. Lerner & L. Steinberg (Eds.), *Handbook of adolescent psychology*. New York: John Wiley & Sons, Inc.

Little, T. D., Preacher, K. J., Selig, J. P., & Card, N. A. (2007). New developments in latent variable panel analyses of longitudinal data. *International Journal of Behavioral Development, 31*, 357–365.

Lu, L., & Kao, S.-F. (2013). The reciprocal relations of pressure, work/family interference, and role satisfaction: Evidence from a longitudinal study in Taiwan. *Human Resource Management, 52*, 353–373.

McArdle, J. J. (2009). Latent variable modeling of differences and changes with longitudinal data. *Annual Review of Psychology, 60*, 577–605.

Millsap, R. E., & Olivera-Aguilar, M. (2012). Investigating measurement invariance using confirmatory factor analysis. In R. H. Hoyle (Ed.), *Handbook of structural equation modeling* (pp. 380–392). New York: The Guildford Press.

Muthén, B., Asparouhov, T., Hunter, A. M., & Leuchter, A. F. (2011). Growth modeling with nonignorable dropout: Alternative analyses of the STAR*D antidepressant trial. *Psychological Methods, 16*, 17–33.

Mychasiuk, R., & Benzies, K. (2012). Facebook: An effective tool for participant retention in longitudinal research. *Child: Care, Health and Development, 38,* 753–756.

Newman, D. A. (2003). Longitudinal modeling with randomly and systematically missing data: A simulation of ad hoc, maximum likelihood, and multiple imputation techniques. *Organizational Research Methods, 6,* 328–362.

Paxton, P., Curran, P. J., Bollen, K. A., Kirby, J., & Chen, F. (2001). Monte Carlo experiments: Design and implementation. *Structural Equation Modeling: A Multidisciplinary Journal, 8,* 287–312.

Ployhart, R. E., & Vandenberg, R. J. (2009). Longitudinal research: The theory, design, and analysis of change. *Journal of Management, 36,* 94–120.

Ribisl, K. M., Walton, M. A., Mowbray, C. T., Luke, D. A., Davidson, W. S., II, & Bootsmiller, B. J. (1996). Minimizing participant attrition in panel studies through the use of effective retention and tracking strategies: Review and recommendations. *Evaluation and Program Planning, 19,* 1–25.

Rubin, D. B. (1976). Inference and missing data. *Biometrika, 63,* 581–592.

Schafer, J. L., & Graham, J. W. (2002). Missing data: Our view of the state of the art. *Psychological Methods, 7,* 147–177.

Scott, C. K. (2004). A replicable model for achieving over 90% follow-up rates in longitudinal studies of substance abusers. *Drug and Alcohol Dependence, 74,* 21–36.

Selig, J. P., & Little, T. D. (2011). Autoregressive and cross-lagged panel analysis. In B. Laursen, T. D. Little, & N. A. Card (Eds.), *Handbook of developmental research methods* (pp. 265–278). New York: Guilford Press.

Singer, J. D., & Willett, J. B. (2003). *Applied longitudinal data analysis: Modeling change and event occurrence.* New York: Oxford University Press.

Sullivan, C. M. (1996). Retaining participants in longitudinal community research: A comprehensive protocol. *The Journal of Applied Behavioral Science, 32,* 262–276.

Tourangeau, R. (1999). Remembering what happened: Memory errors and survey reports. In A. A. Stone, C. A. Bachrach, J. B. Jobe, H. S. Kurtzman, & V. S. Cain (Eds.), *The science of self-report: Implications for research and practice* (pp. 29–47). Mahwah, NJ: Lawrence Erlbaum Associates.

Tu, Y. K., Gunnell, D., & Gilthorpe, M. S. (2008). Simpson's paradox, Lord's paradox, and suppression effects are the same phenomenon—the reversal paradox. *Emerging Themes in Epidemiology, 5,* 1–9.

Uy, M. A., Foo, M. D., & Aguinis, H. (2009). Using experience sampling methodology to advance entrepreneurship theory and research. *Organizational Research Methods, 13,* 31–54.

Vandenberg, R. J. (2000). A review and synthesis of the measurement invariance literature: Suggestions, practices, and recommendations for organizational research. *Organizational Research Methods, 3,* 4–70.

Wainer, H., & Brown, L. M. (2006). Three statistical paradoxes in the interpretation of group differences: Illustrated with medical school admission and licensing data. *Handbook of Statistics, 26,* 893–918.

Wang, D.-S., & Shyu, C.-L. (2009). The longitudinal effect of HRM effectiveness and dynamic innovation performance on organizational performance in Taiwan. *The International Journal of Human Resource Management, 20,* 1790–1809.

Wang, M., & Bodner (2007). Growth mixture modeling: Identifying and predicting unobserved subpopulations with longitudinal data. *Organizational Research Methods, 10,* 635–656.

Widaman, K. F., Ferrer, E., & Conger, R. D. (2010). Factorial invariance within longitudinal structural equation models: Measuring the same construct across time. *Child Development Perspectives, 4,* 10–18.

Widaman, K. F., & Reise, S. P. (1997). Exploring the measurement invariance of psychological instruments: Applications in the substance use domain. In K. J. Bryant, M. Windle, & S. G. West (Eds.), *The science of prevention: Methodological advances from alcohol and substance abuse research* (pp. 281–324). Washington, DC: American Psychological Association.

Wu, M. C., & Carroll, R. J. (1988). Estimation and comparison of changes in the presence of informative right censoring by modeling the censoring process. *Biometrics, 44,* 175–188.

6 Experimental Method in HRM Research

Huadong Yang and Julie Dickinson

After reading this chapter, we expect you to be able to:

1. Understand the added value of using experimental methods in HRM research;
2. Recognize the core elements in designing an experiment;
3. Gain an understanding of the meaning of control in experiments;
4. Be familiar with using the vignette technique as a way of manipulation.

---

1. INTRODUCTION

This chapter provides some general information about the experimental method for studying HRM-related topics and introduces a specific technique—the vignette technique—to manipulate independent variables in experimental designs. It starts with the contributions that the experimental method can make to HRM research. Then we introduce the key characteristics of the experimental method. Next we highlight the vignette technique as a way of manipulating independent variables in experimental designs and provide an example to show how to use this technique in HRM studies. The chapter concludes with a discussion of the advantages and challenges of using experimental methods in HRM research.

2. VALUE OF THE EXPERIMENTAL METHOD IN HRM RESEARCH

One of the most important research questions in the HRM field is the relationship between HRM and performance, both in terms of employee and organizational outcomes. Although this question has been the main interest of researchers since the beginning of HRM studies, the answers have not been clear so far. Guest (2012, p.11), in his review on HRM and performance, concluded: "After hundreds of research studies we are still in no position to assert with any confidence that good HRM has an (positive) impact on organizational performance."

In diagnosing why there is no robust conclusion that can be drawn from existent literature concerning HRM and performance, many scholars (Guest, 2011; Gerhart, 2007; Wright, Gardner, Moynihan, & Allen, 2005) have pointed to the methodological shortcomings in the majority of HRM studies. The question of the relationship between HRM (either in terms of HRM practice or HRM process) and performance (in terms of employee and organizational outcomes) concerns *a cause-and-effect relationship;* that is, we assume that HRM is the cause and enhanced performance is the outcome. However, the research designs and methods commonly used in the HRM field rely on cross-sectional survey studies (see Chapter 1 for more information). Cross-sectional survey studies are powerful in identifying associations among variables, but they have drawbacks for establishing a cause-and-effect relationship. In comparison, the experimental method is a scientific approach that is designed to test for a cause-and-effect relationship. Using the experimental method, researchers can observe the effects of systematically changing one of more variables under controlled conditions (Christensen, 2007). Concerning the relationship between HRM and performance, if researchers are able to make HRM vary systematically in a controlled situation, any changes regarding individual and organizational performance can then be attributed to the cause of HRM.

The above example is hypothetical and oversimplifies the complicated HRM practice. The ideas behind this hypothetical example, however, reveal the added value of conducting experiments in the field of HRM. With the experimental method, researchers can study HRM practices and processes in a controlled situation. Such a setup creates an opportunity for researchers to check whether HR-related factors really have an effect on employee and organizational outcomes and examine the cause-and-effect relationship between HRM and performance directly. The extent to which researchers can accurately state that the independent variable *A* causes a change in the dependent variable *B* is termed *internal validity*. In this regard, the experimental method offers a chance to generate a high internal validity.

3. KEY CHARACTERISTICS OF THE EXPERIMENTAL METHOD

By definition the experimental method is designed to explore a cause-and-effect relationship between the independent variable and the dependent variable. The advantage of examining the cause-and-effect relationship makes the experimental method suitable to address the research question of the relationship between HRM and performance. Therefore, the experimental method has particular value for HRM studies. The challenge faced by HRM researchers, however, is how to apply the experimental method to the HRM field, where research issues are often practically oriented and complex. To tackle this challenge we first need to understand the key characteristics of the experimental method.

In the experimental method researchers observe or measure the changes in outcome variables (or dependent variables) under two conditions: (1) the *independent variable* needs to be arranged to vary systematically, and (2) other variables that might have an effect on the dependent variables need to be kept constant in a controlled situation. The first condition is managed by means of *manipulating* the independent variable and the second by means of *controlling* extraneous variables. Put differently, "manipulation of independent variables" and "control of extraneous variables," are the two key characteristics of the experimental method. In the following part, we will discuss these two characteristics in detail.

Manipulation of Independent Variables

The term *manipulation* refers to the experimenters administering one treatment of the independent variable to one group of individuals and another treatment of the independent variable to a second group of individuals. By doing so, the experimenters aim to vary the independent variable systematically. Manipulation of the independent variables in the experimental method is different from measures of the independent variables in a questionnaire survey in two ways. First, manipulation is arranged by researchers deliberately and intentionally to capture the different levels of the independent variable. Measures in the questionnaire survey, in contrast, tend to manifest the "variation" of the independent variable as it might be in reality and are not preset by researchers. Second, the independent variable in the experimental method is manipulated as an ordinal variable (e.g., presence versus absence; a weak condition versus a strong condition), but the independent variable in the questionnaire survey is operationalized as an interval variable (e.g., 1 = strongly disagree; 5 = strongly agree).

For instance, an HR manager is interested in how recruitment team members' skills on social media tools (e.g., LinkedIn, Facebook) may have an effect on their efficiency in approaching potential candidates. If the questionnaire survey method is used, the focus in the research design would be on constructing the reliable and valid scales to measure such skills accurately and distributing the questionnaires around a representative sample to capture the full variation of members' skills. If the experimental method is used, the research concerns would be on manipulating the levels of skills. For example, one group of participants would receive a training workshop aimed at increasing members' skills on social media tools. A second group would not receive such training. This arrangement allows researchers to create a level difference in the independent variable of "skills on social media tools." This example shows that the questionnaire method is good at capturing the realistic variation of the independent variable. By contrast, with the experimental method researchers intentionally "create" different levels of the independent variable and then "observe" its consequential effect on the dependent variable.

There are two basic ways of experimentally manipulating an independent variable. By *instructional manipulation*, one group of participants receives a set of instructions and another group receives another set of instructions. Instructional manipulation tries to generate different anticipations between the experimental group and the control group and prepare participants in those two groups with different mind-sets before conducting their task. The priming technique is a good example of instructional manipulation. In a study in which Shantz and Latham (2011) were interested in how subconscious processes had an influence on employee job performance, they used the priming technique as an instructional manipulation to elicit participants' subconscious goal-settings. Employees who worked in a call center as fund-raisers were recruited to participate in their study. The subconscious goals were operationalized by presenting a piece of information either on a paper that had the backdrop photograph of a woman winning a race (the experimental group) or on a paper that had no backdrop photograph (the control group). Their assumption was that the backdrop photograph of a woman winning a race subconsciously directs participants toward goal-oriented behavior more than the backdrop with no photograph. So the backdrop photograph serves as a kind of instructional manipulation. The results showed that participants in the experimental group on average had a better job performance (e.g., the amount of money raised) than those in the control group.

The second way of experimentally manipulating an independent variable is *event manipulation*. By event manipulation, the experimenters change the events that participants experience to create a systematic variation of the independent variable. In comparison with instructional manipulation, event manipulation is more realistic and has a stronger effect on participants. However, in HRM studies event manipulation is often costly. Researchers need to negotiate with the organization on many barriers. Intervention is a good example of event manipulation. For example, Frayne and Geringer (2000) performed an intervention program in which a self-management training workshop was administered to 30 sales employees at a life insurance company (the experimental group). In their study self-management training consisted of lectures, group discussions, and case studies. The training program contained four weekly sessions, each two hours long, and was offered during normal work hours. There was no such training for the control group ($n = 30$). The findings showed that participants in the experimental group who received training in self-management skills had better job performance than those in the control group.

Note that the goal of manipulation is to create a systematic variation in the independent variable. A *manipulation check* is usually carried out to verify that the manipulation of the independent variable is consistent with what the researchers believe it to be reflecting (Bryman, 1989). In other words, manipulation checks ensure that there is a systematic variation of the independent variable. In the example of the effects of skills in social media tools on recruiters' job performance, the researcher would need to carry out a manipulation check after the participants had received a relevant training workshop by asking participants to demonstrate their skills in using social media (for instance, by using a scale measuring their expertise on social media tools). If the participants in the training group demonstrate more expertise in social media tools than the participants who do not receive such training, then the HR manager is assured that he or she has succeeded in creating a systemic variation of the independent variable.

Control of extraneous and confounding variables

Another key characteristic of the experimental method is the control of extraneous and confounding variables. An extraneous variable is a name given to any variable other than the independent variable that may have an influence on the dependent variables. A confounding variable refers to a variable that correlates with both the independent variable and the dependent variable, which in turn creates a spurious relationship between the independent variable and the dependent variable. Both an extraneous variable and a confounding variable[1] provide another explanation for the cause-and-effect relationship between the independent variable and the dependent variable; thus, the researcher cannot draw the conclusion that observed effects in the dependent variable are caused only by the independent variable. In other words, the extraneous or confounding variables threaten the internal validity that researchers strive for in the experimental method.

In any experiment there are extraneous and confounding variables that need to be controlled. They differ from experiment to experiment. Cook and Campbell (1979) have identified an overall list of such variables that usually need to be controlled in conducting experiments in the field of social sciences. Below is a summary that highlights some of those variables:

History. Between the premeasurement and the postmeasurement of dependent variables, many events other than the independent variables can occur, which may cause the changes in the dependent variables.

Maturation. Changes in the dependent variables resulting from factors internal to individual biological and psychological conditions rather than the experimental manipulations may contribute to the observed outcome.

Mortality. Participants often drop out of an experiment before it is completed. Those participants who leave the experiment may differ from those who stay, making it more difficult to draw comparisons between the different groups.

Instrumentation. The dependent variables are assessed with different instruments over time. For example, the measurement of product quality may become more accurate and sophisticated over time, which gives another explanation for the changes of the dependent variable of product quality.

Selection. If there is a preexisting difference between groups, this difference rather than experimental manipulation may account for the changes of the dependent variables.

Demand Characteristics. In any experiment participants receive information from many cues, such as the way the experimenters greet them, the instructions given to them, and the experimental settings. These cues, called the demand characteristics, may influence participants' motivation and expectations, which in turn accounts for the changes in the dependent variable.

In summary, two features—*manipulation of the independent variables* and *control of extraneous variables* distinguish the experimental method from other research methods and allow researchers to examine a cause-and-effect relationship between the independent variable and the dependent variable. In others words, the way of manipulating the independent variable and the way of controlling extraneous and confounding variables determine the quality of an experimental method. Below we will first discuss the issues of control in the experimental design and then introduce the vignette technique as a way of manipulating the independent variables in HRM studies.

4. TWO APPROACHES TO CONTROL IN THE EXPERIMENTAL METHOD

Two general approaches to "control" are usually performed to eliminate the effect of the extraneous and confounding variables in the experimental method. The first approach is to incorporate one or more of the available control techniques. The second approach is through appropriate design of the experiment. Below we provide some basic knowledge on those two approaches with the purpose of demonstrating how control is performed in the experimental method. More sophisticated knowledge regarding control of extraneous and confounding variables can be found in Christensen's (2007) work and Cook and Campbell's (1976) work.

Available Control Techniques

Randomization is one of the most valuable techniques available to exert control in the experimental method. A complete randomization means that participants are randomly drawn (i.e., possible participants have a known and equal chance of being drawn) and their assignment to any particular group (i.e., participants could be assigned to any one of the groups set up) is also random (Sekaran & Bougie, 2010). Randomization can control for both unknown and known extraneous variables related to participants and make sure that there are no other divergent characteristics except for the manipulated variable across different groups that can be attributed to the changes in the dependent variables.

Despite the advantages of randomization, this technique is not always feasible in practice, especially in organizational studies. *Matching* is then used as an alternative technique of control for extraneous and confounding variables. Matching is to equate participants on the known characteristics across different groups. In the example of examining the effect of skills on social media tools, if we know recruiters' previous experience on social media has an effect on their recruitment performance, we then need to make participants' previous experience on social media "equivalent" across different groups. For instance, we can collect information on members' experience on social media beforehand and use it as criteria when assigning the participants into different groups.

Note that randomization and matching are just two examples of the available techniques for controlling extraneous and confounding variables. Many more complicated techniques, such as the counterbalancing technique to eliminate the order effect of experimental treatments, the deception technique to eliminate participants' effects, and the blind technique to eliminate experiments' effects, can be found in Christensen's (2006) work.

Research Design in the Experimental Method

Research design refers to the outline or plan that sets up the specific procedures to be used in an empirical study to examine research hypotheses. A purpose of the research design in the experimental method is to control extraneous and confounding variables efficiently. A true experimental design needs to meet three conditions: (1) randomly assigning participants; (2) including both the experimental group and the control group; and (3) recording information both before and after treatment (Cook & Campbell, 1976). By randomization the first condition eliminates those extraneous variables related to participants. In the second condition, whatever happens with the experimental group also happens with the control group except for the manipulation of the independent variable. The third condition reveals the net effect of the experimental manipulation. All three conditions together make sure that the only difference between the experimental group and the control group lies in the manipulation of the independent variable. Figure 6.1 below illustrates a classic true experimental design, which is also referred to as an "equivalent control group experiment with pre- and

		Time		
Participants	Pre-test	$\longrightarrow$	Post-test	
Random	O_1	Manipulation	O_2	Experimental Group
assignment	O_3	Without Manipulation	O_4	Control Group

Figure 6.1   A classic true experimental design

post-testing" (Bryman, 1989). The net effect of manipulation can be calculated in the formula: treatment effect = $[(O_2 - O_1) - (O_4 - O_3)]$.

When experiments are done in an artificial or contrived environment (namely, lab experiments), it is relatively easy to conduct a true experimental design. However, when experiments are done in the natural environment in which work goes on as usual but manipulations are given to one or more groups, it is almost impossible to perform a true experimental design. For example, when an experiment is conducted in an organizational setting, the employees have already worked in the organization. It is usually impossible to reassign them randomly into the experimental group and the control group, violating the condition of a true experimental design.

If an experimental design cannot meet all three conditions that are required for a true experiment, it then falls into the category of *quasiexperimental design*. In a quasiexperiment, participants are not randomly assigned to different treatments, there is no control group that corresponds to the experimental group, or a pretest cannot be conducted. Depending on the extent to which the three conditions of a true experimental design are violated, the quasiexperimental designs take different forms. If a quasiexperiment contains no control group, such research designs are considered *faulty research design*. The simplest faulty quasiexperimental design is *one group posttest only design*, where only the experimental group receives a treatment: X → Y. If researchers are able to collect information on the dependent variable before and after experimental manipulation, a *one-group before-after design* is then formed: Y_1 → X → Y_2. When a control group is made available in a quasiexperiment, such designs are considered *true quasiexperimental designs*. An example of such a design, *after-only design*, in which the experimental and the control groups' posttest scores are compared to assess the effect of experimental manipulation, is provided in Figure 6.2 below.

Due to the lack of rigidity in "controls," a quasiexperiment is not as powerful as a true experiment in establishing a cause-and-effect relationship. However, in a real organizational setting, the three conditions required for a true experiment are unlikely to be met. Imagine that a HR manager is interested in how high commitment HRM (HCHRM) practices have an effect on employee performance. The existent organizational structure makes it impossible to randomly assign employees into different experimental treatments. By using a quasiexperimental design, the HR manager can exercise

	Manipulation	Measures of Dependent Variables
Experimental group	X	Y
Control group		Y

Figure 6.2   After-only design in a true quasiexperimental design

the HCHRM practices to employees in one department (as the experimental group) and continue exercising the conventional HRM practices in other departments (as the control group). This "naturally occurring quasiexperiment" offers the opportunity of ascertaining the effect of the "intervention." Quasiexperiments on this point are very appealing to HR researchers and practitioners. Readers who are interested in quasiexperimental design can refer to Cook and Campbell's (1976) classic work for more information.

5. USING VIGNETTES AS A MANIPULATION TECHNIQUE IN HRM STUDIES

Above we discussed the control approach in the experimental method. As explained, in addition to the control, the other key characteristic of the experimental method is the *manipulation of the independent variable*. In this chapter we introduce using the vignette technique for manipulating independent variables in HRM studies.

Definition of Vignette

A vignette, also called a scenario, is a short description of a social situation that contains precise references to what are thought to be the most important factors in the decision-making or judgment-making process of respondents (Alexander & Becker, 1978). In a vignette study, instead of direct questions, one or more brief stories that are familiar to respondents are used as stimuli to elicit respondents' reactions.

Below is an example of a vignette used by Yang, van de Vliert, and Shi (2007) in studying how employees choose sides between two superiors in a workplace conflict. They described the conflict below to their participants:

Imagine you are a personnel officer in a Personnel Department of a company. You have two superiors, Arca and Barc. Arca coordinates the departmental selection work and Barc coordinates the departmental appraisal work. You do both selection work supervised by Arca and appraisal work supervised by Barc. Right now you are in charge of selecting a trainer for the Computer Department, part of whose work will also have to be coordinated by Barc because training often follows naturally from appraisal.

According to the job description at least five years of experience as a trainer is necessary for that position. Additionally, in a meeting, the general manager has put forward the problem that the current director of the Computer Department has no successor and suggested that it would be a great case of personnel planning if the trainer selected had the potential to become the director in good time.

Three candidates A, B, and C, have sent their applications to the Personnel Department. Arca strongly recommends candidate A to you because Arca likes A and wants to gradually change the Computer Department's work approach with the help of A. But A has only one year of relevant experience as a trainer and has little potential to become the next director. Arca, who comes from the same town as you do, has been your supervisor over the past ten years. Indeed Arca taught you a lot, not only in your work but also in your private life.

Barc strongly recommends candidate B to you because B has six years of relevant experience as a trainer, and also because Barc thinks that B certainly has enough managerial potential to eventually become the director of the Computer Department. You are hardly familiar with Barc, who entered your department just half a year ago. Before that, you had heard about Barc but never had any contact.

Characteristics of Vignettes

As indicated by this example, in the vignette technique respondents react to concrete and real-life situations rather than abstract statements. It creates greater realism for respondents (Wason & Cox, 1996), especially if the research topics are about controversial issues such as choosing sides in a conflict. Because of the concrete and real-life situations, the vignettes are more likely to elicit participants' true responses than the direct and abstract questions used in the survey studies. Besides, vignettes provide standardized background information to all respondents (Weber, 1992). In the example above, all respondents need to indicate whom they would like to support regarding the personnel selection case. If the research topics are sensitive, standardizing the information given to participants becomes an important issue. To some extent, standardization in this case can be understood as a kind of control: it rules out the irrelevant situational factors that may result in the variation of dependent variables. In the example of choosing sides, if the researchers fail to standardize the information that describes the conflict setting, participants may think of different conflict situations and their responses may be influenced by many irrelevant factors such as, What are the two superiors fighting for? How long have they known each other? Is the dispute an important issue to the company?

Another characteristic of the vignette technique is that it allows researchers to systematically vary the independent variable (Alexander & Becker, 1978). By altering words or sentences in the vignette that are related to the theoretical concerns, researchers manipulate the independent variable. In the example above, one of the independent variables is "interpersonal relationship," two levels of which were manipulated by changing the sentences from "*Arca, who comes from the same town as you do, has been your supervisor over the past ten years. Indeed Arca taught you a lot, not only in your work but also in your private life.*" (representing a close relationship) to "*You are hardly familiar with Barc, who entered your department just half a year ago. Before that, you had heard about Barc but never had any contact.*" (representing a distant relationship).

Finally, the vignette technique can reduce the social desirability or impression management of respondents. Because vignettes use concrete and detailed descriptions of social situations as stimuli, it is less likely that respondents will notice which words or sentences are used to operationalize the independent variable. The technique thus reduces yes-saying bias (Kennedy & Lawton, 1996). This characteristic makes the vignette particularly suitable in researching controversial and sensitive managerial issues.

Types of Vignettes

Two types of vignettes can be distinguished in management research. The first type is called the constant-variable-value vignette, in which all respondents read the same "short stories" and are exposed to the identical "situations" (Cavanagh & Fritzsche, 1985). The advantage of this type of vignette lies in the standardization of the information related to background. An event or a case that is familiar to respondents is presented to respondents as stimuli. The familiarity between the respondents' real-life experience and the situation described in the vignette helps respondents to place themselves into the studied "situation," thus making it easier to elicit a concrete perception and an accurate judgment from the respondents. Findings from the constant-variable-value vignette in this regard have a strong practical implication. This type of vignette is extensively used in management studies.

The second type of vignette is referred to as the contrastive vignette (Burstin, Doughtie, & Raphaeli, 1980), which combines ideas from the experimental designs with the sample survey procedures (Wason, Polonsky, & Hyman, 2002). As the definition implies, the contrastive vignette highlights the characteristics of systematically varying the independent variables, which makes it suitable as a manipulation technique. In the contrastive vignette, respondents are randomly assigned to different versions of the same basic vignette.

Sanders and Yang's (under review) study on employee HR attribution is an example of using the contrastive vignette as a way of manipulating independent variables. Based on Bowen and Ostroff's theoretical work on HR attribution (2004) and Kelly's attribution theory (1972), Sanders and Yang assumed that the high commitment HRM practices would have a stronger effect on employees' affective organizational commitment if employees attributed HR practices in terms of high distinctiveness, high consistency, and high consensus (the HHH pattern, attributing to management) than in terms of low distinctiveness, high consistency, and low consensus (the LHL pattern, attributing to employees themselves) or high distinctiveness, low consistency, and low consensus (the HLL pattern, attributing to context and situation). Using vignettes, they manipulated low and high levels of distinctiveness, consistency, and consensus systematically as follows.

Participants who were randomly assigned to the HHH pattern read the following vignette about HR attribution: "*You notice in your company that HRM in comparison to other companies provides **better** employment conditions, that the different HR practices like recruitment & selection, reward and training **are aligned to** each other, and that rules and policies from the HR department **are comprehended in the same way** among your colleagues.*"

In comparison, participants who were randomly assigned to the LHL pattern read: "*You notice in your company that HRM in comparison to other companies **provides quite similar** employment conditions, that the different HR practices like recruitment & selection, reward and training **are aligned to** each other, and that rules and policies from the HR department are **comprehended in a different way** among your colleagues.*"

And participants in the HLL pattern were given the following vignette: "*You notice in your company that HRM in comparison to other companies provides **better** employment conditions, that the different HR practices like recruitment & selection, reward and training **are not aligned** to each other, and that rules and policies from the HR department **are comprehended in a different way** among your colleagues.*"

In this example, researchers managed to create two levels (low versus high) of the attributional dimensions (distinctiveness, consistency, and consensus) by changing some key words systematically (e.g., are aligned to → not aligned to; same → different). Note that each version is used as a reference for others. In other words, it does not make any sense to focus only on one version of the vignettes. If one single version is evaluated, one may draw the conclusion that it lacks "mundane realism"—the setting and circumstances are not likely to be found in the real world (Bryman, 1989). However, manipulations in this type of vignette achieve their effects by comparing different versions, aiming at achieving "experimental realism"— differences should be observed across different experimental groups.

To assure the "experimental realism," manipulation checks become necessary in using the contrastive vignette. In the example mentioned above, participants were asked about their understanding of vignettes regarding distinctiveness, consistency, and consensus (e.g., To what extent do you think your colleagues perceive the HR practices in the same way as you do? 1 = *totally disagree*; 5 = *totally agree*). The scores of the manipulation checks across the three vignettes were then compared to make sure that participants understood the attributional patterns as they were intended.

Some Tips in Creating and Using Vignettes

Weber (1992) and Wason *et al.* (2002) have provided the detailed recommendations of how to design and use a vignette. Four points related to HRM studies are highlighted below.

First, vignettes should be developed based on a solid theoretical foundation. Although the stimulus to which participants respond in the vignette studies are concrete and real situations, these "real situations" should be developed and modified with the guidance of theories. By relying on theories, researchers can make a distinction between the factors in which researchers are interested and other irrelevant factors. Manipulations focus on the research relevant factors. In Sanders and Yang's study, the three attribution dimensions could have led to eight combinations, however only three combination were taken into account. They could do so because they based their choices on Kelly's attribution model (1972): only the three informational patterns make theoretical sense on the cause-and-effect relationships.

Second, make the vignette believable and fitted to the respondents. Respondents in the vignette studies are asked to place themselves into the situation described, so that the situation can trigger participants' responses. One of the assumptions here is that the situation described needs to be realistic and has been experienced by participants. Vignettes will fail in their purpose if the participants have never experienced the situation described. For example, students might be asked to respond to a management vignette that concerns selecting a top-level HR manager; yet such a vignette will not make any sense to students. It is very difficult for students to place themselves into that situation and give a response accordingly.

Third, it is better to revise a well-developed vignette than to invent a completely new vignette. To develop a valid and reliable vignette is a time- and cost-consuming business. If possible, researchers should rely on and further revise the existing vignettes. There are two advantages in doing this. The first advantage is that using the existing vignettes can reduce researchers' efforts in creating a real-life situation since such vignettes have often been tested in terms of their relevance to management practices and reality. Researchers can then focus more on manipulating the factors in which they are interested. The second advantage is that the use of the same or similar vignettes makes a cross-study comparison possible. With the same vignette, background information is standardized in the same way and the differences in outcomes can be directly traced to the manipulated factors. Research findings can then be compared across different studies. To some extent, this can be understood as a validation process of a set of vignettes.

Fourth, conduct manipulation checks. Manipulation in the vignette studies is done by means of differentiating semantic elements, such as "different/ similar," "better/worse," etc., and is usually considered a weak manipulation. Researchers, however, try to demonstrate that even such a weak manipulation of the independent variable can still account for some variances in the dependent variables (Prentice & Miller, 1992). If this weak manipulation can be replaced by a strong one, we would expect a stronger effect. Since the independent variables are manipulated in a rather weak way in the vignette studies, it is important to make sure that participants do recognize the different treatments. Manipulation checks become a gatekeeper, which assures that participants who are randomly assigned to different groups have a different experience about the situation described.

Apply the vignette technique as a way of manipulation in the experimental methods: How does it work in practice?

John, a PhD student, is interested in investigating the professional identity of HR practitioners. Through literature review and pilot interviews with HR practitioners, he has developed his research assumption that the way in which HR practitioners view their profession will have a fundamental influence on their workplace behavior. When HR practitioners view their work as an essential part of management aimed at helping an organization to achieve its goals, they will behave as an agent of the organization and try to maximize organizational interests if there is a conflict between management and employees. By contrast, when HR practitioners view their profession as a linking pin between management and employees, they will behave as a mediator, trying to help management and employees to resolve their problem if a conflict arises between the two parties.

John decides to test his assumption by using the experimental method. He plans to manipulate HR practitioners' professional identities by using vignettes as the instructional manipulation. The concept of HR professional identity is operationalized with two levels: HR work as a managerial professional versus HR work as a peacemaker. He plans to recruit HR practitioners as participants. One group of participants will read a vignette in which the HR work is described from the view of management. The other group will read a vignette in which the HR work is described as workplace mediator, trying to help management and employees to reach a joint agreement. John also decides to focus the dependent variable on conflict handling behavior. Since conflict handling is a sensitive issue for HR practitioners, John thinks that it may be a good idea to use the constant-variable-value vignette, and he presents a real workplace conflict between managers and employees to elicit respondents' conflict handling behavior.

John is going to present his research design at the department research seminar next week. He is nervous about the feedback from his supervisor and other colleagues. Can he convince them that the experimental method is worthwhile to try? What are the advantages of using the vignette technique?

6. CHALLENGES OF ADOPTING THE EXPERIMENTAL METHOD IN HR STUDIES

Relationship between Internal and External Validity

Establishing a cause-effect relationship between the independent variable and the dependent variable is essential for HRM studies. As explained in the beginning of this chapter, a well-conducted experiment can achieve a high internal validity and establish the cause-effect relationship. Using the experimental method, researchers can systematically vary the independent variable and efficiently control the effects of extraneous variables. Under such conditions, the observed changes of the dependent variable can be accurately attributed to the independent variable.

Internal validity, however, does not address the issue of whether the research findings can be generalized beyond the specific confines of the settings in which the study was undertaken. The term *external validity* is used to describe the extent to which the results of an experiment can be applied to and across different persons, settings, and times. It would be ideal if a study could achieve both high internal validity and high external validity. However, the problem is that there tends to be an inverse relationship between internal validity and external validity (Kazdin, 1980). In other words, high internal validity embedded in a well-conducted experiment often means low external validity in terms of generalizing research findings. Below we discuss the issues related to external validity in terms of applicability, settings, and time.

Applicability refers to whether researchers can generalize the results from one group studied to groups not studied. Organizational members (e.g., employees, managers) are the target population in HRM studies. Applicability can be a serious issue of generalizability in HRM studies if university students without working experience are recruited as participants. In relation to this issue, some journals in the field of organizational studies, such as *Journal of Organizational and Occupational Psychology*, ask authors to "clearly demonstrate that the data obtained can be generalized to working populations" (http://onlinelibrary.wiley.com/journal/10.1111/(ISSN)2044–8325/homepage/ForAuthors.html).

Organizational settings are dynamic and sophisticated and thus difficult to create in a lab experimental setting. This raises another concern related to external validity: How can researchers transcend the boundaries of a study? Schwab (2005) suggests that this issue should be discussed through a thoughtful identification of similarities and differences between the experiments conducted and the environments in which the results may apply.

Experimental studies, particularly lab experiments, are often conducted during one time period. However, organizational conditions keep changing. The findings obtained during the period of study may not be held true as organizational conditions change. This is especially the case when studying intervention and using intervention programs as a way of manipulating the independent variable. The topics discussed in Chapter 5 about longitudinal designs may deserve more attention when designing an experimental study in organizations.

Challenges in Future Research

The experimental method is certainly needed in the field of HRM studies. Actually, HRM research has benefitted from employing the experimental method in studying selection, training, and performance appraisal, etc. (Cook & Campbell, 1976). Now, as HRM research moves to complicated topics, such as the bundles of HR practices, high performance HRM systems, and HRM process, the experimental method seems to lose fashion. In our opinion the new research topics set a challenge for designing complicated experiments. In relation to this point, we would like to conclude this chapter by highlighting three challenges that HRM researchers need to overcome in future studies.

The first challenge is to employ rigorous research designs combining lab experiments with field experiments in HRM studies. A well-designed lab experiment can achieve a good internal validity but is weak in terms of external validity. In contrast, a well-conducted field experiment often has a good external validity but struggles with accurately manipulating the independent variables and strictly controlling extraneous variables. Rather than debating which approach is suitable for HRM studies, researchers need to experiment with how to combine those two approaches in their designs and conduct multiple studies to answer research questions. For example, researchers can start with a vignette-based study in the lab setting and then follow through with a field experiment with the aim to generalize the research findings in real-life organizations.

The second challenge is to come up with an alternative way to efficiently deal with control in experiments in HRM studies. HRM research topics tend to become more and more complicated. Researchers are interested in not only more than one variable but also the connections between variables. Such demands require a new way to manage control in the experimental designs. If researchers still follow the conventional view to treat control, it will become impossible to use the experimental method in HRM research. For example, in studying the effect of HR bundles, different HR practices connect with each other, thus creating a complicated system. How to control variables at a system level? Exploratory work is much appreciated in this direction. It benefits not only HR studies but also the social sciences in general.

The third challenge is to produce sound research designs for studying the HR process. As the rise of HCHRM, the study of the HR process such as HR attribution, the meaning of HR practices to employees and to line managers has been added to the research agenda in the field of HRM studies (Sanders, Shipton, & Gomes, 2013). Although some theoretical work has been done to address the process issue, little methodological concern has been raised and discussed. Most empirical work is conducted by means of questionnaire surveys. There is a strong urge to employ and develop other research methods to validate the research findings and uncover the so-called black box or missing link between HRM content and performance. New ventures in experimental design in this area are certainly encouraged.

NOTE

1. The focus of this section is on discussing the control techniques. We thus do not differentiate the extraneous variables from the confounding variables.

REFERENCES

Alexander, C., & Becker, H. (1978). The use of vignettes in survey research. *Public Opinion Quarterly, 42,* 93–104.

Bowen, D. E., & Ostroff, C. (2004). Understanding HRM-firm performance linkages: The role of "strength" of the HRM system. *Academy of Management Review, 29,* 203–221.

Bryman, A. (1989). *Research methods and organizational studies.* Oxon, UK: Routledge.

Burstin, K. D., Doughtie, E. B., & Raphaeli, A. (1980). Contrastive vignette technique: An indirect methodology designed to address reactive social attitude measurement. *Journal of Applied Social Psychology, 10,* 147–165.

Cavanagh, G., & Fritzsche, D. (1985). Using vignettes in business ethnics research. In L. E. Preston (Ed.), *Research in corporate social performance and policy* (pp. 279–293). Greenwich, CT: JAI Press.

Christensen, L. (2007). *Experimental methodology* (10th Ed.). Boston, MA: Allyn & Bacon.

Cook, T. D., & Campbell, D. T. (1976). The design and conduct of quasi-experiments and true experiments in field settings. In M. D. Dunnette (Ed.), *Handbook of industrial and organizational psychology* (pp. 223–326). Chicago, IL: Rand McNally.

Frayne, C., & Geringer, M. (2000). Self-management training for improving job performance: A field experiment involving salespeople. *Journal of Applied Psychology, 85,* 361–372.

Gerhart, B. (2007). Modeling HRM and performance linkage. In P. Boxall, J. Purcell, & P. Wright (Eds.), *The Oxford handbook of human resource management* (pp. 552–580). Oxford, UK: Oxford University Press.

Guest, D. (2011). Human resource management and performance: Still searching for some answers. *Human Resource Management Journal, 21,* 3–13.

Kazdin, A. E. (1980). *Research design in clinical psychology.* New York: Harper & Row.

Kelley, H. H. (1972). Causal schemata and the attribution process. *American Psychologists, 28,* 107–128.

Kennedy, E. J., & Lawton, L. (1996). The effects of social and moral integration on ethical standards: A comparison of American and Ukrainian students. *Journal of Business Ethics, 15,* 901–911.

Prentice, D. A., & Miller, D. T. (1992). When small effects are impressive. *Psychological Bulletin, 112,* 160–164.

Sanders, K., Shipton, H., & Gomes, J. (2012). Call for paper: Are HRM processes important? *Human Resource Management.*

Sanders, K., & Yang, H. The HRM process approach: The influence of employees' HR attribution on the commitment-based HRM–employee outcome linkages. (Under review)

Sekaran, U., & Bougie, R. (2010). *Research methods for business* (5th ed.). Sussex, UK: Wiley.

Shantz, A., & Latham, G. P. (2013). The effects of primed goals on employee performance: Implications for human resource management. *Human Resource Management, 50,* 289–299.

Shwab, D. (2005). *Research methods for organizational studies* (2nd ed.). Mahwah, NJ: Lawrence Erlbaum.

Wason, K. D., & Cox, K. C. (1996). Scenario utilization in marketing research. In D. Strutton, L. E. Pelton, & S. Shipp (Eds.), *Advances in marketing* (pp. 155–162). Texas: Southwestern Marketing Association.

Wason, K. D., Polonsky, M. J., & Hyman, M. R. (2002). Designing vignette studies in marketing. *Australasian Marketing Journal, 10,* 41–58.

Weber, J. (1992). Scenarios in business ethics research: Review, critical assessment and recommendations. *Business Ethics Quarterly, 2,* 137–160.

Wright, P., Gardner, T., Moynihan, L., & Allen, M. (2005). The relationship between HR practices and firm performance: Examining causal order. *Personnel Psychology, 58,* 409–446.

Yang, H., Van de Vliert, E., & Shi, K. (2007). When a favorable relationship leads initial outsiders to take sides: A cross-cultural study among Chinese and Dutch. *Journal of Cross-Cultural Psychology, 38,* 438–457.

7 Cross-Cultural Research

Yuan Liao, Jian-Min Sun, and David C. Thomas

After reading this chapter, we expect you to:

1. Understand the strengths and weaknesses of cross-cultural research in HRM;
2. Recognize the four main challenges in conducting cross-cultural studies;
3. Understand the ways of surmounting such challenges;
4. Be able to design an appropriate study to address a cross-cultural research question.

---

1. INTRODUCTION

Cross-cultural research investigates similarities and differences between cultures. In the context of human resource management (HRM), cross-cultural studies investigate and compare HR activities and practices such as selecting, training, evaluating, and retaining employees across cultures and nations (Thomas & Lazarova, in press). National culture has become an important topic in HRM research because it influences not only the policies, practices, and processes of HRM, but also the effectiveness of a particular HRM practice in a given country (Newman & Nollen, 1996). As the number of international and multicultural organizations increases, as does the speed at which they are growing and broadening their borders, global human resource management is facing the challenge of conducting the appropriate HR activities in different countries. The best HR practices in one country are not always the best practices in the rest of the world (Harris, 2008; Harvey, 1997; Mendonca & Kanungo, 1996). Each country has its own institutions, values, beliefs, social structures, and norms, all of which have a profound impact on HR practices. A successful and popular HR practice in the U.S. may be inconsistent with another country's social and cultural factors and thus is inapplicable, let alone effective, in a new cultural environment. Conducting cross-cultural research in HRM helps researchers explore indigenous HR practices in various countries, compare the effectiveness of HR practices in different cultures, understand what cultural values or other contextual factors account for the differences across cultures, identify best HR practices in multinational corporations (MNCs), and establish HRM strategies in international firms. In the age of a war for global talent, these results provide HR practitioners, particularly those working in the MNCs, with specific and practical guidelines concerning how to design and implement an effective HRM system in order to better attract, engage, and retain talent employees when their business operation enters into different cultural contexts.

Culture is a shared system about the understanding and interpretation of behaviors. It is usually learned during the socialization process and can be passed down to the next generation (Smith, Bond, & Kağitçibasi, 2006). Culture is a complex concept with many elements, such as language, customs and norms, values and beliefs systems, institutions, economic development, legal and political structures, climate, and so on. This complexity imposes challenges to quantifying culture in a consistent way. A recent review identified 121 instruments that have been used to measure culture in the last half a century (Taras, Rowney, & Steel, 2009). Because of the complexity of the construct of culture, researchers often oversimplify the definition and operationalization of culture and use nation as a proxy. In a review of cross-cultural organizational research, Schaffer and Riordan (2003) reported that 79% of cross-cultural organizational studies published between 1995 and 2001 used country as a proxy for culture. Even when a more refined framework of culture was used to explain the impact of culture in their theory, about half of the studies still used country as a proxy in their empirical analyses. This practice not only fails to explicate the complexity of the definition of culture, but also ignores the variance within cultures and assumes all members within a society are the same (Au, 1999).

Using country as a proxy and treating culture as a single variable limits our ability to fully understand the mechanisms underlying the relationship between culture and HRM practices and strategies. Unpacking the effect of culture has been called for by many scholars and has become a key focus in cross-cultural research in psychology and management in the last decade. Of the many ways of operationalizing culture, one of the most widely used is to define it in terms of values. Since Hofstede's (1980, 2001) landmark work in national cultural values, cultural values have become the most popular cultural element on which researchers draw. Several other frameworks of cultural values, such as the Schwartz Values Survey (SVS; Schwartz, 1992) and the Global Leadership and Organizational Behavior Effectiveness (GLOBE) project (House, Hanges, Javidan, Dorfman, & Gupta, 2004), have been developed. These frameworks propose somewhat different cultural values. Hofstede (1980) initially distinguished four value dimensions at the national level; namely, individualism-collectivism, power distance, masculinity-femininity, and uncertainty avoidance. Later, this framework was extended by adding more value dimensions such as long-term versus short-term orientation (Hofstede & Bond, 1988; Minkov & Hofstede, 2012). The Schwartz Values Survey (Schwartz, 1992) identified ten value types, which are summarized as two bipolar dimensions at the individual level. A separate analysis revealed seven value types, which are summarized as three bipolar dimensions at the national level (Schwartz, 1994). The most recent national-level cultural value framework, the GLOBE project (House *et al.*, 2004), identified nine dimensions based on Hofstede's original idea. Although the SVS and GLOBE frameworks identified different value dimensions, they both include values conceptually similar to the four values defined in Hofstede's work. Defining culture in terms of values allows researchers to establish conceptual frameworks of how culture influences HRM practices (e.g., Aycan, 2005) that unpackage general cultural and national differences into more specific and fundamental constructs. Many empirical studies in cross-cultural HRM research have drawn on these cultural values to explore the underlying causes of effective HRM practices across nations (e.g., Chiang & Birtch, 2010; Fey, Morgulis-Yakushev, Park, & Björkman, 2009; Peretz & Fried, 2012).

Three major domains of HRM research with a cross-cultural or international focus can be identified in the literature: single-country studies, cross-cultural comparison studies, and expatriate studies. Single-country studies focus on HR practices in a particular, usually non-U.S., country. These studies either adopt the North American research paradigm, or describe indigenous HR activities in the country with an *emic* approach. This emic approach assumes that concepts are embedded in the specific culture and are only meaningful when defined and measured in the specific cultural context (Chan, 2008; Gudykunst, 1997). This approach also argues that definition and measurement of a construct developed in one culture should not simply be applied to another culture. Cross-cultural comparison studies, on the other hand, often use an *etic* approach to compare the magnitude of and relationships among constructs between cultural groups, assuming these constructs are defined and measured in a similar fashion (Chan, 2008). Expatriate studies mainly discuss expatriates' psychological adjustment and performance-related issues in an intercultural context. All three domains have received considerable attention and made significant progress in the past decades. Each domain has its own research methods and approaches. The current chapter focuses on research methods that are relevant to the first two types of studies.

Although research methods in cross-cultural studies have been extensively discussed in the fields of psychology and management (see Leung & Van de Vijver, 2008; Matsumoto & Van de Vijver, 2011; Schaffer & Riordan, 2003), debates and discussions about the conceptualization and methodological issues and challenges are still going on in today's academic dialogues (e.g., Cascio, 2012; Chan, 2008; Leung, 2008; Tsui, 2007). For instance, the fundamental questions of what culture is and how to measure culture appropriately have been discussed extensively, yet each approach has its own strengths and weaknesses. The debate on the emic versus etic approach raises concerns of accurately defining, measuring, and comparing constructs across different cultures. Clarifying all these issues goes beyond the scope of the current chapter. Instead, we highlight four main issues embedded in cross-cultural research; namely, the emic versus etic approach, cross-cultural equivalence issues, level of analysis (see the discussion in *institutional embeddedness* in Chapter 1 of this volume), and causal inferences. In this chapter we first discuss the added value of cross-cultural studies to HRM research and its general strengths and weaknesses. We then describe each of the four issues and discuss their associated challenges in the context of cross-cultural HRM research, and recommend ways to overcome these difficulties.

2. STRENGTHS AND WEAKNESSES

Compared with other research methods discussed in this book, cross-cultural research is not only a method but also a research paradigm that provides numerous advantages in comparison to more traditional research (i.e., single-country studies of HRM conducted in the U.S.). First, cross-cultural research examines potential relationships between culture and HRM practices and strategies, which may in turn shed light on the explanation of the influence of HRM in organizational performance. Second, cross-cultural research tests the boundary of theories by comparing the effectiveness of the same practice across cultures. Since many HRM studies originated in the U.S., testing models and frameworks outside of this cultural boundary moves the theoretical development of HRM forward. In practice it helps identify universal best HR practices that ultimately improve organizational performance or establish HRM models in international firms. Third, recognizing indigenous HR practices advances our understandings of HRM around the globe and helps organizations design appropriate HR practices to serve local employees when entering a new cultural context. Fourth, cross-cultural research incorporates the influence of multiple levels. The effectiveness of HR systems can be influenced by societal-level factors such as cultural values, economic development, and political systems; organizational-level factors such as competitiveness of the environment; and individual-level factors such as employees' motivations. A well-designed cross-cultural study allows researchers to simultaneously investigate effects *at* and *across* different levels.

The nature of cross-cultural research also imposes some weaknesses and challenges to this paradigm. First, conducting a cross-cultural study is more time consuming and resource demanding. It usually requires a focal culture expert on the research team and involves data collection in multiple countries. Large-scale cross-cultural research even requires data collection from more than 20 countries, and coordination within the research team can be challenging. Second, it is difficult to choose a research approach to balance the local and universal concerns. Most studies adopt either an emic or etic approach when studying culture and overlook the bias induced by a single approach. Third, since cross-cultural studies either compare or imply differences between countries, one central question is whether employees interpret work-related measures in an equivalent manner (Riordan & Vandenberg, 1994). Uncritically assuming the phenomena under investigation are equal across cultures results in conceptual, methodological, or measurement nonequivalence, which in turn leads to misinterpretation of the results and invalid conclusions. Even objective measures sometimes suffer the problem of cross-cultural nonequivalence. For example, measures of financial performance of subsidiaries such as profitability and return of assets might be distorted by transfer pricing, which makes the financial performance across subsidiaries incomparable (Cogin & Williamson, in press). Also, the complexity of ownership of some sites, such as joint ventures and alliances, creates difficulties to match data on financial performance from different sources (Cogin & Williamson, in press). Fourth, although the embedded level of analysis provides insightful explanations on how culture influences HRM, researchers sometimes confuse the levels of analysis or use inappropriate data transformation across levels. Lastly, cross-cultural studies are quasiexperimental designs that limit the ability to draw causal conclusion. In the following, we focus on the latter four issues that are critical in cross-cultural research.

3. CHALLENGES IN CONDUCTING CROSS-CULTURAL HRM RESEARCH

As mentioned previously, there are many challenges in conducting cross-cultural HRM research and it is impractical to discuss all of them thoroughly in one chapter. In this section, we highlight four main issues embedded in cross-cultural research; namely, the emic versus etic approach, cross-cultural equivalence issues, level of analysis, and causal inferences. We describe each of the issues, discuss their associated challenges in the context of cross-cultural HRM, and recommend ways to overcome these difficulties.

Emic versus Etic Approach

The emic approach examines a phenomenon in the context of a specific culture and tries to understand the phenomenon from the perspective of members within that culture (Berry, 1990; Gudykunst, 1997). Some of the single-country studies in HRM are emic in nature when they investigate indigenous HR policies and practices in a particular country. For example,

Hamaaki, Hori, Maeda, and Murata (2012) reexamined the traditional practices of seniority-based wages and lifetime employment in the Japanese employment system and found that these practices have been declining due to the economic and social movements since early 2000s. Although emic studies identify and explain indigenous HR practices within a particular culture, they usually make explicit or implicit narrative comparisons between the focal culture and results from other cultures (Schaffer & Riordan, 2003). On the other hand, since the U.S. research paradigm is currently dominant in the field, many studies conducted in a non-U.S. country still follow the U.S. paradigm and apply the concepts and theories developed in the U.S. to their focal culture. These studies are not emic, but *imposed etic* (Berry, 1989, 1990). Many of these studies investigate whether Western HR practices are effective in a new cultural context. For example, Du and Choi (2010) studied how pay for performance was related to employees' organizational commitment and interpersonal helping at the organizational level in China, and Selvarajan and Cloninger (2012) hypothesized that multisource performance appraisal resulted in higher perceived fairness of performance appraisal among Mexican employees. The etic approach assumes that a construct is universally defined and can be meaningfully compared across cultures (Chan, 2008). Most of the cross-cultural comparison studies adopt an etic approach, define and measure the key constructs in the same way, and compare the levels of and the relationships among these constructs. For example, when comparing how interpersonal affect may bias performance ratings between the U.S. and India, Varma, Pichler, and Srinivas (2005) used the same measure of key variables in both samples and found evidence of a moderating effect of culture: American supervisors separated their liking for a subordinate from actual performance, whereas Indian supervisors inflated ratings for low performers when assigning performance ratings. Because the constructs are operationalized in the same way across cultures, results of etic studies are believed to be more generalizable (Ronen & Shenkar, 1988).

The debate between the emic versus etic approach has been going on for decades. The emic approach allows a more in-depth analysis of cultural impact, but the generalizability of the findings to other cultural contexts is limited. While the etic approach allows researchers to conveniently compare HR practices and their effectiveness between cultures, it discourages researchers from recognizing the uniqueness of HR practices within each culture and fully exploring the influence of culture in HRM. Assuming the constructs are understood in the same way across cultures masks the true differences in more fundamental cultural factors and results in uncritical adoption of HR practices in other cultures. Since effective global HRM requires managers to understand both universal and local issues, considering both issues paints a clearer picture in cross-cultural research. A *derived etic* approach that combines both emic and etic approaches has been recommended to blend shared and unique aspects of a construct and is believed to capture a construct more accurately (Schaffer & Riordan, 2003). Applying this approach also helps identify constructs that originate from a non-U.S. culture but can be extended and applied to other cultures, and thus further develop a concept or a framework from a non-Western perspective. For example, Bond developed a Chinese Value Survey (CVS) rooted in Chinese culture and administered the survey to students in 23 countries. Results yielded four value dimensions, three of which replicated Hofstede's (1980) value dimensions. The fourth CVS value was unique to Hofstede's original cultural value frameworks, but effectively distinguished nations with a future orientation from nations with a past and present orientation (Chinese Culture Connection, 1987). This dimension was labeled as long-term versus short-term orientation and added as a fifth universal dimension into Hofstede's framework (Hofstede & Bond, 1988).

Although the derived etic approach has the advantage of considering both etic and emic aspects, it is not without risk. Farh, Earley, and Lin (1997) developed an indigenous instrument measuring organizational citizenship behavior in the Chinese context and identified five factors. They compared the five dimensions of the Chinese citizenship behavior scale with those identified by Organ (1988) and Podsakoff, MacKenzie, Moorman, and Fetter (1990) in the U.S. and found that three dimensions were similar between the two scales and appeared to be the etic dimensions. Two dimensions from the Chinese scale, namely, interpersonal harmony and protecting company resources, seemed to be the emic aspects of citizenship behavior in the Chinese context. However, in a reexamination of this widely used Chinese scale, Zhao, Wu, Sun, and Chen (2012) argued that these two dimensions in fact measured the construct of deviant behavior instead of cultural-specific aspects of citizenship behavior. Their findings challenged the conclusion of Farh *et al.* (1997) concerning the indigenous characteristics of Chinese citizenship behavior. Therefore, researchers should be cautious drawing conclusions about emic aspects of a construct when their results indicate differences in this construct between cultures.

Cross-Cultural Equivalence

In the area of global HRM studies, constructs developed and investigated in domestic research have been largely applied in new cultural contexts. Researchers who directly compare measurement results across cultures share three assumptions. The first assumption is that the concepts developed in one culture (usually U.S.) also exist in other cultures. The second assumption is that the concept can be captured by the same instrument across different populations. The third assumption is that people from various cultures share the same frame of references and response set when answering survey questions, and thus their scores on the instrument reflect their true levels on the measured constructs (Schaffer & Riordan, 2003). These assumptions ignore the potential of nonequivalence in constructs and compromise the meaningfulness of comparisons. Researchers will be comparing apples with oranges if equivalence is not established first. Challenges to equivalence occur in different stages of cross-cultural research, including conceptualization, data collection, and data analysis. In the following, we discuss conceptual, methodological, and measurement equivalence and present ways to achieve such equivalence.

Conceptual Equivalence

Conceptual equivalence refers to whether the concept under investigation is defined in the same way across cultures. This refers to the emic versus etic approach discussed previously. The emic approach assumes that a concept can only be accurately understood within its cultural context, whereas the etic approach suggests the meaning of a concept can be shared across cultures. When researchers adopt an etic approach, caution needs to be taken to ensure that people from different cultures understand the concept in the same way. For example, while employment security is a key component of high commitment work systems in Western societies, it is not perceived as an indication of an employer's trust and commitment to company employees in China (Xiao & Björkman, 2006). A significant problem is that some researchers may lack the knowledge of a foreign culture and thus impose understanding and interpretation of the concepts from their own cultural perspective. Collaborating with researchers from the targeted cultures helps identify emic meaning of a concept and achieve conceptual equivalence. In fact, cross-cultural research alliances have been called for in order to improve the validity of cross-cultural studies (Graen, Hui, Wakabayashi, & Wang, 1997).

Methodological Equivalence

Methodological equivalence mainly concerns the consistency of procedures when a study is conducted in multiple countries. Cross-cultural research usually requires collaboration from researchers in different countries and thus induces biases that are not common in single-cultural studies. These biases lead to incomparable meanings of observed items and latent constructs across cultures and induce confounding to identified cultural differences. Biases can happen in the instrument preparation, sampling of participants, and administration of the study. In the following we discuss issues in instrument selection and development, scale translation, matching participants, and administration of surveys that should be dealt with if methodological equivalence is to be achieved.

Selecting an appropriate instrument in cross-cultural research goes beyond choosing a valid and reliable scale. Since a concept may be defined in various ways across cultures, a valid and reliable scale in one country may not accurately capture the same concept in other cultures. Researchers should consult content experts in the targeted cultures to ensure conceptual equivalence of a scale, or choose instruments that have been validated in the target cultures. Developing indigenous items and scales improves the validity and reliability of the instrument in a particular culture, but different scales may result in difficulties of comparison across cultures. Schaffer and Riordan (2003) recommended a best practice of derived etic approach to include both etic and emic items. According to their suggestion, if a concept has both shared and distinct meanings between two cultures, then a scale comprised of items tapping the universal aspects and items tapping the specific aspects may be developed to better capture the concept in such a cross-cultural comparison.

Semantic equivalence is another challenge to cross-cultural HRM studies since there is a good chance that questionnaires will be administrated in different languages. Semantic inconsistencies may lead to differences in responses to the questionnaire and thus induce confounding to true cultural differences. Back-translation (Brislin, 1970) is the most widely used procedure to ensure language equivalence. One bilingual translates the original survey to the local language, and another bilingual, without seeing the original survey, translates the instrument back to the original language. Then the back-translated version is compared with the original version and any discrepancies in meanings are discussed in order to arrive at an accurate translation. Further procedures can be carried out to improve the accuracy, appropriateness, and interpretability of the translated instrument. For instance, researchers can recruit native speakers from the focal country and ask them to compare each pair of original and translated items. Researchers also can assess test-retest scores on the two-language versions of the survey with bilingual people (Sperber, Devellis, & Boehlecke, 1994). In addition to back-translation, it is recommended to use short, simple sentences, avoid using phrases that are common in one culture but not familiar to other cultures, and use examples to explain complex ideas when translating an instrument (Brislin, 1986; Schaffer & Riordan, 2003). Researchers should be aware that some words or terminologies, such as the indigenous concepts of *mianzi* in Chinese culture and *wasta* in Arab nations (Smith, 2008), may not be accurately translated to another language. Researchers should also note that even when the translation is perfect, the same scale may tap different concepts across cultural groups and conceptual equivalence is not guaranteed. Although careful selection of instruments and accurate translation increase the conceptual equivalence of constructs across cultures, testing measurement equivalence is necessary and usually the first step in data analysis. We discuss this topic under measurement equivalence ahead.

Another aspect of methodological equivalence is that the demographics of participants between cultural groups should be comparable. For example, Hofstede (1980) surveyed employees from one multinational company and it was assumed that these participants were comparable in terms of their age, gender, work experience, job position, and other demographics. Bui, Ituma, and Antonacopoulou (2013) sampled both academic and nonacademic staff from one university in the UK and one in Vietnam. The two universities were comparable in terms of their reputation, structure of schools, and size of employees. Stratified random sampling was used to draw representative samples from each university. The two samples were similar in terms of their education, tenure, and job roles. However, in HRM research some samples may not be comparable. If employees from high-tech companies are surveyed in one culture and employees from manufacture factories are surveyed in another culture, these two samples may differ in age, gender composition, socioeconomic status, and so on. The differences in these demographics may contribute to any differences found between the two cultures and thus confound the results. If it is not possible to match samples, or when samples representing the cultures are preferred over matched samples, then key variables should be measured and later controlled for in data analysis in order to rule out possible alternative explanations for cultural differences.

Administration of surveys may also introduce bias into cross-cultural studies and jeopardize methodological equivalence. Since surveys are likely to be distributed by different researchers across cultures, inconsistencies in procedures may impair methodological equivalence. For example, if a survey is mailed to participants in Country A, is put online and the link to the survey e-mailed to participants in Country B, and is directly distributed by the company's HR division in Country C, or if the cover letter of the survey is written in different ways across cultures, response rates may differ because of a systematic bias. Schaffer and Riordan (2003) recommended developing a data collection protocol, providing explicit and consistent instructions and examples and implementing uniform procedures across cultures to reduce biases in administration.

Measurement Equivalence

Another major challenge cross-cultural researchers are faced with is measurement equivalence across cultural groups. As mentioned previously, conceptual equivalence refers to whether or not the concept under study is defined in the same way across cultures. In technical terms, conceptual equivalence is satisfied when the same measure captures the same underlying construct across cultural groups and measurement equivalence is achieved. In some HRM research, variables are measured in a standard and objective way, especially variables regarding HR practices on the organizational level, and thus statistically establishing measurement equivalence on these measures across cultural groups is not required. For example, Peretz and Fried (2012) gathered indices of performance appraisal policies and practices such as the percentage of employees evaluated, number of sources of raters, and organizational outcomes such as average yearly turnover percentage and average annual absenteeism measured in days. Fey *et al.* (2009) measured training in terms of number of days instead of quality of training and measured performance appraisal as the portion of the workforce that regularly received performance evaluation. The meaning of these variables (percentages, number of days) is not affected by culture and therefore equivalence can be assumed. However, some other variables, especially psychological traits and attitudes at the individual level (e.g., justice perception or organizational commitment) may contain different meanings in various cultures and thus are more likely to suffer measurement nonequivalence. In the following we present two approaches to establish equivalence, multi-group confirmatory factor analysis (CFA) and meta-analytic structural equation modeling (MASEM). Multi-group CFA is suitable for studies with a small number of countries (e.g., two or three), and MASEM is suitable for studies with a large number of countries.

Little (1997) described a multi-group CFA approach to examine construct comparability between groups. This technique provides a standard procedure and meaningful comparisons of indices, and has been widely used (see reviews Schmitt & Kuljanin, 2008; Vandenberg & Lance, 2000). In this approach, a factor structure is conceptualized *a prior* and tested simultaneously across cultural groups. Then constraints are added to test whether or not the factor loadings, intercepts, factor variances and covariances, as well as error variances are invariant across cultural groups. If these invariances are supported, then the measurement is claimed to be equivalent across cultures. In practice, however, studies that achieve invariance in factor loadings and intercepts are considered to provide adequate evidence of measurement equivalence. In technical terms, three nested models, configural invariance, metric invariance, and scalar invariance, need to be tested for this purpose.

The *configural invariance model* is the baseline model for comparisons. In this model, the same factor structure is tested simultaneously across all groups. No equivalence between groups is assumed and no constraints are added. If this model does not fit, it means the factor structure fails to hold in at least one cultural group and indicates some items are not appropriate measures of the latent construct in that cultural group(s). Researchers should then investigate the items in the measure to check the appropriateness of each item. After the configural invariance model is established, the next step is to test whether each factor loading is equivalent across cultures. In the *metric invariance model,* factor loadings of the same items are constrained to be equal across the cultural groups. If this model yields an acceptable model fit and the model fit does not deteriorate significantly from the baseline model, it suggests that the relationships between the items and the latent construct are the same across cultures. The metric invariance model provides evidence for construct validity but does not guarantee the means of the latent factors are comparable between cultural groups. Researchers who are interested in comparing the mean differences among cultures should further test scalar invariance in order for such comparisons to be meaningful. The *scalar invariance model* addresses the questions of whether observed mean differences in the measurement items across cultures can be attributed to mean differences in the latent construct. The scalar invariance model is based on the metric invariance model with constraints on the intercepts of the items. If this model fits and the model fit does not deteriorate significantly compared with the metric invariance model, it indicates participants across cultures use similar response sets and the means on the latent construct across cultures are comparable. The same procedure is described in more technical terms in Chapter 7 of this volume, and the full procedure for testing measurement equivalence with multi-group CFA can be found in many methodology papers (e.g., Jöreskog, 1971; Steenkamp & Baumgartner, 1998). Computer programs such as Amos (Arbuckle, 2006), EQS (Bentler, 2008), and Mplus (Muthén & Muthén, 1998–2010) are available for testing measurement equivalence using this approach. Multi-group SEM is usually used to compare structures and relationships across cultures after measurement equivalence has been established by multi-group CFA.

When a large number of cultural groups are involved, using CFA to establish measurement equivalence is inefficient and the MASEM approach is recommended instead. Cheung, Leung, and Au (2006) described using MASEM to establish measurement equivalence across 40 cultural groups. Two steps are performed in MASEM. The first step tests the homogeneity of correlation matrices across cultural groups. If the correlation matrices are homogeneous, then the data can be pooled together for analysis in step two. Note that the first step does not test whether the factor structure holds across cultures as does the configural model in the multi-group CFA approach. Instead, it tests whether the interrelationships among the items are the same across cultures. In step two, the proposed model is fitted against the pooled correlation matrix. If the proposed model fits the data well, then scholars can conclude that the model achieves measurement equivalence across cultures. Technical details can be found in the appendix of Cheung *et al.* (2006). The MASEM approach is usually followed by multi-level CFA to assess factor structures or multi-level SEM to estimate relationships among latent constructs with nested data (e.g., Dyera, Hangesa, & Hall, 2005; Mehta & Neale, 2005).

Level of Analysis

In cross-cultural HRM research, three levels of analysis are possible: individual, organizational, and cultural. Individual-level studies investigate the levels of or relationships among individual characteristics, such as employees' motivation, work engagement, commitment, individual performance, and so on. Organizational-level studies investigate the levels of or relationships among organizational characteristics, such as organizational age, size, sector, organizational climate, performance management practices, organizational performance, and so on. Cultural-level studies investigate the levels of or relationships among cultural characteristics, such as cultural values and beliefs, GDP, national indices of trust and corruption, and so on. This type of study usually requires a large sample of countries.

Sometimes constructs at different levels are labeled with the same term but are operationalized in different ways across levels. For example, individual performance is usually measured by an employee's task outcome, whereas organizational performance is usually assessed by a firm's financial outcomes such as profitability and return on asset. Similarly, culture by definition is a country-level construct and countries' standings on the value dimensions can be obtained from indexes such as Hofstede's framework and GLOBE. On the other hand, culture can be operationalized as dispositional values at the individual level using scales such as Horizontal and Vertical Individualism and Collectivism scale (Triandis & Gelfand, 1998). Constructs measured at a lower level may be aggregated to a higher level for analysis when indices of the higher level variables are not available. For instance, values measured at the individual level may be aggregated to the cultural level for analysis, and results from this kind of analysis should be interpreted at the cultural level. Hofstede's (1980) national value dimensions were obtained by factor analysis of national aggregated individual scores (i.e., country means of items). Thus the results should be interpreted as how countries or nations differ along the value dimensions, not how people differ along the dimensions. However, some higher level constructs (e.g., organizational performance) are more than the aggregation of the lower level constructs (e.g., individual performance) and changes in the lower level constructs do not necessarily translate to the higher level correspondents (DeNisi, 2000). Therefore researchers should be cautious about the appropriate level of the constructs when theorizing or measuring them.

In addition, researchers should not assume that characteristics at one level will hold at other levels. Uncritically assuming and applying cultural-level characteristics to the individual level leads to what is called ecological fallacy (Robinson, 1950). For example, Hofstede has repeatedly emphasized that his national value dimensions only correlated across nations instead of organizations or individuals. In fact, the variables that define these values do not correlate meaningfully at the individual level and as a result these values neither describe individuals nor explain individual behavior (Hofstede, 1980; Minkov & Hofstede, 2011). Furthermore, Hofstede assumed that individualism and collectivism formed a bipolar single dimension, with high individualism equivalent to low collectivism. However, studies have suggested that individualism and collectivism values are two separate dimensions at the individual level (Oyserman, Coon, & Kemmelmeier, 2002). These findings suggest different construct structures across levels.

Because cross-cultural HRM research involves multiple levels, research questions in this area may have a multi-level structure that examines how characteristics on a higher level influence characteristics on a lower level. For example, an employee is embedded in an organization, which in turn is embedded in a country. The employee's workplace behavior (e.g., risk taking) can be a function of all three levels: it can depend on the employee's personality of openness to new experience, the organizational culture of encouraging innovation, and the country's cultural value of openness to change. Characteristics on a higher level can influence the magnitude of variables or the strength of relationships between variables on a lower level. For example, Peretz and Fried (2012) studied the relationship between performance appraisal practices and the organizational outcomes of absenteeism and turnover. This relationship between HR practices and organizational outcomes are at the organizational level. They further investigated how cultural practices such as power distance moderated the above relationship. Since cultural practices are cultural-level characteristics that affect the strength of a relationship at the organizational level, their research question addressed a cross-level issue. Similarly, cultural-level characteristics influence relationships at the individual level. For example, receiving an unfair job evaluation from supervisors decreases employees' motivation, but this relationship becomes weaker as the degree of a country's power distance increases because people in high power distance cultures tend to accept messages from authority figures.

When data have a multi-level or hierarchical structure, multi-level modeling (hierarchical linear modeling) is recommended for analysis of effects across levels. Since data are nested in nature (e.g., employees are nested within organizations, which in turn are nested within cultures), multi-level analysis aims to partition the observed variance into lower level (e.g., individual psychological traits) and higher level (e.g., cultural values) components. Technical discussions in multi-level analysis can be found in Chapter 3 in this volume and other research methods books (e.g., Goldstein, 2011; Hox, 2010; Raudenbush & Bryk, 2002). Computer programs such as HLM (Raudenbush, Bryk, & Congdon, 2004) and Mplus (Muthén & Muthén, 1998–2010) are available for multi-level modeling.

Causal Inferences

Cross-cultural HRM research faces the challenge of drawing causal conclusions. Most of the current HRM studies are correlational in nature, in which both independent and dependent variables are measured by questionnaires and their relationships are investigated. It is therefore technically inappropriate to make causal inferences based on these studies alone. Experimental studies, on the other hand, manipulate the level of the independent variables, randomly assign participants to different levels of independent variables, and measure their responses on the dependent variables while controlling other variables to be equal. In cross-cultural studies, the independent variable of interest is usually culture. However, researchers cannot manipulate culture or randomly assign participants into different cultural groups. Therefore, although experimental studies make stronger causal inference than correlational studies, they are rare in the cross-cultural HRM area. Chapter 6 in this volume is devoted to a discussion of experimental designs in HRM and readers should refer to that chapter for more information.

Generally speaking, the conclusion of a causal relationship is more convincing when results from multiple data sources and different research methods converge. Scholars have recently called for using both correlational and experimental studies in a complementary fashion (e.g., Chan, 2008). Using a triangulation approach (see Chapter 2 in this volume) and combining survey and experiments in cross-cultural HRM research will strengthen causal inferences. Readers should refer to Chapter 2 for a discussion of mixed methods research. Other than using multiple research methods, Leung and Van de Vijver (2008) recommended several ways to strengthen the causal inferences of correlational studies in cross-cultural research. In the following we summarize systematic contrast strategies and covariate strategies.

Systematic Contrast Strategies

Systematic contrast strategies are usually carried out in the sampling stage and try to rule out possible confoundings by strategically choosing cultural groups. Many of the current cross-cultural studies sample only two cultural groups and draw conclusions about one cultural dimension on which the two cultural groups are different. Since two cultures can differ in many respects, interpretations of any differences found are ambiguous. Systematic contrast strategies suggest several ways to reduce this ambiguity. For example, instead of choosing two countries that are on the extremes of one cultural dimension, researchers can use a *multiple contrast strategy* and choose three countries that represent high, medium, and low levels on a cultural dimension. If the expected cultural differences show the same order, then researchers are more confident in drawing conclusions about the focal cultural dimension. For example, to study the influence of cultural power distance, researchers may choose New Zealand to represent egalitarian culture, Malaysia to represent hierarchical culture, and France in the middle, based on Hofstede's country rankings. More countries can be included in this approach and their ranking on the cultural dimension and ranking on the dependent variables are compared to see whether they correspond. Researchers can also use a *systematic sampling strategy* to deliberately select countries to rule out specific confounding variables. Countries that are different on the focal cultural dimension but similar on confounding variables are selected. Alternative explanations based on the confounding variables can be ruled out if the expected cultural difference still emerges. Using China, France, and Demark for example; China is higher on both collectivism and power distance dimensions than France, according to Hofstede's rankings. If both collectivism and power distance may encourage the implementation of a particular HR practice, then it will be ambiguous as to which dimension is responsible for the difference found between China and France. On the other hand, France and Demark are very similar in the ranking of individualism, but France is higher in power distance. If the same pattern of differences is found between France and Demark, then researchers are more confident in attributing the observed differences in HR practice to the value of power distance.

Covariate Strategies

Covariate strategies are usually carried out in the measurement and data analysis stages to empirically partial out the effect of alternative variables. It requires the measurement of contextual variables, which are variables that may explain observed cultural differences. They include country variables such as cultural values and GDP, organizational variables such as technology level and organizational size, and individual variables such as personality and education level. When contextual variables are not included and cultural differences are found, it is simply concluded that these differences are due to the contextual variables hypothesized without empirically testing whether the proposed contextual variables indeed account for such cultural differences. This type of study is pervasive in comparative studies involving two or three countries. For example, Fey *et al.* (2009) proposed that power distance affected the effectiveness of performance appraisal such that performance appraisal worked better in low power distance than high power distance cultures. They sampled Finland and the U.S. as representatives of low power distance cultures and Russia as a representative of high power distance cultures based on Hofstede (1980) and GLOBE (House *et al.*, 2004) frameworks, and compared the strength of the relationship between performance appraisal and employee abilities among the three countries. However, the scores of power distance of the three countries were not included in their data analysis. Although this approach has been applied by many studies, it suffers a major weakness of being unable to identify the true causes of observed cultural differences. For example, differences observed between the U.S. and China can be attributed to their differences in cultural values such as individualism-collectivism and power distance, or to their GDP or political systems. Without ruling out other possible causes or empirically testing the effect of the proposed variables, researchers may draw misleading conclusions. Therefore, including contextual variables improves the validity of the conclusions and strengthens causal inferences.

In the *simple covariate approach,* the hypothesized contextual variable such as a cultural element is measured and controlled for in data analysis. If the cultural difference diminishes or disappears after the contextual variable is entered into the equation, it indicates the hypothesized contextual variable is responsible for the observed cultural difference. An extension of this approach is to test whether the contextual variable mediates the moderating effect of country. If mediation is supported, it indicates the observed differences between cultures are explained by the contextual variable. That is, culture influences the outcomes through the mechanism of the contextual variable. For example, Shao and Skarlicki (in press) investigated the relationship between customer mistreatment and sabotage toward the customers who mistreated them and found the relationship was stronger among service employees in Canada than in China. They further showed that employees' value of individualism at the individual level fully accounted for (i.e., mediated) the moderating effect of country on the relationship between customer mistreatment and sabotage. Their results indicated that Canadian employees were more likely to sabotage after receiving unfair treatment from customers because they were higher on individualism values and thus were more likely to react with "direct, active, and target-specific actions." In the *complex covariate approach,* the hypothesized contextual variable and possible confounding variables are both measured and included in the data analysis. If the hypothesized contextual variable still explains significant amount of variance in outcomes after confounding variables are controlled, it suggests the contextual variable is a cause of the cultural differences. An example is described in the box below.

Conducting a cross-cultural HRM study: How does it work in practice?

Jane is a PhD student who is interested in how individualism-collectivism value influences preference for pay for individual performance. She recruited a group of participants from an individualist culture (Australia) and another group from a collectivist culture (China) and measured their endorsement of individualism-collectivism value at the individual level. She speculated that performance versus learning orientation might also affect the preference for pay for individual performance, and thus measured this variable as a covariate. In the data analysis, Jane regressed the outcome variable on country (a categorical variable), individualism-collectivism value, and performance versus learning orientation and found that individualism-collectivism value explained a significant amount of variance in the outcome. Jane concluded that employees with individualism value prefer pay for individual performance more than employees with collectivism value.

---

4. CONCLUSION

Cross-cultural research in HRM advances our knowledge in selecting, training, and compensating employees in the age of globalization. However, researchers conducting such studies are faced with difficulties in both conceptualization and methodology. This chapter has focused on issues and challenges associated with cross-cultural comparative studies in HRM research. We first presented strengths and weaknesses of cross-cultural study design, then discussed possible biases that threaten the validity of such studies and presented strategies to overcome them. Among the conceptual and methodological concerns with cross-cultural studies, we have highlighted four issues: the emic versus etic approach, cross-cultural equivalence, level of analysis, and causal inferences. We described the debate between emic and etic approaches and recommended a combined approach. In terms of equivalence, we discussed conceptual, methodological, and measurement equivalence. We also discussed the level of analysis issues in cross-cultural studies and emphasized that the relationships and frameworks identified at one level cannot be assumed to be the same at another level. Finally, we described strategies to strengthen causal inferences in correlational studies, given that most cross-cultural studies are quasiexperimental in nature. We hope this chapter provides a brief introduction to the many challenges in cross-cultural comparative studies in HRM.

REFERENCES

Arbuckle, J. L. (2006). Amos (Version 7.0) [Computer Program]. Chicago: SPSS.
Au, K. (1999). Intra-cultural variation: Evidence and implications for international business. *Journal of International Business Studies, 30*, 799–812.
Aycan, Z. (2005). The interplay between cultural and institutional/structural contingencies in human resource management practice. *International Journal of Human Resource Management, 16*, 1083–1119.
Bentler, P. M. (2008). *EQS 6 Structural Equations Program Manual*. Encino, CA: Multivariate Software Inc.
Berry, J. W. (1989). Imposed etics—emics—derived etics: The operationalisation of a compelling idea. *International Journal of Psychology, 24*, 721–735.
Berry, J. W. (1990). Imposed etics, emics, and derived etics: Their conceptual and operational status in cross-cultural psychology. In T. N. Headland, K. L. Pike, & M. Harris (Eds.), *Emics and etics: The insider/outsider debate*. Newbury Park, CA: Sage.
Brislin, R. W. (1970). Back-translation for cross-cultural research. *Journal of Cross-Cultural Psychology, 75*, 3–9.
Brislin, R. W. (1986). The wording and translation of research instruments. In W. J. Lonner & J. W. Berry (Eds.), *Field methods in cross-cultural research* (Vol. 8, pp. 137–164). Beverly Hills, CA: Sage.
Bui, H. T. M., Ituma, A., & Antonacopoulou, E. (2013). Antecedents and outcomes of personal mastery: Cross-country evidence in higher education. *International Journal of Human Resource Management, 24*, 167–194.
Cascio, W. F. (2012). Methodological issues in international HR management research. *The International Journal of Human Resource Management, 23*, 2532–2545.
Chan, D. (2008). Methodological issues in international human resource management research. In M. M. Harris (Ed.), *Handbook of research in international human resource management* (pp. 53–76). New York: Lawrence Erlbaum Associates.
Cheung, M. W.-L., Leung, K., & Au, K. (2006). Evaluating multilevel models in cross-cultural research: An illustration with social axioms. *Journal of Cross-Cultural Psychology, 37*, 522–541.
Chiang, F. F. T., & Birtch, T. A. (2010). Appraising performance across borders: An empirical examination of the purposes and practices of performance appraisal in a multi-country context. *Journal of Management Studies, 47*, 1365–1393.
Chinese Culture Connection. (1987). Chinese values and the search for culture-free dimensions of culture. *Journal of Cross-Cultural Psychology, 18*(2), 143–164.

Cogin, J. A., & Williamson, I. O. (In press). Standardize or customize: The interactive effects of HRM and environment uncertainty on MNC subsidiary performance. *Human Resource Management*.

DeNisi, A. S. (2000). Performance appraisal and control systems: A multilevel approach. In K. Klein & S. Kozlowski (Eds.), *Multilevel theory, research, and methods in organizations* (pp. 121–156). San Francisco, CA: Jossey-Bass.

Du, J., & Choi, J. N. (2010). Pay for performance in emerging markets: Insights from China. *Journal of International Business Studies, 41,* 671–689.

Dyera, N. G., Hangesa, P. J., & Hall, R. J. (2005). Applying multilevel confirmatory factor analysis techniques to the study of leadership. *The Leadership Quarterly, 16,* 149–167.

Farh, J.-L., Earley, P. C., & Lin, S. C. (1997). Impetus for action: A cultural analysis of justice and organizational citizenship behavior in Chinese society. *Administrative Science Quarterly, 42,* 421–444.

Fey, C. F., Morgulis-Yakushev, S., Park, H. J., & Björkman, I. (2009). Opening the black box of the relationship between HRM practices and firm performance: A comparison of MNE subsidiaries in the USA, Finland, and Russia. *Journal of International Business Studies, 40,* 690–712.

Goldstein, H. (2011). *Multilevel statistical models* (4th ed.). Chichester, UK: Wiley.

Graen, G. B., Hui, C., Wakabayashi, M., & Wang, Z. (1997). Cross-cultural research alliances in organizational research. In P. C. Earley & M. Erez (Eds.), *New perspectives on international industrial/organizational psychology*. San Francisco, CA: New Lexington Press.

Gudykunst, W. B. (1997). Cultural variability in communication. *Communication Research, 24,* 327–348.

Hamaaki, J., Hori, M., Maeda, S., & Murata, K. (2012). Changes in the Japanese employment system in the two lost decades. *Industrial & Labor Relations Review, 65,* 810–846.

Harris, M. M. (2008). Introduction. In M. M. Harris (Ed.), *Handbook of research in international human resource management* (pp. 1–4). New York: Lawrence Erlbaum.

Harvey, M. (1997). Focusing the international personnel performance appraisal process. *Human Resource Development Quarterly, 8*(1), 41–62.

Hofstede, G. (1980). *Culture's consequences: International differences in work related values*. Beverly Hills, CA: Sage.

Hofstede, G. (2001). *Culture's consequences: Comparing values, behaviors, institutions, and organizations across nations* (2nd ed.). Thousand Oaks, CA: Sage.

Hofstede, G., & Bond, M. H. (1988). The Confucius connection: From cultural roots to economic growth. *Organizational Dynamics, 16,* 5–21.

House, R. J., Hanges, P. J., Javidan, M., Dorfman, P. W., & Gupta, V. (2004). *Culture, leadership, and organizations: The GLOBE study of 62 societies*. Thousand Oaks, CA: Sage.

Hox, J. J. (2010). *Multilevel analysis: Techniques and applications* (2nd ed.). New York: Routledge.

Jöreskog, K. G. (1971). Simultaneous factor analysis in several populations. *Psychometrika, 36,* 409–426.

Leung, K. (2008). Methods and measurements in cross-cultural management. In P. B. Smith, M. F. Peterson, & D. C. Thomas (Eds.), *The handbook of cross-cultural management research* (pp. 59–73). Thousand Oaks, CA: Sage.

Leung, K., & Van de Vijver, F. J. R. (2008). Strategies for strengthening causal inferences in cross cultural research: The consilience approach. *International Journal of Cross Cultural Management, 8*(2), 145–169.

Little, T. D. (1997). Mean and covariance structures (MACS) analyses of cross-cultural data: Practical and theoretical issues. *Multivariate Behavioral Research, 32,* 52–76.

Matsumoto, D., & Van de Vijver, F. J. R. (Eds.). (2011). *Cross-cultural research methods in psychology*. New York: Cambridge University Press.

Mehta, P. D., & Neale, M. C. (2005). People are variables too: Multilevel structural equations modeling. *Psychological Methods, 10*, 259–284.

Mendonca, M., & Kanungo, R. N. (1996). Impact of culture on performance management in developing countries. *International Journal of Manpower, 17*, 65–75.

Minkov, M., & Hofstede, G. (2011). The evolution of Hofstede's doctrine. *Cross-Cultural Management: An International Journal, 18*, 10–20.

Minkov, M., & Hofstede, G. (2012). Hofstede's fifth dimension: New evidence from the World Values Survey. *Journal of Cross-Cultural Psychology, 43*, 3–14.

Muthén, L. K., & Muthén, B. O. (1998–2010). *Mplus user's guide* (6th ed.). Los Angeles, CA: Muthén & Muthén.

Newman, K. L., & Nollen, S. D. (1996). Culture and congruence: The fit between management practices and national culture. *Journal of International Business Studies, 27*, 753–779.

Organ, D. W. (1988). *Organizational citizenship behavior: The "good soldier" syndrome*. Lexington, MA: Lexington Books.

Oyserman, D., Coon, H. M., & Kemmelmeier, M. (2002). Rethinking individualism and collectivism: Evaluation of theoretical assumptions and meta-analyses. *Psychological Bulletin, 128*, 3–72.

Peretz, H., & Fried, Y. (2012). National cultures, performance appraisal practices, and organizational absenteeism and turnover: A study across 21 countries. *Journal of Applied Psychology, 97*, 448–459.

Podsakoff, P. M., MacKenzie, S. B., Moorman, R. H., & Fetter, R. (1990). Transformational leader behaviors and their effects on followers' trust in leader, satisfaction, and organizational citizenship behaviors. *Leadership Quarterly, 1*, 107–142.

Raudenbush, S. W., & Bryk, A. S. (2002). *Hierarchical linear models: Applications and data analysis methods* (2nd ed.). Newbury Park, CA: Sage.

Raudenbush, S. W., Bryk, A. S., & Congdon, R. (2004). HLM 6 for Windows [Computer software]. Skokie, IL: Scientific Software International, Inc.

Riordan, C. M., & Vandenberg, R. J. (1994). A central question in cross-cultural research: Do employees of different cultures interpret work-related measures in an equivalent manner? *Journal of Management, 20*, 643–671.

Robinson, W. S. (1950). Ecological correlations and the behavior of individuals. *American Sociological Review, 15*, 351–357.

Ronen, S., & Shenkar, O. (1988). Clustering variables: The application of nonmetric multivariate analysis techniques in comparative management research. *International Studies of Management & Organization, 18*(3), 72–87.

Schaffer, B. S., & Riordan, C. M. (2003). A review of cross-cultural methodologies for organizational research: A best-practices approach. *Organizational Research Methods, 6*, 169–215.

Schmitt, N., & Kuljanin, G. (2008). Measurement invariance: Review of practice and implications. *Human Resource Management Review, 18*, 210–222.

Schwartz, S. H. (1992). Universals in the content and structure of values: Theoretical advances and empirical tests in 20 countries. In M. P. Zanna (Ed.), *Advances in experimental social psychology* (Vol. 24, pp. 1–65). San Diego, CA: Academic Press.

Schwartz, S. H. (1994). Beyond individualism/collectivism: New dimensions of values. In U. Kim, H. C. Triandis, C. Ka itçibasi, S. C. Choi, & G. Yoon (Eds.), *Individualism and collectivism: Theory applications and methods* (pp. 85–119). Newbury Park, CA: Sage.

Selvarajan, T. T., & Cloninger, P. A. (2012). Can performance appraisals motivate employees to improve performance? A Mexican study. *The International Journal of Human Resource Management, 23*, 3063–3084.

Shao, R., & Skarlicki, D. P. (In press). Service employees' reactions to mistreatment by customers: A comparison of North America and East Asia. *Personnel Psychology.*

Smith, P. B. (2008). Indigenous aspects of management. In P. B. Smith, M. F. Peterson, & D. C. Thomas (Eds.), *The handbook of cross-cultural management research* (pp. 319–332). Thousand Oaks, CA: Sage.

Smith, P. B., Bond, M. H., & Ka itçibasi, C. (2006). *Understanding social psychology across cultures: Living and working in a changing world.* London: Sage.

Sperber, A. D., Devellis, R. F., & Boehlecke, B. (1994). Cross-cultural translation: Methodology and validation. *Journal of Cross-Cultural Psychology, 25,* 501–524.

Steenkamp, J. B. E. M., & Baumgartner, H. (1998). Assessing measurement invariance in cross-national consumer research. *Journal of Consumer Research, 25,* 78–107.

Taras, V., Rowney, J., & Steel, P. (2009). Half a century of measuring culture: Review of approaches, challenges, and limitations based on the analysis of 121 instruments for quantifying culture. *Journal of International Management, 15,* 357–373.

Thomas, D. C., & Lazarova, M. B. (In press). *Managing people globally: Essentials of international human resource management.* Thousand Oaks, CA: Sage.

Triandis, H. C., & Gelfand, M. J. (1998). Converging measurement of horizontal and vertical individualism and collectivism. *Journal of Personality and Social Psychology, 74,* 118–128.

Tsui, A. S. (2007). From homogenization to pluralism: International management research in the academy and beyond. *Academy of Management Journal, 50,* 1353–1364.

Vandenberg, R. J., & Lance, C. E. (2000). A review and synthesis of the measurement invariance literature: Suggestions, practices, and recommendations for organizational research. *Organizational Research Methods, 3,* 4–69.

Varma, A., Pichler, S., & Srinivas, E. S. (2005). The role of interpersonal affect in performance appraisal: evidence from two samples—the US and India. *International Journal of Human Resource Management, 16,* 2029–2044.

Xiao, Z., & Björkman, I. (2006). High commitment work systems in Chinese organizations: A preliminary measure. *Management and Organization Review, 2,* 403–422.

Zhao, H., Wu, J., Sun, J.-M., & Chen, C. W. (2012). Organizational citizenship behavior in Chinese society: A reexamination. *International Journal of Human Resource Management, 23,* 4145–4165.

8 HRM Research Methods
Where We Are and Where We Need to Go

Cai-Hui (Veronica) Lin and Karin Sanders

After reading this chapter, we expect you to be able to:

1. Describe the state-of-science and development trajectories of the research methods utilized in the HRM-performance relationship studies;
2. Identify the problems in the current methodological practices;
3. Understand the promises and challenges of the research methods discussed in this volume;
4. Become familiar with the different stakeholders in the field of HRM research and understand how they are connected with each other.

---

1. INTRODUCTION

The field of Human Resource Management (HRM) research has been subject to heavy methodological criticisms for a long time. As pointed out in Chapter 1, various common research designs pertinent to the strength and causal relationship between HRM and performance have been taken issue with. Many of these issues have been repeatedly discussed by scholars, such as cross-sectional (Boselie, Dietz, & Boon, 2005; Wright, Gardner, Moynihan, & Allen, 2005), single-actor (Gerhart, Wright, McMahan, & Snell, 2000; Gerhart, Wright, & McMahan, 2000; Huselid & Becker, 2000), and single-level research design (Boselie *et al.*, 2005; Klein & Kozlowski, 2000). As scientific progress is premised on rigorous research methods with sound design, accurate measurement, and appropriate analytic techniques, these critiques threaten the validity and legitimacy of the current HRM research (see Welbourne, 2012; Sanders, Bainbridge, Kim, Cogin, & Lin, 2012; Sanders, Cogin, & Bainbridge, *this volume*). Indeed, after nearly three decades of inquiry, methodological limitations have been considered directly responsible for the inability of HRM scholars to answer the core question, What is the relationship between HRM and performance? (Guest, 2011; Wall & Wood, 2005).

Given the important role sound methodology plays in HRM research, it's time for HRM researchers to improve their research design, validate the measures, and apply advanced analytic techniques. To achieve this, they need to be equipped with knowledge and skills of when and how to use the available advanced methods. This book aims to contribute in this aspect. The preceding six chapters each introduced an advanced research method or research approach. After reading them, we hope the readers will be more confident in applying these methods. Before we move forward with the advanced methods, however, it might be meaningful to systematically take stock of what research methods have already been used in the field. Such an audit would inform the state-of-science of HRM research methods, indicate where the field currently is in terms of research design, and suggest what changes are needed in the future (Casper, Eby, Bordeaux, Lockwood, & Lambert, 2007; Scandura & Williams, 2000). A chronological review would further assist in judging the trajectories the field is following and predicting the direction the field is heading. To accomplish this task we draw on a research project conducted by Sanders and colleagues (2012). One prominent feature of this research is that it not only described the frequencies of the method adoption in HRM research, but also flagged the trend of changes over time. Based on this study (Sanders *et al.*, 2012), we outline the research methods employed in mainstream journals between 1996 and 2010 in studies that have examined the relationship between HRM and performance (see Section 2 of this chapter).

In light of the results of the systematic review, we then discuss the promises of the advanced research methods introduced in this book in overcoming the common methodological limitations in the HRM literature (Section 3). Since research design always involves a dilemmatic trade-off among multiple choices (McGrath, 1982), we also present the challenges that are intrinsic to each of these methods so that researchers are aware of both the strengths and weaknesses of a research method. Finally, acknowledging that researchers' methodological choice is not only a matter of preference but also constrained (or enabled) by many other factors, we call for joint actions from all the stakeholders of HRM research to facilitate significant changes in the field. We argue that without collaborative efforts, substantial methodological progress in the HRM field would be extremely difficult, if not impossible (Section 4).

2. THE STATE-OF-SCIENCE OF HRM RESEARCH METHODS

To present the state-of-science of the methodological choices made in HRM research and reveal the trajectories the field has been following, Sanders and colleagues (2012) thoroughly investigated the methods employed in the HRM-performance literature. Studies from six leading management journals and three field-specific HR journals were selected over a 15-year time frame (1996–2010). Since HRM researchers have increasingly come to the agreement that it is the combination of multiple HR practices that influences employee and organizational performance (Hayton, Piperopoulos, & Welbourne, 2011; Martín-Alcázar, Romero-Fernández, & Sánchez-Gardey, 2008; Wright & Boswell, 2002), Sanders *et al.* (2012) focused on research that examined the effect of *multiple* HR practices in relation to individual, group, and organizational outcomes. A total of 179 empirical studies that fulfilled their selection criteria were identified.

Under the umbrella of multiple HR practices-performance relationship, the studies included in their investigation covered five basic research models, although many studies involved a combination of two or more of these basic models. The first research model answers the question: What is the *direct effect* of multiple HR practices on performance? This strand of research is characterized by researchers' endeavors to identify an effective set of HR practices and empirically test the direct relationship between multiple HR practices and their outcomes. Examples include Delaney and Huselid (1996) and Tsui, Pearce, Porter, and Tripoli (1997). Overall, 141 out of the 179 studies (79%) investigated the direct relationship between HRM and performance. The second research model is concerned with the question: *When* are multiple HR practices more (or less) effective? This strand of research holds the view that the effectiveness of HRM is contingent upon contextual factors. Organizational strategy, for instance, is one factor that is often studied (e.g., Guthrie, Spell, & Nyamori, 2002; Youndt, Snell, Dean, & Lepak, 1996). Forty-nine studies (27%) examined the moderating effect of some variables in the HRM-performance relationship. The third research model asks the question: *How* do HR practices relate to performance? The last few years have witnessed a surge of research addressing the intermediate linkage between HRM and performance measures (e.g., Chuang & Liao, 2010; Gong, Law, Chang, & Xin, 2009; Kaše, Paauwe, & Zupan, 2009). This body of research provides insights into the causal mechanisms of how and why HRM contributes to performance. Forty-five studies (25%) in the sample researched the intermediate variables linking HRM and performance. In the fourth research model, HRM is treated as endogenous; namely, another variable affects performance *through* HR practices. For example, Bae and Lawler (2000) argued that an organization's management values regarding HRM and its overall strategy determine its HRM strategy, which further influences the organization's performance. In 16 studies (9%) HRM worked as a *mediator*. In the fifth research model, the effect of another variable is facilitated or inhibited by HRM. That is, HRM works as a *moderator*. Eighteen studies (10%) were based on this model (e.g., Shaw, Dineen, Fang, & Vellella, 2009; Shaw, Gupta, & Delery, 2005). Sanders *et al.* (2012) found that over time the proportion of studies examining the direct relationship between HRM and performance was declining, whereas there was a growing interest in examining how HR practices related to performance via mediation designs. This trend echoed the call from many scholars for a diversion of research attention to opening up the "black box" between HRM and performance (e.g., Becker & Gerhart, 1996; Lepak, Takeuchi, Erhardt, & Colakoglu, 2006).

In terms of general research method, single-method research comprised 95% of the sample. The prevalence of quantitative studies (91%) over qualitative studies (4%) and mixed methods studies (5%) was palpable. Specifically, most quantitative studies (162 out of the 163 quantitative studies) adopted a survey approach. Case studies (7 studies) and interviews (8 studies) were used infrequently. Researchers' overdependence on single-method research design dismisses the opportunity to compensate for the inherent weakness of one method with the strengths of another (Jick, 1979). What is discouraging is that there was a declining proportion of qualitative research, due in part to a move away from case-study research.

With regard to more specific research designs, Sanders *et al.* (2012) found that multi-level research was underrepresented in the sample (13 out of the 179 studies); 93% of the studies adopted a single-level research design. The preponderance of single-level research design suggested that HRM researchers largely failed to bridge macro and micro research (Wright & Boswell, 2002). By failing to do this, they risked erroneously attributing high-level phenomena to low level or vice versa (Rousseau, 1985). There was, however, evidence that multi-level research was gaining popularity and that the proportion of multi-level studies was increasing over time.

Although it is suggested that longitudinal data and experiments allow stronger inference of the direction of causality (Guest, 2011; Little, Card, Preacher, & McConnell, 2009; Wright *et al.*, 2005), 96% of the studies used cross-sectional data. Only one study in the sample was an experimental study. The limited number of longitudinal studies and experimental studies weakened the ability of researchers to infer the direction of causality between HR practices and performance. Furthermore, Sanders *et al.* (2012) found no evidence of an increasing proportion of longitudinal research.

In terms of measurement, more than half of the studies (59%) relied on data from the same source, which meant the same respondent answered questions on both HR practices and performance. Therefore, common method variance (CMV, Podsakoff, MacKenzie, Lee, & Podsakoff, 2003) posed a threat to the validity of the research results. It invoked suspicion that the significant relationship between multiple HR practices and performance may in fact be a methodological artifact. Disappointingly, no evidence was found of a change in preference for multiple informants for either the measurement of HR practices or performance.

In summary, the systematic review of Sanders *et al.* (2012) points to the following concerns in HR research: overreliance on a single method, particularly surveys; a dearth of a multi-level perspective; the prevalence of cross-sectional research design; and infrequent measurement drawn from multiple respondents. These limitations undermine HRM researchers' confidence in asserting that HRM makes an impact on performance. As a result, no conclusive answers exist to the following questions: (1) Does adoption of HR practices lead to superior performance? (2) If HRM leads to superior performance, how large is the effect size? Due to the importance of these two questions to the practitioners and the ambiguity of the answers, the diffusion of HRM research results to the practitioners is much impeded (Wall & Wood, 2005; Welbourne, 2012). To enhance the impact of HRM research, significant changes in research methods are needed to improve research validity. More adoption of advanced research methods is desired, which promises to overcome the limitations in the HR literature.

3. PROMISES AND CHALLENGES OF ADVANCED RESEARCH METHODS

This book introduced mixed methods research, multi-level and multi-actor research, social network analysis, longitudinal research, experimental methods, and cross-cultural studies in HRM. In each chapter the authors discussed the advantages of that method, when it is appropriate to use it, and how to use it. They also illustrated the common decision points researchers will encounter at various stages of a research project, using examples either from published literature or from their own research experiences. Although we advocate these research methods and recognize their high values, we do also point out the challenges associated with them to the readers. In this section, we summarize the promises and challenges of each research method to give the readers an overview (see Table 8.1). Strategies for researchers for efficiently employing these methods are also developed.

In Chapter 2 (Bainbridge & Lee) a mixed methods approach was introduced. Johnson, Onwuegbuzie, and Turner (2007, p. 123) define mixed methods research as "the type of research in which a researcher or team of researchers combines elements of qualitative and quantitative research approaches for the broad purpose of breadth and depth of understanding and corroboration." The strength of this approach lies in its capacity to address complex research problems by combining the "best of both worlds." Mixed methods draw upon the capacity of qualitative research to provide a contextualized deep understanding (Creswell, 1998), and quantitative research to develop generalizable findings. To the extent that results from the two methods converge, researchers can be more confident in the validity of their research, instead of attributing the research results to a methodological artifact (Bouchard, 1976).

Despite of these advantages, the authors of Chapter 2 recognize the demands of mixed methods. First, due to a broader scope of data collection and analysis, mixed methods research is complex. It sets higher demands on researchers' domain-specific knowledge, methodological expertise, project-management competency, and skills in integrating findings from

Table 8.1   Promises and challenges of the research methods introduced in this book

	Promises	Challenges
Mixed methods research (Chapter 2)	• Accessibility to complex research questions • Deep understanding AND generalizability • Triangulation • High impact of research	• Complexity • Time • Unrealistic expectations of payoff • Compatibility of paradigms • Bilingual language
Multi-level and multi-actor research (Chapter 3)	• Bridging macro and micro research (multi-level) • Avoiding ecological and atomistic fallacy (multi-level) • Incorporating the perspectives of multiple stakeholders (multi-actor) • Avoiding common method variance (multi-actor)	• Alignment among the levels of theory, measurement, and analysis • Selection of data source • Adequate sample size at each level
Social network research (Chapter 4)	• Superiority in modeling interaction and interdependency • Modeling actor and relational effects at the same time • Can be used at various levels of analysis as well as across levels of analysis	• The conflict between tracking respondents and ensuring confidentiality • High participant rate needed • Additional ethical issues to be addressed • Complex and time-intensive analysis
Longitudinal research (Chapter 5)	• Stronger causal inference • Modeling change over time • Differentiation of time-varying and time-invariant factors	• Time frame • Number of assessments • Spacing of assessments • Recruitment, tracking, and retention of participants
Experimental methods (Chapter 6)	• Stronger causal inference – Controlling for confounding variables and ruling out alternative explanation	• Generalizability • Manipulation of a set of HR practices
Cross-cultural research (Chapter 7)	• Tests the boundary of theory • Delineates universal and culture-specific HR practices • Incorporates the influence of multiple levels	• Emic vs. etic approaches • Cross-cultural equivalence • Level of analysis • Causal inference

different research methods. Second, the greater breadth and depth of data collection and analysis involved implies a greater time commitment to the project. Third, the promise of mixed methods can lead researchers to create overly complex research designs and develop unrealistic expectations of the contribution that mixed methods can make to addressing research problems and smoothing the path of publication. Similarly, Creswell (2011) lists 11 key controversies and questions in mixed methods research. Although there are preliminary answers to some of these concerns, most are still being debated. The compatibility of paradigms and worldviews and the necessity of adopting a bilingual language in mixed methods research are two that are still being discussed. As Howe (2004) comments, the "natural home" of qualitative methods is "within an interpretivist framework" (pp. 53–54), whereas quantitative methods seem to be endorsed more by the positivists. If methods are linked to paradigms, can paradigms be mixed (Holmes, 2006)? Or should methods be delinked from paradigms (Johnson & Onwuegbuzie, 2004)? Different voices exist on this question (Creswell & Plano Clark, 2007, 2011; Greene & Caracelli, 1997). Also, when writing up a research report, there remains an open question as to whether researchers should adopt a bilingual language to accommodate the tastes of both qualitative and quantitative researchers (Creswell, 2011).

Chapter 3 (Mäkelä, Ehrnrooth, Smale, & Sumelius) discussed issues deserving attention in multi-level and multi-actor quantitative research. This research design has both theoretical and methodological strengths. Theoretically, multi-level research has the potential to integrate macro- and micro-level research and provide a holistic understanding of HRM (Rousseau, 1985; Wright & Boswell, 2002), while multi-actor research is justified by an emerging trend in HRM research that endorses a key-actor approach (Rupidara & McGraw, 2011) or stakeholder approach (Tsui, Ashford, St. Clair, & Xin, 1995). Methodologically, multi-level research avoids the ecological and atomistic fallacy common at single level of analysis and enables researchers to model more complex cross-level phenomenon, while multi-actor research can address the much criticized problem of common method variance (CMV).

Challenges in conducting multi-level research arise from the need to correctly identify level of theory, level of measurement, and level of analysis (Rousseau, 1985). First, researchers need to clearly identify their level of theorization. In strategic human resource management (SHRM), for example, some researchers assume that a set of HR practices is used across all employees in a firm, whereas Lepak and Snell (1999, 2002) propose that different employment modes are adopted for different types of human capital. With the former assumption, the level of theory is the organization, whereas with the latter, the appropriate level of theory is the employment mode. Even when the level of theory is clear, measurement can be problematic because unit membership may be ambiguous (Mathieu & Chen, 2011). Resolution of this problem requires close cooperation with organizational insiders who can provide more information that helps researchers to make sound decisions. Finally, the level of data analysis has to be in alignment with the level of theory and data. To ensure the theory-data-analysis alignment, adequate sample size at each level needs to be obtained. Various possible external constraints, such as a fixed number of entities at a certain level, or unwillingness of organizations to participate in research, could hinder the successful development of a project.

In Chapter 4 (Kaše) social network research, a method that has been underutilized in HRM research, was presented. Social network research addresses "a social phenomenon (or social phenomena, *author added*) composed of entities connected by specific ties reflecting interaction and interdependence" (Carpenter, Li, & Jiang, 2012, p. 1329). Because the assumption of social network theory is that individuals are not independent but embedded in relational networks, social network analysis is extremely well suited for modeling the interactions and interdependence among different entities. It allows researchers to model actor and relational effects at the same time and at various levels as well as across levels.

Challenges of conducting social network research reside primarily in the process of data collection and analysis. First, the dual goals of tracking respondents and keeping them anonymous at the same time are difficult. Multitime passwords are recommended as one way of addressing this problem. Second, to capture the relational ties within a network, a high participation rate is desirable as missing data can be highly problematic. Obtaining support from the top management of a focal organization thus becomes vital to the success of social network data collection. Close cooperation with the management, however, opens some ethical issues (Cross, Kaše, Kilduff, & King, 2013). Finally, in terms of data analysis, because observations from network data violate the independence assumption and are thus subject to autocorrelation problem (Krackhardt, 1988), it requires different analytic approaches. Due to its distance from traditional regression analysis, analysis of network data is complex and time-consuming.

Chapter 5 (Bednall) reviews longitudinal research designs. Longitudinal research overcomes the shortcomings of cross-sectional design by permitting a stronger inference of the direction of causality (Little *et al.*, 2009; Wright *et al.*, 2005). It allows researchers to model the change of variables over time and determine what factor causes the difference in change. A further strength of longitudinal research is the ability to allow researchers to distinguish the effects of time-varying and time-invariant factors.

Challenges of conducting longitudinal research are firstly those concerned with determining the time frame of data collection, number of assessments, and spacing of assessments. Sound decisions are based on researchers' reasonable assumption about the rate of changes. However, in HRM research it can be demanding to determine the time needed for HRM to result in change in individual, group, or organizational performance, especially when different indicators of performance are involved (Combs, Crook, & Shook, 2005;

Dyer & Reeves, 1995). The attrition of participants in the phase of data collection poses another challenge. Various strategies for the recruitment, tracking, and retention of participants are suggested. As far as data analysis is concerned, missing data is an issue that needs to be addressed carefully. Chapter 5 outlines strategies for dealing with different types of missing data depending on whether the data is missing completely at random (MCAR), missing at random (MAR), or missing not at random (MNAR).

In Chapter 6 (Yang & Dickinson) the application of experimental methods into HRM research was discussed. The merit of experimental methods is that they allow researchers to claim a cause-and-effect relationship more confidently by manipulating the independent variables and controlling for confounding variables. Thus, experimental methods are one route for enhancing the internal validity of a study. Because it is not easy to randomly manipulate real HR practices in organizational settings, in this chapter the authors particularly concentrated on discussing the vignette technique. A vignette asks respondents to react to specific, recognizable situations (Wason & Cox, 1996). This allows researchers to systematically manipulate the focal factors in a study (Alexander & Becker, 1978).

Although in theory experimental study provides a powerful tool to test the causal relationship between HRM and performance, its potential has not been fully utilized by HRM researchers. The concern that the results produced in the lab or by a vignette study might not generalize to the field probably has hindered its widespread use. Another reason might be that as SHRM research has gained popularity, researchers have turned their attention toward HRM systems (Lepak, Liao, Chuang, & Harden, 2006). The manipulation of a set of HR practices is far more complex than manipulating a single HR practice.

Chapter 7 (Liao, Sun, & Thomas) introduced cross-cultural research in HRM. Cross-cultural research has received more attention against the backdrop of intensified globalization. Cross-cultural HRM research focuses on the impact of culture on the adoption and effectiveness of HR practices. It explores indigenous HR practices in various cultures, compares effectiveness of HR practices in different cultural contexts, and provides a better understanding of the influence of cultural factors on HR practices and effectiveness. As a result, it helps multinational corporations (MNCs) to navigate through diverse international environments.

Challenges of cross-cultural research in HRM lie in the selection of research approaches, establishment of cross-cultural equivalence, potential confusion of levels of analysis, and difficulties in drawing causal inferences. A derived etic approach was recommended to combine both emic and etic aspects of culture. In terms of cross-cultural equivalence, the authors outlined ways to ensure conceptual, methodological, and measurement equivalence. Different levels of analysis embedded in cross-cultural studies sometimes lead to confusions of levels and inappropriate data transformation across levels. However, a well-designed study should be able to incorporate the impact from different levels and establish a comprehensive model. Finally, since most cross-cultural studies are quasiexperimental in nature, systematic contrast strategies and covariate strategies were recommended to strengthen causal inferences by strategically choosing countries or statistically controlling confounding variables and ruling out alternative explanations.

Strategies for Researchers

The advanced methods discussed in this book hold clear advantages over the single-method, single-actor, single-level, and cross-sectional research designs that prevail in the current HRM research. But their utilization also comes with challenges that can make their application a daunting task. How to balance the advantages and challenges of a research method or multiple research methods in a research project? Below we develop some strategies for researchers. We recommend that researchers undergo the evaluation process described below before embarking on a project. Using the hypothetical description of Marjan's PhD research, we illustrate how these methodological considerations might be addressed.

The first step is to determine the primary research purpose and evaluate the nature of the research question. Adequate research designs are always driven by the question being asked (Bono & McNamara, 2011). This implies a consideration of the nature of the research question at the very beginning of a project. For example, is the research question causal or associative? The answer has clear implications for the research design. For instance, if the purpose is to examine the coexistence of a pay-for-performance practice and a promotion-from-within system, the question is associative. In contrast, the question of whether HRM is effective in terms of enhancing employee and organizational performance is causal. Other potential questions might include: Are different stakeholders' interests involved in the research question under investigation? Can a single actor's answer be a valid representation of different stakeholders' opinions or perceptions? Answers to these questions suggest the degree of applicability of a multi-actor research design.

Second, based on the evaluation of the nature of the research question, a researcher should attempt to identify the components of an *ideal* research design. If the research question is causal, an experimental study or a longitudinal study is superior to a cross-sectional survey in inferring causality. If the question is associative and the variables are relatively stable over time, a cross-sectional design may be sufficient. If the question asks how HR policies are shaped, based on the upper echelon theory (Hambrick & Mason, 1984) one can assume that it is the judgment of the most senior HR manager who makes the decision on HR design. Consequently, the best informant would be that HR manager. If a researcher assumes that the final HR policies are a result of political struggles among different parties, a multi-actor research design is superior to a single-actor research design. Researchers are directed to review Cook and Campbell's (1976) chapter for experimental research and Mitchell's (1985) checklist for correlational research as a guide to avoiding pitfalls in research design. At the stage of determining the ideal study design, one is encouraged to consider a match between his or her research question and the various aspects of research designs regardless of the resources available. A comprehensive consideration would avoid opportunities being dismissed prematurely.

Finally, researchers should assess the available resources and make necessary compromises. For example, a longitudinal study with time intervals of a year might not be the best choice for a PhD student. Or due to the difficulty of accessing multiple respondents, a multi-actor research design has to be abandoned. Despite all kinds of such constraints, researchers should make an effort to match their research designs with their research question as much as possible. For example, one could try to obtain multiple actors for a portion of the sample if it's not possible for the whole. Then the researcher can compare the conclusions drawn from this sample with that from the whole sample. This would give some hints about how much discrepancy there could be between using a single actor and multiple actors. By comparing the compromised research design with the ideal, researchers can determine the study limitations that can suggest paths for future research.

Choosing a research design: How does it work in practice?

Marjan is a PhD candidate interested in teachers' informal learning. From her own experiences Marjan knows the importance of teachers who are eager to learn and improve their teaching capabilities. Marjan's overarching research question is, How can HRM, especially training and performance appraisal and HRM strength, as was introduced by Bowen & Ostroff (2004; see also Bednall, Sanders, & Runhaar, in press) promote informal learning of teachers over time? The idea behind this question is that HRM content such as training and performance appraisal are positively related to informal learning. If teachers can understand what is expected from them, this will strengthen the positive effect of HRM content. Because this question assumes that the change in HRM leads to the change in teachers' informal learning, Marjan determines that it is causal in nature. A random experimental study or longitudinal study would be ideal options to address this question.

To get more contextualized understandings of her research question and inform her later research design, Marjan interviewed teachers, team leaders, and HR professionals at different schools and got several insights from these interviews. During the interviews she learned that one of the schools would implement a new HRM system in a few months; this gave her the unique opportunity to conduct a quasiexperimental study. Although she wanted to combine the quasiexperimental method with a longitudinal research design to strengthen the causal inference, her scholarship is only for three years. A multiple-wave longitudinal study seems not likely. Finally, she made the choice to do a two-wave data collection from the quasiexperimental study with a six-month interval. Then she could have the data within one year. In writing up her thesis, Marjan found that the insights she got from the interviews greatly helped her in the interpretation of the results from the two-wave quasiexperimental study.

4. JOINT ACTIONS TO MOVE THE FIELD FORWARD

While this book acquaints the readers with advanced research methods, a question can be asked whether simply becoming familiar with these tools is sufficient to change the methods used by the HRM field. Planned behavior theory (Ajzen, 1985, 1991) suggests that an individual's intention to act is a confluence of his or her attitude toward certain behavior, his or her perception of the norms held by significant others regarding that behavior, and his or her perceived control of that behavior. Similarly, researchers' methodological choices are not only influenced by their own skills. They are also shaped by the climate of the whole scholarly community and the support researchers obtain from within and outside the community. If a strong climate exists in the HRM scholarly community that proper research methods are desirable, researchers are more likely to conform. Furthermore, as advanced research methods are often more complex in terms of research design and data collection, to the extent that researchers can get support from interested organizations, they are more likely to implement the complex research designs.

Because the factors that influence researchers' decisions to employ advanced research methods involve a number of stakeholders, joint actions from all stakeholders are called for to enable significant changes in the field. As we believe that an action plan is only feasible when most stakeholders' missions or goals are compatible with each other within the framework of that plan, below we briefly discuss some important missions or goals of the stakeholders and make recommendations as to how these missions or goals might be realized.

HRM researchers (including PhD candidates) need to discover and create knowledge on the management of people and work. The most quantifiable measurement of knowledge output probably is publication. This might explain why publication is one of the most important criteria in the decision making concerning faculty recruitment, pay increases, and promotion. We expect that either being intrinsically or extrinsically motivated, HRM researchers would make an effort to maximize their knowledge output, which is reflected in their publications.

Business schools shoulder the responsibility to disseminate knowledge to students and, further, to society. This mission can be better served when researchers who obtain insights from the latest research feed these insights back to their teaching. By employing faculty who are good at doing research and thereby enhancing teaching quality, business schools can realize their mission. With that said, the missions of business schools and researchers are congruent.

Journal editors are charged with the task of increasing journals' impact factor and expanding their reach to readers. To accomplish these tasks a journal needs to encourage high-quality submissions. High-quality research is characterized by important research questions, rigorous research methods, and valid findings. Research with these features is cited and read more frequently (Arvey & Campion, 1998). It also provides more value to practitioners and, therefore, has a higher probability to reach practitioners. To increase the number of high-quality publications in their journals, editors are nevertheless dependent on researchers' efforts to conduct high-quality research.

Organizations focus on surviving, making a profit, and competing with other companies to keep or strengthen their market position. Management based on scientific evidence that overcomes the sole reliance on intuition, unsystematic experience, unexamined ideologies, and idiosyncratic situational cues is essential to support this goal (Charlier, Brown, & Rynes, 2011). There is evidence demonstrating that organizations whose HR professionals read academic research have higher financial performance (Terpstra & Rozell, 1997). Although research finds a large knowledge gap (Rynes, Colbert, & Brown, 2002; Sanders, Riemsdijk, & Groen, 2008) and discrepant interests (Deadrick & Gibson, 2007) between academics and managers, the latter would benefit from a recognition that organizational performance can be supported by research.

Recommendations

Based on the above discussion of each stakeholder's mission or goal, we develop the following recommendations.

Highlight the importance of valid research methods. Journal editors should *explicitly* highlight the importance of valid research methods via editorials emphasizing the importance of valid methods, special issues discussing research methodology, or in authors' submission guidelines. For example, *Academy of Management Journal* notes in an editorial (Bono & McNamara, 2011) that many papers using cross-sectional design are rejected because they are not sufficient in answering their research questions that implicitly address issues of change. *Human Resource Management* expresses its disfavor with experiments using student samples. Similarly, *Journal of International Business Studies* discourages empirical studies employing student samples unless strong justification can be provided. *Personal Psychology* particularly welcomes multi-level research that includes individual, team, and organizational levels. By highlighting the importance of valid research methods and publishing rigorous research, journals heighten their impact and widen their reach. They also benefit organizations by providing reliable research evidence and improving managers' decision quality.

Promote implications for practice in published research/research outputs. Researchers need to listen to managers and HR professionals from organizations to understand their concerns (Deadrick & Gibson, 2007). Research questions generated from practitioners' concerns will be better valued and embraced by them. Journal editors as gatekeepers for the published articles can ask researchers to explicitly articulate the practical implications of their research. *Human Resource Management* is one of the few high-impact research-based journals that is practicing this. Submitters to *Human Resource Management* are asked to explain the implications of their research to practitioners. Editors of practitioner-oriented journals can go even further. *Harvard Business Review* seeks research "whose practical application has been thought through in clear jargon-free language." Their editors clearly ask the question "How much does this idea benefit managers in practice?" (http://hbr.org/guidlines-for-authors-hbr). It requires HR researchers not only to conduct practice-relevant research, but also to write in "practice-based language" that is understandable to the managers (Deadrick & Gibson, 2007, p. 137). By emphasizing the practical value of research, academic efforts and results will be more appreciated by practitioners.

Evidence-based management is a decision-making process combining critical thinking with the use of the best available scientific evidence and business information (Rousseau & Barends, 2011). It requires managers to seek systematic evidence from the best available academic research and translate principles based on the evidence into practice. An appealing promise of evidence-based management is that it consistently helps attain organizational goals (Rousseau, 2006). Research shows that organizations using evidence-based management gain a seven percent profit increase (Lovallo & Sibony, 2010). Therefore, organizations are encouraged to pursue evidence-based management. Because organizations aiming at evidence-based management are aware of the value of research, we expect that they are more willing to participate in research, since participation in research increases the salience of the logic behind evidence and exposes organizations directly to scientific information (Rousseau, 2006). Organizations' interest in research evidence and in participating in research will consequently benefit researchers and reduce the difficulty in accessing organizations.

Add engagement with organizations to researchers' promotion schemes. In the current promotion schemes of most business schools little or no attention is paid to the collaboration researchers have with organizations. Adding engagement with organizations into researchers' promotion schemes will stimulate collaborations. It would motivate researchers to actively seek collaboration opportunities with organizations and, at the same time, promote their thinking on the practical values of their studies. Although, beyond the scope of this chapter, how to measure the degree of engagement is definitely an issue that deserves consideration in practice.

In summary, the above recommendations serve two goals: to raise the awareness of researchers that advanced research methods are encouraged, and to facilitate the collaboration between the scholarly community and the practitioners. The former can be realized primarily by journal editors who set high standards on valid research methods and further by business schools that place value on researchers who produce valid knowledge. The achievement of the latter on the one hand requires researchers and journals to enhance the practical value of their research; on the other hand it calls for organizations to embrace evidence-based management to make scientific decisions. Business schools can facilitate the collaboration process by motivating researchers through promotion schemes. If these recommendations can be implemented, more advanced research methods will be applied and more valid HR research will be spawned. Organizations will gain insights from valid research results, increasing trust in HR research and enhancing opportunities for collaboration in the research process. In turn, academic research will be spurred, exploring more relevant questions. Research and practice inform and stimulate each other, which will move the HRM research to a higher level. This is where we need to go.

REFERENCES

Ajzen, I. (1985). From intentions to actions: A theory of planned behavior. In J. Kuhl & J. Beckmann (Eds.), *Action control: From cognition to behavior* (pp. 11–39). Heidelberg: Springer.

Ajzen, I. (1991). The theory of planned behavior. *Organizational Behavior and Human Decision Processes. 50*, 179–211.

Alexander, C. S., & Becker, H. J. (1978). The use of vignettes in survey research. *The Public Opinion Quarterly, 42*, 93–104.

Arvey, R. D., & Campion, J. E. (1998). Being there: Writing the highly cited article. *Personnel Psychology, 51*, 845–848.

Bae, J., & Lawler, J. J. (2000). Organizational and HRM strategies in Korea: Impact on firm performance in an emerging economy. *Academy of Management Journal, 43*, 502–517.

Bednall, T., Sanders, K., & Runhaar, P. (in press). Stimulating informal learning activities through perceptions of performance appraisal quality and HRM system strength: A two-wave study. *Academy of Management Learning & Education.*

Becker, B. & Gerhart, B. (1996). The impact of human resource management on organizational performance: Progress and prospects. *Academy of Management Journal, 39*, 779–801.

Bono, J. E., & McNamara, G. (2011). Publishing in AMJ-part 2: Research design. *Academy of Management Journal, 54*, 657–660.

Boselie, P., Dietz, G., & Boon, C. (2005). Commonalities and contradictions in HRM and performance research. *Human Resource Management Journal, 15*, 67–94.

Bouchard, T. J., Jr. (1976). Unobtrusive measures: An inventory of uses. *Sociological Methods and Research, 4*, 267–300.

Bowen, D. E., & Ostroff, C. (2004). Understanding HRM–firm performance linkages: The role of the "strength" of the HRM system. *Academy of Management Review, 29,* 203–221.

Carpenter, M. A., Li, M., & Jiang, H. (2012). Social network research in organizational contexts: A systematic review of methodological issues and choices. *Journal of Management, 38,* 1328–1361.

Charlier, S. D., Brown, K. G., & Rynes, S. L. (2011). Teaching evidence-based management in MBA programs: What evidence is there? *Academy of Management Learning & Education, 11,* 222–236.

Casper, W. J., Eby, L. T., Bordeaux, C., Lockwood, A., & Lambert, D. (2007). A review of research methods in IO/OB work-family research. *Journal of Applied Psychology, 92,* 28–43.

Chuang, C.-H., & Liao, H. (2010). Strategic human resource management in service context: Taking care of business by taking care of employees and customers. *Personnel Psychology, 63,* 153–196.

Combs. J. G., Crook, T. R., & Schook, C. L. (2005). The dimensionality of organizational performance and its implications for strategic management research. *Research Methodology in Strategy and Management, 2,* 259–286.

Cook, T. D., & Campbell, D. T. (1976). The design and conduct of quasi-experiments and true experiments in field settings. In M. Dunette (Ed.), *Handbook of industrial and organizational psychology* (pp. 223–326). Skokie, IL: Rand McNally.

Creswell, J. W. (1998). *Qualitative inquiry and research design: Choosing among five approaches.* Thousand Oaks: Sage.

Creswell, J. W. (2011). Controversies in mixed methods research. In N. K. Denzin & Y. S. Lincoln (Eds.), *The Sage handbook of qualitative research* (pp. 269–299). Los Angeles: Sage.

Creswell, J. W., & Plano Clark, V. L. (2007). *Designing and conducting mixed methods research.* Thousand Oaks, CA: Sage.

Cross, R., Kaše, R., Kilduff, M., & King, Z. (2013). Bridging the gap between research and practice in organizational network analysis: A conversation between Rob Cross and Martin Kilduff. *Human Resource Management, 52*(4), 627–644.

Deadrick, D. L., & Gibson, P. A. (2007). An examination of the research-practice gap in HR: Comparing topics of interest to HR academics and HR professionals. *Human Resource Management Review, 17,* 131–139.

Delaney, J. T., & Huselid, M. A. (1996). The impact of human resource management practices on perceptions of organizational performance. *Academy of Management Journal, 39,* 949–969.

Dyer, L., & Reeves, T. (1995). Human resource strategies and firm performance: What do we know and where do we need to go? *International Journal of Human Resource Management, 6,* 656–670.

Gerhart, B., Wright, P. M., & McMahan, G. C. (2000). Measurement error in research on the human resources and firm performance relationship: Further evidence and analysis. *Personnel Psychology, 53,* 855–872.

Gerhart, B., Wright, P. M., McMahan, G. C., & Snell, S. A. (2000). Measurement error in research on human resources and firm performance: How much error is there and how does it influence effect size estimates? *Personnel Psychology, 53,* 803–834.

Gong, Y., Law, K. S., Chang, S., & Xin, K. R. (2009). Human resources management and firm performance: The differential role of managerial affective and continuance commitment. *Journal of Applied Psychology, 94,* 263–275.

Greene, J. C., & Caracelli, V. J. (1997). *Advances in mixed-method evaluation: The challenges and benefits of integrating diverse paradigms.* San Francisco, CA: Jossey-Bass.

Guest, D. E. (2011). Human resource management and performance: Still searching for some answers. *Human Resource Management Journal, 21*, 3–13.

Guthrie, J. P., Spell, C. S., & Nyamori, R. O. (2002). Correlates and consequences of high involvement work practices: The role of competitive strategy. *International Journal of Human Resource Management, 13*, 183–197.

Hambrick, D. C., & Mason, P. A. (1984). Upper echelons: The organization as a reflection of top managers. *Academy of Management Review, 9*, 193–206.

Hayton, J. C., Piperopoulos, P., & Welbourne, T. M. (2011). Celebrating 50 years: 50 years of *knowledge sharing:* Learning from a field moving forward. *Human Resource Management, 50*, 697–714.

Holmes, C. A. (2006). *Mixed (up) methods, methodology and interpretive frameworks.* Paper presented at the Mixed Methods Conference, Cambridge, UK.

Howe, K. R. (2004). A critique of experimentalism. *Qualitative Inquiry, 10*, 42–61.

Huselid, M. A., & Becker, B. E. (2000). Comment on "Measurement error in research on human resources and firm performance: How much error is there and how does it influence effect size estimates?" by Gerhart, Wright, McMahan, and Snell. *Personnel Psychology, 53*, 835–854.

Jick, T. D. (1979). Mixing qualitative and quantitative methods: triangulation in action. *Administrative Science Quarterly, 24*, 602–611.

Johnson, R. B., & Onwuegbuzie, A. (2004). Mixed methods research: A research paradigm whose time has come. *Educational Researcher, 33*, 14–26.

Johnson, R. B., Onwuegbuzie, A., & Turner, L. (2007). Toward a definition of mixed methods research. *Journal of Mixed Methods Research, 1*, 112–133.

Kaše, R., Paauwe, J., & Zupan, N. (2009). HR practices, interpersonal relations, and intra-firm knowledge transfer in knowledge-intensive firms: A social network perspective. *Human Resource Management, 48*(4), 615–639.

Klein, K. J., & Kozlowski, S. W. J. (2000). *Multi-level theory, research and methods in organizations: Foundations, extensions, and new directions.* San Francisco, CA: Jossey-Bass.

Krackhardt, D. (1988). Predicting with networks: Nonparametric multiple regression analysis of dyadic data. *Social Networks, 10*(4), 359–381.

Lepak, D. P., Liao, H., Chuang, Y., & Harden, E. E. (2006). A conceptual review of human resource management systems in strategic human resource management research. In J. J. Martcchio (Ed.), *Research in personnel and human resources management* (Vol. 25, pp. 217–271). Emerald Group Publishing Limited.

Lepak, D. P., & Snell, S. A. (1999). The human resource architecture: Toward a theory of human capital allocation and development. *Academy of Management Review, 24*, 31–48.

Lepak, D. P., & Snell, S. A. (2002). Examining the human resource architecture: The relationships among human capital, employment, and human resource configurations. *Journal of Management, 28*, 517–543.

Lepak, D. P., Takeuchi, R., Erhardt, N. L., & Colakoglu, S. (2006). Emerging perspectives on the relationship between HRM and performance. In R. J. Burke & C. L. Cooper (Eds.), *The human resources revolution: Why putting people first matters* (pp. 31–54). Burlington: Emerald Group Publishing.

Little, T. D., Card, N. A., Preacher, K. J., & McConnell, E. (2009). Modelling longitudinal data from research on adolescence. In R. M. Lerner & L. Steinberg (Eds.), *Handbook of adolescent psychology.* New York, NY: John Wiley & Sons.

Lovallo, D., & Sibony, O. (2010, March). The case for behavioral strategy. *McKinsey Quarterly*, 1–14.

Martín-Alcázar, F., Romero-Fernández, P. M., & Sánchez-Gardey, G. (2008). Human resource management as a field of research. *British Journal of Management, 19*, 103–119.

Mathieu, J. E., & Chen, G. (2011). The ethology of the multilevel paradigm in management research. *Journal of Management, 37,* 610–641.

McGrath, J. (1982). Dillemmatics: The study of research choices and dilemmas. In J. E. McGrath, J. Martin, & R. A. Kulla (Eds.), *Judgment calls in research* (pp. 69–102). Newbury Park, CA: Sage.

Mitchell, T. R. (1985). An evaluation of the validity of correlational research conducted in organizations. *Academy of Management Review, 10,* 192–205.

Podsakoff, P. M., MacKenzie, S. B., Lee, J.-Y., & Podsakoff, N. P. (2003). Common method biases in behavioral research: A critical review of the literature and recommended remedies. *Journal of Applied Psychology, 88,* 879–903.

Rousseau, D. M. (1985). Issues of level in organizational research: Multi-level and cross-level perspectives. *Research in Organizational Behavior, 7,* 1–37.

Rousseau, D. M. (2006). 2005 presidential address: Is there such a thing as "Evidence-Based Management"? *Academy of Management Review, 31,* 256–269.

Rousseau, D. M. & Barends, E. G. R. (2011). Becoming an evidence-based HR practitioner. *Human Resource Management Journal, 21,* 221–235.

Rupidara, N. & McGraw, P. (2011). The role of actors in configuring HR systems within multinational subsidiaries. *Human Resource Management Review, 21,* 174–185.

Rynes, S. L., Colbert, A. E., & Brown, K. G. (2002). HR professionals' beliefs about effective human resource practices: Correspondence between research and practice. *Human Resource Management, 41,* 149–174.

Sanders, K., Bainbridge, H., Kim, S., Cogin, J., & Lin, C.-H. (2012, August). *Strategic human resource management research: A content analysis.* Paper presented at the 72nd annual meeting of the Academy of Management, Boston, MA.

Sanders, K., van Riemsdijk, M., & Groen, B. (2008). The gap between research and practice: A replication study on the HR professionals' beliefs about effective human resource practices. *International Journal of Human Resource Management, 19,* 1975–1987.

Scandura, T. A., & Williams, E. A. (2000). Research methodology in management: Current practices, trends, and implications for future research. *Academy of Management Journal, 43,* 1248–1264.

Shaw, J. D., Dineen, B. R., Fang, R., & Vellella, R. F. (2009). Employee-organization exchange relationships, HRM practices, and quit rates of good and poor performers. *Academy of Management Journal, 5,* 1016–1033.

Shaw, J. D., Gupta, N., & Delery, J. E. (2005). Alternative conceptualizations of the relationship between voluntary turnover and organizational performance. *Academy of Management Journal, 48,* 50–68.

Terpstra, D. E., & Rozell, E. J. (1997). Sources of human resource information and the link to organizational profitability. *Journal of Applied Behavioral Science, 33,* 66–83.

Tsui, A. S., Ashford, S. J., St. Clair, L., & Xin, K. R. (1995). Dealing with discrepant expectations: Response strategies and managerial effectiveness. *Academy of Management Journal, 38,* 1515–1543.

Tsui, A. S., Pearce, J. L., Porter, L. W., & Tripoli, A. M. (1997). Alternative approaches to the employee-organization relationship: Does investment in employees pay off? *Academy of Management Journal, 40,* 1089–1121.

Wall, T. D., & Wood, S. J. (2005). The romance of human resource management and business performance, and the case for big science. *Human Relations, 58,* 429–462.

Wason, K. D., & Cox, K. C. (1996). Scenario utilization in marketing research. In D. Strutton, L. E. Pelton, & S. Shipp (Eds.), *Advances in marketing* (pp. 155–162). Texas: Southwestern Marketing Association.

Welbourne, T. M. (2012). Research methods in human resource management: Critical knowledge for practitioners and academics. *Human Resource Management, 51*, 1–2.

Wright, P. M., & Boswell, W. R. (2002). Desegregating HRM: A review and synthesis of micro and macro human resource management research. *Journal of Management, 28*, 247–276.

Wright, P. M., Gardner, T. M., Moynihan, L. M., & Allen, M. R. (2005). The relationship between HR practices and firm performance: Examining causal order. *Personnel Psychology. 58*, 409–446.

Youndt, M. A., Snell, S. A., Dean, J. W., Jr., & Lepak, D. P. (1996). Human resource management, manufacturing strategy, and firm performance. *Academy of Management Journal. 39*, 836–866.

Contributors

Hugh T. J. Bainbridge, Ph.D (University of Melbourne) is a senior lecturer in the School of Management, at the Australian School of Business, University of New South Wales. His research interests encompass the effectiveness of human resource practices, employee diversity, and impression formation processes relevant to individuals, groups, and organizations. His current research considers how line managers and HR specialists can improve the participation and employment quality of diverse individuals in the workforce. The results of his research have been published in the *Academy of Management Review, Journal of Applied Psychology, Analyses of Social Issues and Public Policy,* and *Asia Pacific Journal of Human Resources.*

Timothy Colin Bednall, PhD is a postdoctoral research fellow at the School of Management within the Australian School of Business at the University of New South Wales. He graduated with a combined Masters and PhD in Industrial/Organizational Psychology in 2009 from the University of New South Wales. He previously worked at the Australian Red Cross Blood Service and is currently an honorary associate of the School of Management and Marketing at the University of Melbourne. Dr. Bednall's research interests include learning and training, pro-social behavior, human resource management, and advanced research methods.

Julie A. Cogin, PhD is associate professor at the School of Management within the Australian School of Business at the University of New South Wales. Julie's research interests surround the HRM–performance relationship. This includes understanding how components of an HRM strategy can be configured to realize superior organizational outcomes (in both profit and not-for-profit sectors) as well as the impediments to HRM professionals operating as true strategic partners. Julie is also interested in HRM research methods, the progress of the field, and designing research that does not suffer from major methodological problems. Her work has been published in journals such as *Human Resource Management, International Journal of Human Resource Management,* and *Employee Relations.*

Julie Dickinson, PhD is lecturer in Organizational Psychology at the Department of Organizational Psychology, Birkbeck, University of London. She has a BSc in Social Psychology from the London School of Economics and a PhD from Dundee University. Her research addresses the psychological processes supporting pay inequality including perceptions of pay fairness, attitudes to pay secrecy, and the development of economic beliefs in childhood and adolescence. She has published in journals such as the *British Journal of Social Psychology*, the *British Journal of Developmental Psychology*, and *Employee Relations*.

Mats Ehrnrooth, PhD is an associate professor at Hanken School of Economics in Vaasa. His research focuses on human resource management, performance, and related managerial issues in large multinational corporations. He has published, for example, in *Journal of Management Studies, Strategic Management Journal, Journal of International Business, Journal of World Business, Human Resource Management*, and *International Journal of Human Resource Management*.

Robert Kaše, PhD is an associate professor of management at the Faculty of Economics of the University of Ljubljana, Department of Management and Organization, and associate editor of *Human Resource Management*. His current research interests include HRM-performance link, social networks, careers, and knowledge transfer. His work has appeared in journals like *Human Resource Management, International Journal of Human Resource Management, International Journal of Manpower*, and *Organization Science*. He supports interaction between research and practice and is strongly involved in the Slovenian HR Association.

Kristiina Mäkelä, PhD is an associate professor of international business at Aalto University School of Business in Helsinki. Her research focuses on people-related issues in multinational corporations, including those concerning HRM practices, the HR function, knowledge, social capital, and interpersonal interaction. Her work has appeared in more than 20 international peer-reviewed journals and books, including *Journal of International Business Studies, Journal of Management Studies, Human Resource Management, Journal of World Business, International Business Review, Journal of Managerial Psychology, International Journal of Human Resource Management*, and *Organizational Dynamics*, among others. Before entering academia, she worked for more than 10 years in Procter & Gamble, the world-leading consumer-goods multinational.

Ilro Lee is a PhD candidate at the Australian School of Business, University of New South Wales. Before Ilro became a PhD candidate, he was a political consultant to hundreds of political campaigns in the United States. He worked on progressive issue campaigns and high-profile campaigns like

Obama for President. He has extensive experience in running thousands of surveys and polls as well as developing innovative campaign tools that propelled him to be recognized as the "Rising Star of Politics" in 2007. His research interests include SHRM, international business, and healthcare management. He has received an MBA from the University of Maryland, USA.

Cai-Hui (Veronica) Lin is a PhD candidate at School of Management, University of New South Wales. Her research interests include human resource management (HRM) and innovation, research methods in HRM research, international HRM, and leadership. Her dissertation focuses on how HRM can facilitate individual innovative behaviors at the workplace. Prior to her PhD study, Cai-Hui had work experience in the engineering consulting industry in China.

Yuan Liao, PhD is a postdoctoral research fellow in the School of Management at the Australian School of Business, University of New South Wales, Australia. She received her PhD from the Beedie Business School at Simon Fraser University. Her current research interests include regulatory focus, cross-cultural performance management, psychological contract, and cultural intelligence. Her publications have appeared in such journals as *Journal of International Business Studies*, *Journal of Cross-Cultural Psychology*, and *Journal of Business Ethics*.

Karin Sanders, PhD is a professor of Human Resource Management and Organisational Behaviour at the Australian School of Business, University of New South Wales, Sydney, Australia. Her research focuses on the process approach of HRM, in particular the impact of employees' perceptions and attributions of HRM on their attitudes and behaviors. She uses advanced statistical research methods to test a variety of theoretical models. Her research has been published in such scholarly outlets as the *Academy of Management Learning & Education*, *Journal of Vocational Behavior*, *Organizational Studies*, *Asia Pacific Journal of Management*, *International Journal of Human Resource Management*, and *Group and Organization Management*. Together with Dr. Helen Shipton and Dr. Jorge Gomes she is the guest editor for a special issue of *Human Resource Management* titled "Are HRM processes important?" She is associate editor of *Evidence Based HRM*.

Adam Smale, PhD is a professor in the Department of Management at the University of Vaasa, Finland. His research focuses on HRM and knowledge transfer in multinational firm settings and has been published in the *Journal of International Business Studies, International Business Review, Human Resource Management, International Journal of Human Resource Management,* and the *Journal of World Business,* among others.

Jennie Sumelius, Dr.Sc. (econ.), is an assistant professor at the Department of Management and Organization at the Hanken School of Economics in Helsinki. Her research focuses on HRM-related issues in multinational corporations and has been published in *International Business Review, Journal of Management Studies, Human Resource Management*, and *Journal of World Business*, among others.

Jian-Min (James) Sun, PhD is a professor and chair of the Department of Psychology, the director of Human Resource Assessment Center, and adjunct professor at the School of Labor and Human Resource, Renmin University of China. He was a Fulbright scholar at University of Florida in 2007–2008 and has studied and lectured in more than 30 universities worldwide. He has published in journals such as *Strategic Management Journal, Journal of Experimental Social Psychology, Leadership Quarterly, International Journal of Human Resource Management*, as well as many Chinese journals. His research interests include individual differences in personality, attitude, and behavior in organizations, leadership, human resource management and organizational innovation, and cross-cultural management issues.

David C Thomas, PhD is professor of International Business at the Australian School of Business, University of New South Wales, Sydney, Australia. He is the author of 10 books including, most recently, *Essentials of International Human Resource Management: Managing People Globally* (Sage Publications, with Mila Lazarova) and the best-selling *Cultural Intelligence: Living and Working Globally* (2009, Berrett-Koehler Publishers, with Kerr Inkson). His book *Cross-Cultural Management Essential Concepts* (2008, Sage Publications) was the winner of the R. Wayne Pace Human Resource Development book of the year award for 2008. His research on cross-cultural interactions in organizational settings has appeared in numerous journals and he is currently area editor of the *Journal of International Business Studies*.

Huadong Yang received his PhD degree from University of Groningen in the Netherlands. He is now a lecturer at the Department of Organizational Psychology, Birkbeck, University of London. His research focuses on three areas: conflict management, employee professional development, and cross-cultural psychology. His work has been published in journals such as the *European Journal of Personality; Applied Psychology: An International Review; Journal of Cross-Cultural Psychology*, and *European Journal of Work and Organizational Psychology*.

Index